D1615184

A NEST OF CORSAIRS

★ ★

The Karamanli Bashaws of Tripoli in Barbary and their relations with the States, the Consuls and the Travellers of the Christian Powers, 1711 to 1835

Also by Seton Dearden

THE ARABIAN KNIGHT
A biography of Sir Richard Burton

THE GYPSY GENTLEMAN
A biography of George Borrow

LAURENCE OLIPHANT: An Essay

GERTRUDE BELL: An Essay

Edited

LETTERS FROM THE COURT OF TRIPOLI

CURZON'S 'MONASTERIES IN THE LEVANT'

A Nest of Corsairs

THE FIGHTING KARAMANLIS OF TRIPOLI

* * *

Seton Dearden

'Sombres mélodrames, avec cà et là les scènes de comédie les plus bouffonnes. On y trouve a chaque pas des sujets de tragédie ou d'opéra.'

(Augustin Bernard: *Annales Tripolitaines.*)

JOHN MURRAY

Printed in Great Britain by
Butler & Tanner Ltd.,
Frome and London
0 7195 3279 5

FOR BRIDGET SIBYL

CONTENTS

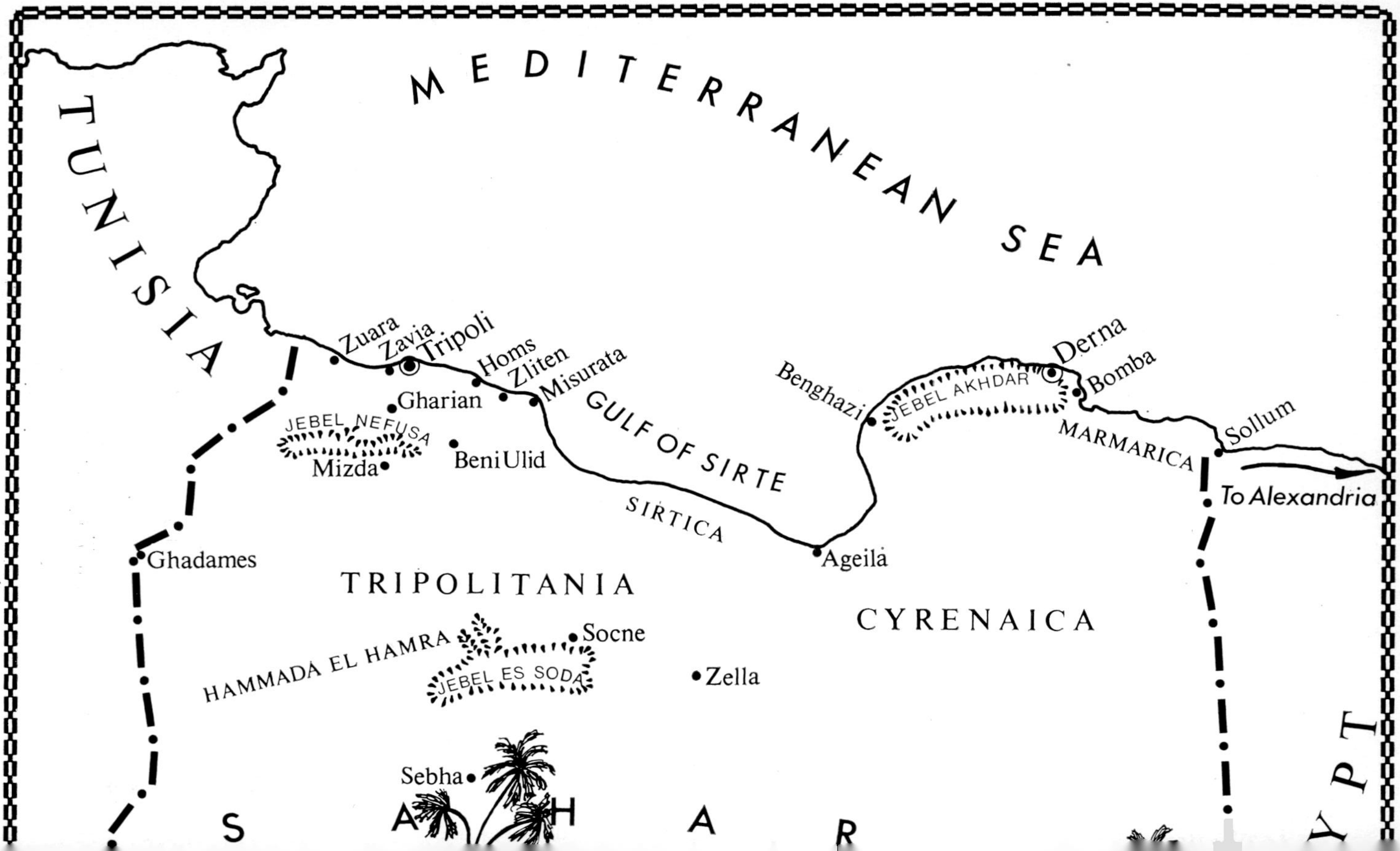

MEDITERRANEAN SEA
TUNISIA
Zuara
Zavia
Tripoli
Homs
Zliten
Misurata
Gharian
JEBEL NEFUSA
Mizda
Beni Ulid
GULF OF SIRTE
SIRTICA
Benghazi
JEBEL AKHDAR
Derna
Bomba
MARMARICA
Sollum
To Alexandria
Ageila
Ghadames
TRIPOLITANIA
CYRENAICA
Socne
HAMMADA EL HAMRA
JEBEL ES SODA
Zella
Sebha
SAHAR
YPT

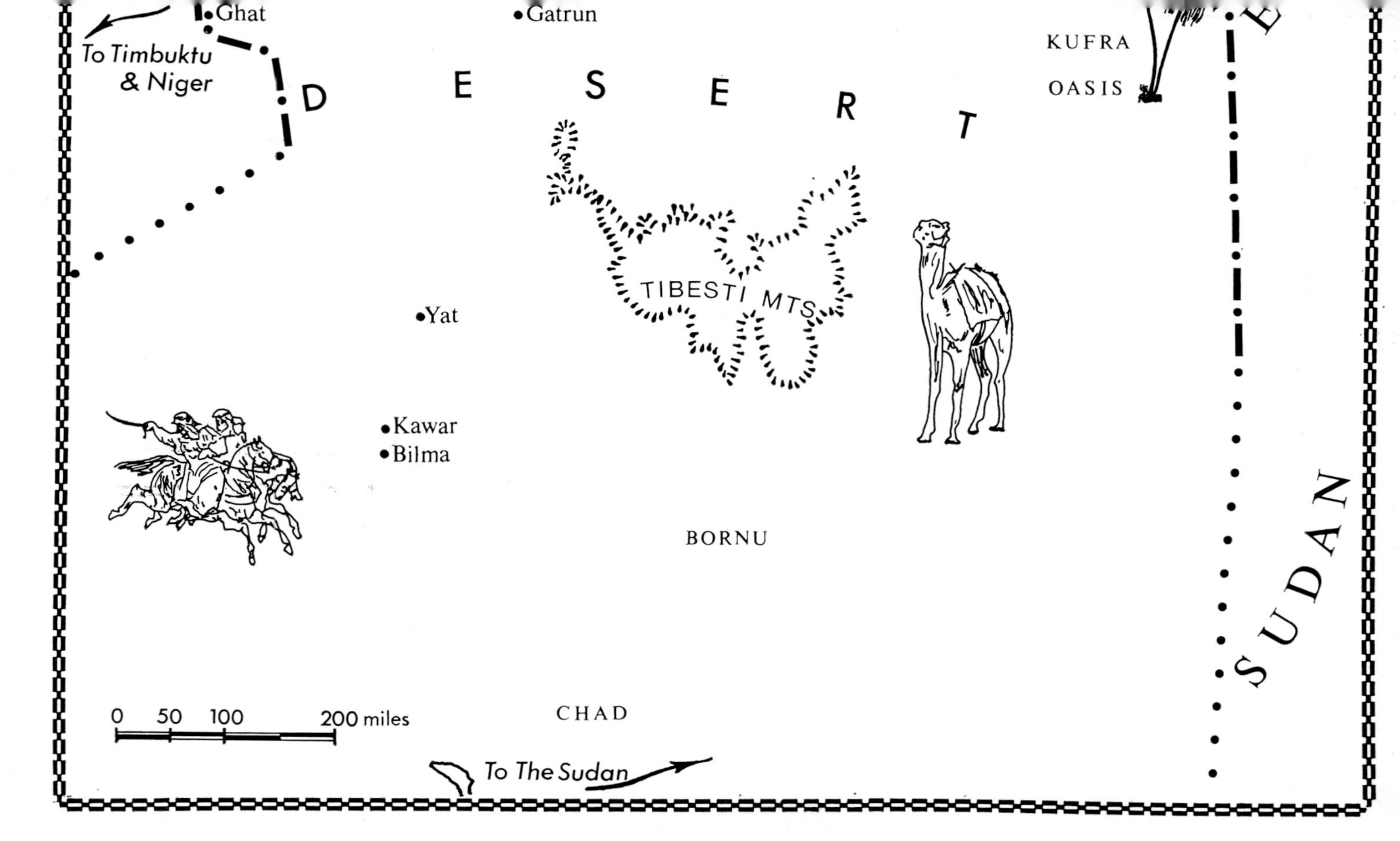
Ghat
Gatrun
To Timbuktu
& Niger
DESERT
KUFRA
OASIS
TIBESTI MTS
Yat
Kawar
Bilma
BORNU
SUDAN
CHAD
0
50
100
200 miles
To The Sudan

ILLUSTRATIONS

Illustrations

ACKNOWLEDGEMENTS

My thanks are due to the following who, at various times, over several years, helped me in collecting material for this book.

The late Sayyid Munir Burshan of Tripoli, editor and journalist who, twenty-five years ago, first aroused my interest in the Karamanli family and recounted to me many of the oral traditions of their early history, took me to the Castle to see the large, mouldering archives of the dynasty—still at that date unsorted. He also showed me the site of the Karamanli house in the *menshia*, where the *janissary* aghas were massacred, and the presumed site of Colonel Warrington's famous garden, and patiently explored with me the available records in Turkish and Arabic, including his own notes taken from the still unpublished Arabic MS. of the local historian of the Karamanli family, ibn Ghalboun.

To Lord Rennell, for much advice and the gift of some useful Warrington papers, and the curious Warrington pedigree, which he had collected.

To M. Roger Chambard, former French consul in Tripoli and linguist, who helped me in my research with advice and material from the French consular archives.

To Ambassador Roberto Gaja, Director General of Political Affairs in Rome and former Italian consul in Tripoli, who took time off from his arduous duties to collect and send me material from the Karamanli archives in Rome.

To Sayyid Mohammed Bouayyed, former Director of the Bibliothèque Nationale in Algiers, who found for me a copy of the very rare memoirs of Madame de Breughel, and to Madame van der Sluys, of the same library, who kindly translated for me from the original Dutch the relevant sections of the Memoirs dealing with the Warrington family.

Finally, I would like to thank Mr. Noel Blakiston of the Public Record Office, and Miss Joan Bailey, of the London Library, for help in tracing documents and books.

FOREWORD

The Barbary Regencies, those former north-African provinces of the Ottoman empire, may have at first sight little claim on the attention of the historian, but, from a combination of circumstances, they survived for nearly three hundred years. They had only a marginal connection with events in Europe and scarcely more with the Ottoman Sultans, though to the end they maintained the Ottoman system of rule and administration. After about a century of direct control from Constantinople, they threw off all but a nominal connection with the Sublime Porte, and went their own way as small principalities, with their elected rulers, independent and autocratic, with their own policies of peace and war. They so remained, as a curious anachronism in a changing world, until the beginning of the 19th century. Their continued existence as a threatening presence off the African shore, on the vital trade routes to the Levant and India, drew them inevitably into the periphery of the struggle for influence and for trade which increasingly developed between the great maritime powers.

While in Algiers and Tunis a series of constantly changing régimes, under contending rulers, succeeded one another so that no clear thread of history can be traced, there emerged in Tripoli in 1711, a leader of unusual talents who founded what was essentially an Arab dynasty, which was to last for one hundred and twenty-five years, providing a long period of relative stability.

It is an account of this family—an early example of Arab independence—which retained the throne of Tripoli so long, and its relations with the European and American nations, their governments, their consuls, and finally their travellers, that forms the theme of this book.

INTRODUCTION: Background

The background to this chronicle of the Karamanli Bashaws is the 18th-century Ottoman Regency of Tripoli in Barbary,[1] a place and period so remote from the main stream of recorded history that a brief description of the country, its peoples and its way of life is necessary, if only to set the scene against which the bizarre events at the Court of Tripoli unfold.

Tripoli, now called by its original Greek name of Libya, comprises that large area of north Africa which lies between Tunisia and Egypt and, from the Mediterranean coastline, extends southwards across the Sahara desert to undefined limits at the gateway to central Africa. Two thousand miles of coast stretch along its northern frontier, and an equal distance between the sea and its southern limits beyond the Tropic of Capricorn. Vast in size,[2] yet sparse in population, its frontiers have been preserved for centuries, not by human contrivance, but by the all-encompassing desert which isolates it from its neighbours, and helps to divide it naturally into its three provinces of Tripolitania, Cyrenaica and the Fezzan.

In the days of horse and camel, the distances separating Tripoli's three provinces must have been formidable. While five hundred miles—three weeks' travel—separated the capital Tripoli, from Derna, the chief town in its eastern province of Cyrenaica, at least a thousand miles—two months' travel—cut off both provinces from the southern province of the Fezzan. Yet, such was the unusual conformation of land and sea that, while these long distances lay between the Bashaw of Tripoli and his Moslem subjects in the provinces, only two hundred miles—three days'

[1] So called to distinguish it from that other Ottoman possession, the town of Tripoli in the Levant.

[2] 2,700,000 square miles of which the desert covers seven-eighths.

sail—separated his Palace from that Christian outpost of Europe—the island of Malta.

Throughout the 18th century, the sea was still the main route for commerce and travel to Tripoli. Few travellers traversed the rough tracks, the only roads which linked the provinces with the capital and with the outer world. An occasional government courier, carrying mail from Damascus and Cairo to the Maghrib, would pick his way along the coast road from Alexandria to Algiers, travelling mostly at night to avoid the Beduin haunting the road; and once a year a column of Turkish troops would march out from Tripoli to collect the periodic tribute from towns and tribes. Once a year also, that unique phenomenon of Islam, the annual caravan of pilgrims to Mecca, emerging from the Maghrib cities in the west, made its way to Cairo, Suez and the holy cities of Arabia.

This annual pilgrimage across the terrain of the northern confines of the Regency, and the corresponding slave caravans which periodically traversed the desert route from central Africa to Tripoli drew, as it were, converging lines which well illustrate the character of the country.

The Maghrib pilgrims, having crossed the Tunisian frontier at a gap between the dying foothills of the Atlas mountains and the sea, found themselves debouching on to a wide plain. To their right, and southwards as they moved slowly along the sea shore, lay an endless flat desert of gravel and salt marsh, where the Sahara, no longer confined, came almost to the sea. Ahead of them lay a dark green line of palm trees, the first of the long string of coastal oases which ran eastwards at intervals for two hundred miles, and contained the principal towns and villages of the central province of Tripoli. For about twenty days, their route took them along these fertile and populated oases, pausing at the towns of Zuara and Tripoli, skirting the deserted ruins of the Roman cities of Sabratha and Leptis Magna.[1] This was an easy section of the long journey ahead. The coastal towns and villages

[1] The two cities, originally Greek settlements, which, with Tripoli, called originally Oea, gave the name 'tripolis' (three cities) to the area.

watered by a series of surface wells contained the gardens of dates and olives, and green fodder for their animals. From Tripoli town, outside whose walls they camped to be joined by more pilgrims, they made their way along a straight stretch of track, still sheltered by palms, to the easternmost town of the province, Misurata. Here they were forced to stay a few days while they prepared for the long and arduous march which lay ahead.

At Misurata, the character of the coastline suddenly changes, leaving the cool, dark line of the palm trees behind and plunging abruptly southwards for nearly a hundred miles through the desert wastes of the great bay of Sirte, a wide sweep of coast, hot, arid and lifeless, where the Sahara desert comes right down to the sea, cutting Tripolitania from Cyrenaica by five hundred miles of sand, salt marshes and steep dry channels of ancient water-courses. For days the caravan crept with difficulty through this desert region until, at the small oasis of Agheila, the coast turned north again towards the Cyrenaican frontier.

From Benghazi, the first town of the province, there began a slow climb from the sea coast to the slopes of the Jebel Akhdar, the mountain range running west to east along the sea's edge, with steep cliffs running down to the water. Here, they passed within view of the capital of the province, Derna, lying below in a small bay. This once again was a pleasant part of the journey; the Jebel Akhdar contained fields of grain and olives, among which they would skirt the tumbled stones of the site of the ancient Greek colony of Cyrene. Then slowly, the character of the land changed again; they left the fertile slopes of the so-called 'green mountain', and entered the rolling waterless hillsides of that area called the Marmarica, which at length brought them to a halt at the steep descent of the Halfaya, from which, at the frontier of Egypt, they could look down on the plains of Egypt and the town of Sollum.

But this journey, hard as it may have seemed to Meccan pilgrims, was as nothing to the travail facing those other caravans which, after crossing the southern frontiers of the Fezzan, coming from the regions of Lake Chad, of Bornu and the areas of the

Niger river, made their unhappy way slowly northwards. These were the long columns of yoked and chained negro slaves, which for centuries had been relentlessly driven northwards to the slave markets of Tripoli.

Assembled at Murzuk, capital of the Fezzan, they were faced with a slow and painful journey across some of the worst country of the vast Sahara desert. After leaving the brackish pools of Murzuk, the last major oasis for many days, they were driven across the sand seas and gravel plains which slowly climb to the great central plateau, the ancient watershed between the coastal provinces and the Fezzan. Here, for days they crawled past the skirts of the black mountains, the *haruj el aswad*, and with little remaining water, began the slow and painful crossing of the dreaded *hammada el hamra*, the endless waterless flat plain, spreading for 40,000 square miles, whose surface was covered with sharp flints which reflected back a merciless sun. Here they left their dead in such numbers that European travellers could follow their route through the trackless waste by the bones lining the wayside.

Such as survived this terrible crossing, now reached a landscape of steep, dry watercourses, whence in geological times, the plateau drained north-eastwards into the gulf of Sirte. Here, the caravans picked their way past patches of green where rain had been conserved by the heaps of broken stone which had once formed the sites of Roman farms and dams. After several days climbing and descending steep rocky banks which form the sides of this series of *wadis*, they at length began a slow descent to the *jefara*, the semi-desert area flanking the coastal oases, and so, by slow degrees through areas populated by the Beduin tribesmen across the last fifty miles of this nightmare journey, to the walls of Tripoli city, and the slave markets of Europe.

Waterless and unproductive as was most of the terrain of this Barbary Regency, it was, in fact, an open door from the Sahara to the sea, and so, from central Africa, through Tripoli to the cities of Europe. Since Tripoli also stood midway between Egypt and the rich cities of the Maghrib, it formed a cross-roads of trade routes which made it strategically more important than the richer provinces of Tunis and Algiers.

So placed, from earliest recorded history, Tripoli has been a site for foreign invasion and occupation. Phoenician, Greek, Roman, Vandal, Byzantine—they have followed one another across the centuries, conquering, but never extirpating, the indigenous Berber tribesmen, the earliest inhabitants of north Africa. Traces of Tripoli's long period of occupation as a Roman province are still in evidence, and until the 7th century, the country, its desert areas watered by the skills of Roman hydrography in the form of dams and aqueducts, was relatively fertile, and at times was so productive that it supplied grain for markets in Europe. But in that century began the first Arab invasions from the Hedjaz, bringing Islam as a religion to the Christian Berbers, and the nomadic way of life to the country. During the successive centuries, the essentially nomadic life of the Arab tribes, who after driving the Berbers into the mountain areas, settled down to occupy all of the provinces, led to a gradual breakdown of water conservation and the return of the desert to its original state. The economy of the country slowly slid to a state of virtual collapse.

From 1510 to 1553, Tripoli had a brief period once more under Christian rule when Ferdinand of Spain captured the town and ceded it to the Knights of Malta. But in 1553, their tenuous hold on the city was broken by the Turkish corsairs, Dragut and Sinan, who were the forerunners of the Ottoman invasion of the western Mediterranean. The corsairs only occupied it for a short time, being unable to hold the city with their limited resources in men. They ceded it to the Sultan of Turkey. It was to remain nominally under the control of the Sublime Porte for the next three hundred years.

The Ottoman system of rule and administration in its widely separated provinces in Asia and Africa was based on that of the Sultan in Constantinople; it was simple and drastic, and was retained by the Karamanli Bashaws during their period of rule, with minor modifications. Some description of it is therefore necessary.

The Sultan appointed the Governors or Pashas of his provinces by *firman* or royal decree, and they were despatched from Constantinople with full powers to rule their provinces, with the stipulation that they sent an annual sum to the treasury and obeyed the Sultan's commands in relation to foreign affairs. They were appointed originally for a period of three years—a precaution against an unwelcome accretion of power or influence in their hands, after which they were either recalled—or re-appointed by the issue of another *firman*.

Like the Sultan, the Pasha was supposed to be guided in affairs of state and in local administration by a Divan, a Council of seniors aided by local notables, and in maritime affairs by a *taiffa*, or corporation of sea captains under the Capudan Pasha, or admiral of the fleet. The principal military aide was the *Bey du Camp*, a Turkish Agha or senior officer, who commanded the *janissary* troops and was, among other duties, responsible for security of the Regency and for the annual tour made for the collection of revenue.

On the civil side, the Pasha's chief minister was the chamberlain or Grand Kehya who controlled the administration of internal affairs and the Pasha's Secretariat, and headed the Divan. He was aided by the Little, or Piccolo, Kehya who supervised, among other matters, the system of Protocol, the secretariat for foreign affairs, and the pay of the Pasha's Palace guards (who though for security were not under the Agha of the *janissaries*). Below these two officers, there was a hierarchy of officials, bearing various titles, who controlled matters of public health, conservation of bread supplies, purchase and sale of slaves and supervision of the locally appointed Mukhtars or chiefs of city and town quarters who reported on sanitation, security and the relations between the religious minorities. On the military side, a series of Aghas, or military officers, helped to administer the police, the customs office, the *janissary* barracks and the liaison with the *Kuloghlis* outside the city.

The civil and criminal law was firmly based on the 7th-century Islamic code, whose framework was the *Qur'an* and the *Traditions of the Prophet Mohammed*—a corpus of regulations which covered all aspects of a Moslem's religious, civic and domestic life.

In serious cases, the administration of the civil law was carried out by the Pasha himself, or by the Grand Kehya, sitting daily in Divan in the audience chamber. The Pasha was assisted by the Mufti, his advisor on any complicated interpretations of Islamic law, and by the Qadi, the religious administrator in all questions affecting inheritance, marriage and divorce. In criminal cases, the Pasha himself was usually the judge; and all judgments, whether right or wrong, had the virtue of being immediate, and with penalties, even death, being frequently administered on the spot.

In one way, the system devised by the Ottoman Turks for the administration of their vast empire of conflicting races and religions, had the virtue of simplicity: 'That which cements all breaches, and cures all these wounds in this Body Politick,' wrote the historian Rycaut, 'is the quickness and severity of their justice . . . which makes almost every crime equal, and punishes it with the last and extremest chastisement, which is death . . .'[1]

Death was the supreme solution to all problems affecting the State. It lay in the Pasha's hands to administer at his will. For in the final issue, as with his master the Sultan, the Divan and its ministers, the interpretations of the Mufti, the judgment of the Qadi, were always subject to the character of the Pasha himself, from whose whims there was no redress. It was perhaps the only method that the unruly peoples of the Sultan's domains could understand. Rycaut again comments:

> In this Government severity, violence and cruelty are natural to it, and it were as great an errour to begin to loose the reins and ease the people of that oppression to which they and their fore-fathers have since their first original been accustomed, as it would be in a Nation free born . . . to change their Liberty into servitude and slavery.

---

[1] Paul Rycaut, *History of the Ottoman Empire.*

Yet the Pasha himself was in reality dependent on the loyalty and quality of the Turkish troops who were the real enforcement of his authority and security of his person. It was the *janissaries* who stood behind him in real control of the Regency.

The Turkish *janissaries* were the creation of the first Ottoman Sultans. Originally they were military pages for the Sultan's protection and were drawn from Christian children, either captured or bought from Asia Minor. Trained for years in Constantinople in complete obedience to the Sultan, converted to Islam and taught the arts of war, they had formed the so-called 'new troops', the *yeni ceri*, spearhead of the first Ottoman victories. But through the centuries, they had inevitably declined in quality. No longer were they taken as children and trained in discipline, obedience and devotion to the Sultans. They were recruited from the streets of Constantinople and the Levantine seaports. By the 17th century, they had degenerated to what a contemporary observer called 'the scum of the People'.[1] Their decline in the Ottoman provinces was perhaps also the result of their way of life. The status of the *janissary*, and the military rules under which he was controlled, gave him a position of mixed licence and constraint. He was exempt from taxation and from any work apart from his military duties; he was free from any sanction of the civil law; yet he was kept in barracks and forbidden to marry. He lived therefore for long periods in a condition of enforced idleness, a prey to ambition and greed. Here, as in the military barracks in Tunis, Algiers and Constantinople lay the seeds of revolt that were eventually to bring the Ottoman system of rule to disaster.

While the *janissaries* were the Pasha's main support for control of the Regency, they were only foot-soldiers. There was an auxiliary force of cavalry available for use in assisting the *janissaries* in the subjugation of the Arab tribes and the collection of revenue in the interior. This, comparable with the Spahis in

[1] Paul Rycaut.

Turkey, was a force of mounted levies called *Kuloghlis*[1] who, in return for their services as unpaid auxiliaries, were exempt from taxation. They were the offspring of civilian Turks who had settled in the Regency and had married Arab women. When not serving with the *janissaries*, they were small landowners and merchants, and consequently had closer contacts with Arabs and Berbers than was possible for the alien Turks. But, though useful, they were suspect to the *janissary* Aghas, as a source of possible trouble. Strict regulations therefore controlled them. They were obliged to live outside the towns, and were forbidden to enter the city of Tripoli without obtaining permission, which was only given when they left their arms outside the gates. They lived, under the control of their own elected Aghas mainly in the palm oases and gardens outside the towns.

The main body of these *Kuloghlis* and their commander, lived outside Tripoli city. Here, about a mile from the south gate and across the foreshore, lay an oasis of palm trees, gardens and villages, known as the *menshia*.[2] Within this oasis, which was the garden of Tripoli, lay a labyrinth of sandy lanes running between hedges of Indian fig, and well-pits where oxen drew the water to irrigate the plots of green peppers and lucerne. Here were the summer retreats of the Tripoli notables in a forest of palm, fig, pomegranate, jasmine and olive trees, where also were the small villages, the houses, the stables, mosques and gardens of the *Kuloghlis*. And here, remote from the heat and turmoil of the city, was the birthplace of the Karamanli Bashaws.[3]

The civil population of the Regency inevitably was a mixture of race and religion—the result of the many invasions and emigrations which had swept over and into the country. Turks, Moors,

[1] From the Turkish 'kul-oghli', meaning 'sons of slaves'; but not a derogatory term, since all the Sultan's officials were called his slaves.

[2] Probably Arabic, and meaning 'place of growth'.

[3] Tradition makes the Karamanli family the offspring of a Turk from Caramania, who came to Tripoli with the pirate Dragut, married an Arab woman, and settled in the *menshia*.

Arabs,[1] Berbers, Jews (of two rites), Moriscos, and negroes, jostled each other in the streets of the towns and villages. With them were Christians, mainly Catholics, from Malta, Sicily, France and Spain. The Turks were the overlords, respected and feared, the Moors were mostly merchants, the Arabs breeders of camels and goats; the Moriscos, a community, much feared for their temperament, of mixed Spanish and Arab blood, were emigrés from the Spanish reconquest of Granada. The Jews were mainly Sephardic who had fled from Spain at the same period as the Moriscos,[2] and the negroes were either slaves or the children of slaves—and many Arabs and Moors had a tincture of negro blood. The settled Christians were few—some Maltese and Italian merchants and seamen, a handful of French and English merchants, and a small, devoted Mission of Catholic Fathers from France who, by the Islamic concept of religious toleration, were permitted to work in Tripoli for the redemption of captives and the religious supervision of the slaves in the Pasha's *bagnios*.

Finally, there were the few European consuls and their dependants, and that strange group of Europeans, mainly Italians, known as the 'renegades'. These men, who must have mixed oddly with the rest of the European community, but who were to play a considerable part in the future of the Regency, were adventurers from seaports, deserters from ships, sometimes escaped criminals, who had renounced their faith and taken Islam and thus obtained lucrative work in the Turkish administration, where they gave their skills and literacy to their masters.

Beyond the towns and villages of the coastal area, in the relatively remote and hilly regions of the Jebel Nefusa[3] and the towns of Gharian and Tarhuna, were settled the Berber tribes, the original inhabitants of the country, who had been driven thither

[1] The word 'Moor' was used by contemporary writers to describe the settled Arab or Berber of the towns. 'Arab' always meant Beduin.

[2] There was another colony of Jews, living in the Berber areas of Gharian, who were refugees from the Ptolemaic persecutions of 200 B.C.

[3] The mountain range running parallel with the coast, about forty-five miles south of Tripoli town.

in the first Moslem invasions of the 8th century. Skilled and stubborn merchants and peasants, they ruled themselves under their own elected councils and, although forced to take Islam, had kept their own language and customs untouched, and had little contact with their Turkish overlords except the payment of their taxes.

The Arab tribes, living in their *diras* or tribal areas, in nearly the same tribal confederations as when they had left Arabia in the 8th century, were spread over all the habitable areas of the desert in all three provinces of the Regency. They were ruled by Beduin law and, apart from the payment of taxes and the sale of camels and horses to them, had little contact with the towns, which, in any case, they were forbidden to enter without permission. They were feared, and rightly so, for they had a constant predilection for reverting to their natural propensity for tribal raiding on villages, caravans and each other. Their control depended entirely on a strong central government and on drastic punishment.

The administration of the three provinces, such as it was, was conducted from the Castle. This large, untidy conglomeration of buildings, surrounded by high walls, rising from bedrock, and resting upon Byzantine and Spanish foundations, stands in the form of a rough quadrilateral at the south-eastern angle of the city walls. Its four bastions are sited to overlook the entrance to Tripoli harbour from the north, to cover the entrance to the city from the south, and thus from the *menshia*, and to face the city below, to the west. Its guns could thus control both the sea and land approaches, and if necessary, the city itself. Two narrow gates in the high walls gave the only access to the interior. One, facing the city, led across a narrow and easily defended ramp, and this was the main entrance; the other, used mainly by the Pasha and the *taiffa*, gave direct access to the shipping at the Marine.

Behind the unscaleable walls of the Castle lay an irregular series of chambers, courtyards, covered passageways, stairs, armouries, kitchens, stables and barracks; there was a small mosque, a hidden strong room for the Treasury, and even an apothecary's shop. Here in close confinement were housed the Pasha, his *harim* of wives and concubines, his personal guards, his Treasury and Secretariat, his garrison of *janissaries* and their servants and, far below floor level, were his dungeons housing never less than a few hundred Christian slaves.

An official visitor calling on the Pasha in Divan, after crossing the narrow causeway leading from the city, passed through the closely guarded entrance and into an office in which sat the Grand Kehya. When his papers had been examined, he was conducted by an armed guard through what seemed a veritable labyrinth of dark passages. He stumbled his way along a crumbling floor with many twists and turns, half blocked by the shadowy figures of guards, past a series of heavy doors, lapped with iron plates, emerging at intervals into small courtyards, open to the sky but barred with iron gratings, surrounded by galleries supported on carved arches bright with tiles. At length he reached the audience chamber, its doors heavily guarded and the entrance surrounded by the numerous supplicants for the Pasha's justice. Within was a large room whose magnificence contrasted oddly with the comparative squalor of its surroundings. Bright with carpets and cushions from Constantinople and gilt chairs from France, its innumerable mirrors reflected the deferential circle of ministers of the Divan and the visitors who stood at a safe distance from the throne. At the far end of the room, on a throne of carpets and tasselled cushions, sat the Pasha himself, his personal guard surrounding him, and his inevitable pipe close at hand.

No one entered the Castle of Tripoli without a sense of gloom and unease.[1] An atmosphere of fear haunted these dark passages

[1] Several European visitors wrote of the feeling of miasma which the Castle passage-ways engendered. Miss Tully (in *Narrative of Ten Years' Residence at Tripoli* by Richard Tully) wrote that they gave her the feeling of leading 'to some dreadful abode for the entombing of the living'. The traveller Mathuisieulx (author of *A Travers la Tripolitanie*) was in the Castle in 1902, when workmen were repairing a water cistern. Some few feet below the soil they uncovered skeletons twisted in strange shapes. '*Prets a remuer dans l'ombre,*' wrote the Frenchman, recoiling from the sight.

and courtyards. For Turks, reared in the shadow of the Grand Serail in Constantinople, this fear was endemic; treachery and distrust were part of the Turkish psychology. It spread everywhere in the Castle of Tripoli. At night, though the iron doors separating the various parts of the Castle were bolted against each other, the heavy entrance gate to the Castle was locked by the *Piccolo Kehya*, and the key handed ceremoniously to the Pasha who slept with it under his pillow.

The Pasha of Tripoli, from the western bastions of the Castle, could look down on the city sprawled below. By the 17th century, Tripoli contained a population of about 30,000. Sited on a rocky outcrop of land which extends into the bay of Tripoli, washed on its northern and eastern flanks by the sea, its south-eastern side covered by the Castle, it was in a strong position for defence, in particular from the direction of the sea, where a series of reefs extend from the harbour mole across the bay, leaving only a narrow entrance for shipping and providing a natural harbour.

Behind high walls, surrounded by a deep ditch, the city spread over several acres. It was roughly divided into Quarters, separated from one another by heavy gates, which were shut at sunset, cutting off from each other the different religious, racial and military sections of the population. Here, between the dwelling houses, the market squares, the caravanserais of the merchants, the military barracks, and the interminable mosques, ran a series of sandy lanes—the only streets—sloping seawards, their centres trenched with ditches down which ran the refuse of the town. The populace, on foot or mounted, picked their way through an untidy huddle of whitewashed buildings which turned blank walls upon the streets, winding past dark archways, the open doors of mosques and openings here and there, to open spaces with bazaars and coffee houses set in the shade of fig trees.

Above the streets, on the flat rooftops and screened by reed mats, the Moslem women, forbidden the streets, led a secret life of their own, calling to each other—their only converse with the outside world—as they dried their clothing or laid out their peppers and figs to ripen in the sun.

About the streets moved the camels and donkeys of the merchants; the Moors in their white woollen cloaks; the Jews in their obligatory black garments; *janissaries* in muslins and silver embroideries; hordes of beggars, and, here and there, followed always by a group of idlers and urchins, the *marabouts* or holy men, both the inspiration and terror of the devout and ignorant Moslems. Occasionally, hurrying on foot or horseback from his house near the Marine gate, came a solitary European consul on his way to a Divan, guarded by two *janissaries* and followed by his dragoman. He might well pass on his way a dismal file of Christian slaves, clanking by in their chains to work, doomed mostly without redemption, to a life of penury and unending toil.

How did they live, this large mixed community, perched on the north African coast, surrounded by deserts, and with few natural resources? Roman skill in perfecting the conservation of rainfall had once made large areas of the country capable of supporting a considerable population. Roman roads had spanned the country and garrisoned forts had guarded the caravan routes from central Africa, down which had formerly passed a stream of merchandise. But, as before stated, Arab and Turkish neglect had led to the inevitable collapse of the system of water conservation, and the return of large areas to natural desert.

Driven thus to rely on its own shrinking resources, the country lived on what was at best a fluctuating and marginal economy: the cultivation of some wheat and barley, olive oil from the Berber areas of the Jebel Nefusa, the sale of meat and hides, the preparation of woollen and leather goods, the occasional sale of dates to Malta and Sicily. On the production and export of these, the country in good years could survive. But in this part of north Africa there were always other forces threatening the economy. The country was subject to periods of severe drought which led to starvation; and there was the constant threat of bubonic plague, endemic in Africa, which not only decimated the population, but closed the port of Tripoli, the only contact for supplies from the outer world. There were times when the country suffered from drought and plague simultaneously.

On this marginal and precarious economy, the Turkish overlords of north Africa, could never have maintained their expensive Courts, paid their *janissaries* and sent their revenues to Constantinople. They needed money from some other source. That source was at hand, and came naturally to a predatory and aggressive race: it was piracy at sea.

Below the Castle walls in Tripoli, to the west, was the small, rock-bound inner harbour in which the Pasha's corsair[1] fleet lay, either fitting for their annual Spring cruises, or laid up for the winter months. Since the 15th century, the North African coast had been a useful base for the activities of corsair vessels. Standing within sailing range of the Mediterranean off Sicily and Malta, and using low lying craft, stripped and specially lightened to afford space for the greatest number of captives and booty, the pirates from Algiers, Tunis and Tripoli could attack the slow and unarmed merchant ships on the trade routes to the Levant. The Barbary Turks were to prove adept at this form of warfare and regarded it as legitimate. They were at war, they declared, with every nation that had not made a peace treaty and financial arrangements with them. This, the great maritime nations such as Britain, France and Holland had been willing to do, and their shipping was relatively unmolested, though not always entirely so. It was the smaller maritime trading nations—Venice, Genoa, Greece, Malta, Sicily, the Papal States and Spain—who suffered. The great maritime States could, with their navies, have combined to suppress the Barbary corsairs at any time, should they have wished to do so. But it was not in their interests. One of the most valuable outlets for merchant shipping in the Mediter-

[1] Legally, the Barbary raiders were corsairs, and not pirates, since they carried letters of *marque* from their governments; but the distinction was small. The words have always been used synonymously.

ranean was the carrying trade operating between its ports, and all maritime nations competed for this. It was therefore essential to London, Paris and the Hague that the smaller nations with their adjacent Mediterranean ports and handy vessels should be suppressed. The cynicism of this manœuvre was emphasised by Louis XIV, who is alleged to have remarked: 'If there had not been an Algiers, I would have had to make one.'

Thus partly legitimised, Mediterranean piracy, whether practised by the Barbary corsairs, or the Greek, Sicilian or Maltese privateers who also, though in smaller numbers, operated in these seas had, by the 17th century, become a carefully conducted business enterprise, embarked on by both Moslem and Christian merchants, from both sides of the Mediterranean, on an agreed scale of share and profit. Slaves were valuable merchandise, and it was not unknown for Moslem and Christian merchants to invest jointly in a piratical enterprise. In all cases this was directed towards the capture of Christian slaves, for Moslems were forbidden by an injunction in the *Qur'an* from making slaves of fellow Moslems.

Strict rules controlled the conduct of the Moslem corsairs at sea. Their activities were under the general supervision of the *taiffa*, or council of sea captains, who themselves came under the direction of the Rais of the Marine, or Capudan Pasha who, by the nature of this complicated task, was frequently a European renegade. From his office at the Marine gate, where he supervised the arrival and departure of all merchant shipping, he worked in close liaison with the European consuls, who acted for nations in treaty relations with the Regency. Through him, the European consuls operated the ingenious system of ships' passes which protected their shipping at sea.

By international agreement, every Mediterranean consul from the Christian States was issued by his government with special passports. These consisted of sheets of paper covered with heavily engraved designs which, after signature, could be divided in half. The bottom sheets of these passes were passed to the Rais of the

Marine, who issued them to the corsair captains before they left port. The top halves were then issued to the captains of merchant vessels by the consul before their ships sailed. If stopped at sea, the captain produced his half of the passport, which the corsair captain could fit to his half. If they fitted the ship was allowed to go on its way undisturbed. It was a simple system for a mainly illiterate people. Other passes were also issued to the corsair captains by the consuls. This left them free to operate if stopped by a warship of the country concerned.

With these documents in hand, and the provisioning and manning of his ship completed, the corsair captain went aboard his vessel and broke a green flag at its masthead, a signal for his crew to go aboard. The composition of a corsair crew was equally ruled by the regulations of the *taiffa*. The crew of each vessel was obliged to include, apart from the captain, or Rais, a scribe or *khoja* to supervise documents, a purser in control of supplies, a trained gunner, some few *janissary* soldiers, and a crew of Moors with some Arabs. No man was allowed to carry aboard more than a musket, a scimitar and dagger, and a small bundle of food. Every inch of space on the small deck was to be reserved for captives and booty.

The cruising areas of the corsairs were carefully laid down by the *taiffa*, and usually lasted for about one month for each vessel during the spring and summer season. Life on board was hard. There was no cover from the elements except a small cabin in which the Rais and his clerk kept the ship's documents. On the open decks, the crew, their captives and the booty lay exposed to sun and sea. Food soon ran short, water began to stink, and the whole ship, as many captives testified, swarmed with vermin.

But if life was hard, so were these men. Their vessels, fast and lying low in the water, would select a position just off the merchant shipping lanes and lie below the horizon, watching for the topsails of a passing ship. When a ship was seen, the corsair came into action. The flag of some harmless neutral country was hoisted at the masthead, the crew concealed themselves below the gunwales, while a helmsman, dressed as a European, stood in view at the tiller.

A course parallel to the ship was then laid so as to allay suspicion, and the corsair vessel would slowly close the distance between the ships. When close enough it would suddenly dart forward and swing alongside its quarry. Then, at a signal, uttering blood-curdling yells to paralyse resistance, the motley and terrifying crew would leap to the bulwarks. The sudden apparition of a savage crew, their fearful cries—'*orribili, spaventosi gridi*' as an Italian slave recollected—would paralyse the crew of a small merchant ship. 'I know not,' wrote the Italian slave, Pananti, 'what chilling hand oppresses the Christian heart on the appearance of the Barbary corsairs; like the head of Medusa it seems to petrify every person on board.'

If there were time, before the actual boarding, a strange agitation would shake the Christians. The captain hurried to jettison the ship's papers to confuse identification; the richer passengers would tear off rings and rich clothing and huddle into old clothes to reduce the price of their possible ransom, and frequently would dirty their hands and faces, so as to be taken for members of the crew.

There was a rush for cover as the corsairs leaped aboard, and resistance from the passengers could meet with death. But the passengers were in most cases treated with comparative gentleness once the corsair crew were in possession, for they were valuable cargo. The ship's papers, if retained, were then examined by the clerk of the Rais. If a passport in the form of a 'top' correctly fitted the engraving on the 'bottom' of the paper held by the corsair, the ship was allowed to proceed on its way unharmed, with all its booty returned. If there was any doubt about the ship's origins and the nationality of those on board, some of the passengers were taken aboard the corsair, the rest with a scratch crew from the corsair, were sent to a selected rendezvous to be taken later into port. Meanwhile the Rais assisted by the *khoja* began an interrogation of the captives, whose names were entered on a list with estimates of their values adjoined. Not infrequently to make them talk, the bastinado was administered. Cast suddenly from the comparative comfort and safety of their normal lives into this nightmare world of slavery the Christians would mostly lie dazed awaiting the awful future which probably lay ahead.

The return to harbour of a Tripoli corsair with its prizes was usually announced by a *feu de joie* of cannon from ship to shore. As the sound echoed in the harbour, the European consuls from their houses by the Marine gate, would mount to their roof-tops with their spy-glasses to fix the flag of the captured ship, which by custom was always flown at the masthead of the corsair vessel, below the striped flag of Tripoli. There is no record of the varied emotions aroused in consular breasts when the strip of bunting swam into focus, and below could be discerned the narrow decks lined with gesticulating Turks and Moors, behind which must have been glimpsed the despairing faces of the captured slaves.

It now became the duty of every consul to collect his documents—the certificates of ships under British, French or Dutch protection—don his ceremonial uniform and proceed, accompanied by his dragoman and clerk, to the great hall of the Divan in the Castle. Here, the consuls were seated in order of precedence at some distance from the Pasha's throne. Behind them stood the ministers of the Divan, the row of sea-captains, the *janissary* and negro guards; behind again, the armourers, clerks, the Moorish merchants and the huddle of Christian prisoners, already wearing their chains.

According to tradition, the Pasha would now be heard arriving in state, preceded by the rhythmic drum-beat and wail of timbrels of his court musicians. A file of stiff *janissaries* in resplendent court uniforms and carrying his staff of Three Horsetails[1] followed, and finally the Pasha himself dressed in silks and diamonds. A

[1] Horsetails, a relic of the nomadic origins of the Ottoman Turks, and a mark of seniority among Governors. The Sultan carried four, his senior Governors three, the rest of the Barbary provinces carried only two. This favour ranked Tripoli with Budapest and Baghdad.

table was set for the Grand Kehya, the armourers approached with their hammers and chisels, and the consuls resumed their seats and examined their papers.

The main purpose of this meeting in full Divan was to establish the legitimacy of the captures. As the name of each slave was called out, there would be cries from the slave for succour, and from time to time a consul would rise, interrupt, and formally claim a slave as under his protection. The consul's papers would be examined, there would be a debate between the consul's clerk and that of the Grand Kehya, and then a sudden gesture from the Pasha either of agreement or refusal; and the slave would sink back in despair, or rise at the formal pronouncement of the Grand Kehya, 'You are free!' and would hold out his limbs for the armourers to strike off his chains.

As with all else, the regulations regarding the validity of captures were complicated and strictly observed.[1] Vessels, crews and passengers of nations in treaty relations either with Tripoli or the Porte were automatically redeemed and all captured property returned. But nationals of these countries, if acting as crews (not passengers) aboard vessels from countries with whom Tripoli considered herself at war, were legitimate prizes, and put to slavery.

Christian slaves of rank or property, who had resources to purchase their redemption, practised various devices to conceal their value and thus reduce their ransom, but the Tripoli Jews were particularly cunning in detecting a slave's true value by examination of hands and person, speech and general demeanour. They were also called in to question other slaves to determine their value in the various trades, so that artificers, accountants, etc., could be set aside to work for the Pasha and his chief ministers.

The life of a Christian slave varied greatly, according to his

[1] The shares from the sale of slaves and booty, including shipping, were divided, according to regulations laid down by the *taiffa*, between the merchant financiers, the captains and crews of the corsair ships. The Pasha, who received a percentage of all sales, also had the right to first choice among the slaves for his own *bagnio*.

skills and the character of his master. Most writers are agreed that they had a better chance of a reasonable life in Moslem hands than had Moslems in the hands of Christians.[1] Both the *Qur'an* and the *Traditions of the Prophet* enjoin on the Moslem kindness to slaves. This was, of course, frequently ignored. While literate and intelligent slaves could often rise to high positions under their masters[2] and indeed, if willing to turn Moslem gain their release from slavery and obtain key posts in the administration, the lot of the ordinary slave, illiterate and slow, could often be hopeless and grindingly cruel. They were kept almost permanently in chains, fed on a subsistence diet and put to continuous labour of the hardest kind.

The fate of the few women prizes can be imagined. Fair and attractive ones fetched a high price and went into the *harims* of the Pasha or his officers, where they were usually fairly well treated; their worst sufferings, apart from boredom, being perhaps their constant almost forcible stuffing with bread soaked in sugar to get them to the most attractive state of corpulence. Others, less favoured, were sold to the Tripoli merchants, who frequently induced them to take Islam and then married them, when they immediately lost their status as slaves. Many disappeared into the shuttered, isolated life of Islam and were never seen again in the outside world.

Yet in spite of their complete servitude, the Christian slaves in North Africa had certain inalienable rights, granted them by religious doctrine, which Moslem slaves in the *bagnios* at Malta, Marseilles or Genoa did not have. They could freely practice their religion, a surprisingly humane and tolerant attitude on the part of their captors which is not generally emphasised in most of the outraged records of Christians who were captured by the corsairs of Tripoli and forced to become slaves.

[1] In 1684, Louis XIV had five hundred Huguenot prisoners marched in chains from Paris to Toulon, where they were condemned to the living death of the galleys. There was small hope for Moslem captives in such hands.

[2] Cervantes was a slave of the Turks; so were Lucas, the English traveller and consul, and the American consuls Eaton and Cathcart.

There were further indulgences allowed in obedience to the *Traditions of the Prophets*. Work for slaves must cease daily three hours before sunset and there was no work at all on Fridays, the Moslem Sabbath. Slaves were also entitled to a small share of prize money allotted to any corsair vessel on which they had worked as carpenters, gunners or armourers. Most important of all, they were allowed, on payment of a small sum to the Treasury, to open taverns for the sale of wine, an enterprise forbidden to Moslems by the *Qur'an*. These small taverns flourished all over the Barbary Regencies, even in the slave *bagnios* themselves, and were very popular with the Moors and *janissaries*.[1]

It was a strange mixture of bondage and licence that characterised the life of the Christian slave in the Moslem world.

While the income from the sale or ransom of white slaves, the plunder from shipping, and the subsidies paid for freedom of passage helped to replenish the Tripoli treasury,[2] another, more marginal, but important source of income came from the sale of black slaves in the Tripoli slave markets. These continued to arrive in a trickle down the hazardous caravan routes from central Africa. But the numbers of this valuable commodity were entirely dependent on the strength of the Pasha's government and the control it maintained over the desert routes. If this control slackened, the income from it correspondingly diminished, and consequently the capital to invest in the corsair cruises became scarce, and they were reduced in number. The result of this was that the pay of the *janissaries* fell into arrears, discipline deteriorated and to complete the vicious circle, security in the desert areas was further neglected. In the final issue, the strength of the Pasha and his ministers and their control over the *janissaries* was the deciding factor.

*   *   *

[1] Cathcart, the American sailor who became a slave in Algiers, was allowed by his captors to run several taverns. He later became consul in Tripoli.

[2] There was a small market for boy slaves in Britain and France, and a ready market for all types of slave in Cairo, Constantinople and Morocco.

Apart from merchants and the occasional traveller, the Regency, during the period of direct Ottoman rule, had little first-hand contact with Europe.

The first European consuls had been accredited to Tripoli in the 17th century. France, with her special interests in the Mediterranean, was the first to realise the necessity of coming to terms with the Barbary States, whose activities she wished to control, but whose existence she wished to preserve. Through the Marseilles Chamber of Commerce she had appointed a consul to Tripoli in 1630. Britain followed in 1658 and, in 1675, when British commerce was still being put at risk, a treaty of peace was extorted from the Pasha, after Charles II's admiral, Sir John Narborough, had burned the corsair shipping in Tripoli harbour.[1]

From this period British and French consuls were resident in Tripoli, and it will be seen that the *leitmotiv* of part of the following history is their struggle for influence and precedence at the Court of Tripoli and for the trade in the Regency. It was soon realised at the Court of St. James that a trading consul of the type operating in European ports was not sufficient for the special conditions in Tripoli, and that such consuls, like the French, should be granted semi-diplomatic status and be paid a salary, with an extra sum for expenditure on so-called 'extraordinaries', for the giving of presents, entertainment and the redemption where necessary of corsair captures. To supplement this income they were allowed to charge consulage fees for British shipping.[2]

With all the coincident hazards of life for Europeans in this primitive and fanatic city—climate, disease, famine, revolution—the consuls were always better treated than their colleagues in Tunis or Algiers. The Calendar of State papers has brief but striking references to the latter. Thus, early in the 17th century, a British consul was cut to pieces by the mob outside the Divan

[1] The signature of this treaty ended the captivity of the last British slaves ever to lie in the Tripoli *bagnios*.

[2] With the signature of the Capitulations with Turkey in 1675, the consuls were further granted some judicial and excutive power over their nationals. The British consul's salary, in 1711 was £360 p.a. plus £250 for 'extraordinaries'.

of the Dey of Algiers. In Algiers again in 1688, when some French warships bombarded the city, the French consul and forty-seven French citizens were, in sight of the ships, blown one by one from the mouth of a cannon.[1]

Consuls in both these Regencies were under constant threat of arrest and subject to humiliation at the hands of the rulers. In Tunis, for example, consuls making official calls on the Dey were obliged to leave their swords behind and crawl under a wooden bar to kiss the Dey's hand.[2] It is not surprising that European visitors sometimes found the Barbary consuls in a lamentable shape. Thus, Mr. Goddard, British consul in Tunis in 1710, was found by a naval visitor to have been kept in chains by the Bey and so ill-treated that he had become a lunatic and 'the recovery of his understanding altogether desperate'. Similarly a visitor to Algiers in 1716 had found the British consul, Le Gros, so menaced and ill-treated that he was 'sitting up in bed with a sword and a brace of pistols by his side, calling for a clergyman to give him the sacraments . . .'

Tripoli had no such records of consular ill-treatment and, in fact, the treatment of Broche the French consul's chancellor, during the heavy bombardment of Tripoli by the French in 1729, shows an intelligent magnanimity only possible in this Regency. As will be seen, there were times when the consuls seemed to dominate the ruler rather than the reverse.

A large, mostly uninhabitable territory, with great distances separating its disparate provinces; a land with a climate made unpredictable by the proximity of sea and desert; a people of mixed racial and religious origins, ignorant and fanatic; a ruler, foreign to the people, trying to rule through a semi-mutinous army; an economy always teetering on the edges of disaster, this in sum, was the Regency of Tripoli at the opening of this chronicle.

[1] R.L. Playfair, *The Scourge of Christendom*. One Frenchman was a priest. When the superstitious Moslems refused to kill him, a Dutch renegade fired the gun.

[2] As late as 1790, Joel Barlow, the American consul, was obliged to kiss the hand of the Dey of Algiers.

I

AHMED KARAMANLI

1711–1745

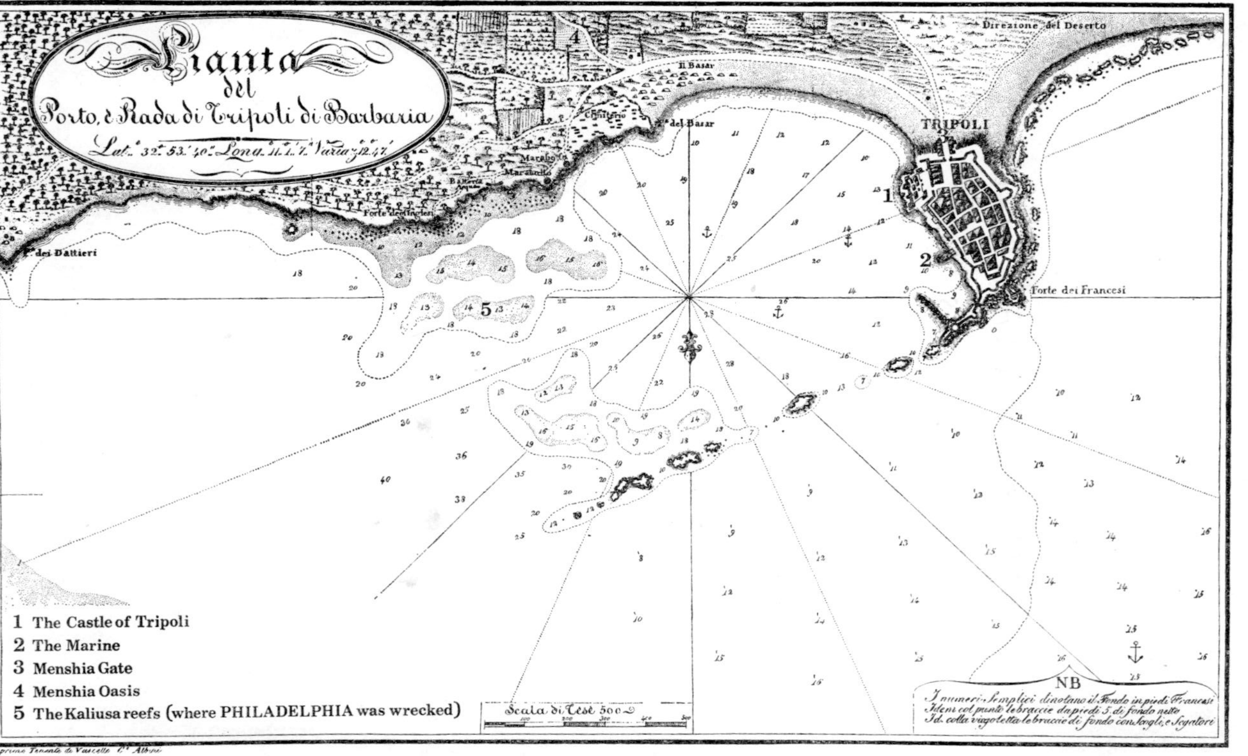

A contemporary map of Tripoli harbour

The struggle for the Throne

If the history of the Karamanli dynasty may be said to begin anywhere, it is on an April day in 1711, when the French consul in Tripoli, Poulard, sat down to write a despatch to his superiors in Marseilles.

As Poulard wrote, in an upper room facing the inner courtyard of the consulate below, he must have looked down at intervals on a huddled crowd of figures below—French merchants, Maltese sailors, Italian priests and some Jews—men, women and children, in all stages of exhaustion and disarray, surrounded by their personal possessions and bundles of food. Between them and the inner doors of the passage leading in from the street, stood the two *janissary* guards traditionally allotted as protection to each consulate, their matchlock guns in their hands, their ears cocked to the tumult in the streets outside. High above the consul's head, from the flat roof of the consulate near the Marine gate, flew the flag of the lilies of France, within view of the city and the ships in the harbour, an indication of sanctuary to fleeing Christians.[1]

It was a scene familiar to any Barbary consul in the 18th century; so familiar, in fact, that the British consul, Benjamin Lodington, from his own consulate a short distance away, listening again, as so often in his long period of service in Tripoli, to the crack of firearms, the rush of feet, the shouts, screams and constant ululation of the women from the adjoining rooftops, does not seem to have recorded the events at all. It is to Poulard, therefore, that we are indebted for the sole, brief eye-witness account of the opening scenes which led to the advent of the Karamanlis.

Poulard, since his arrival in Tripoli three years earlier, had

[1] The assumption by the King of France of the rôle of protector of all Catholic Christians gave the French consul a particularly wide area of responsibility. At this early date, the British consul had no such problems.

watched the situation in the Regency gradually approaching complete anarchy. He had been accredited by his government to Khalil Pasha, the official governor, but on arrival he had found that this post was being disputed by the *janissary* Admiral of the Fleet. Khalil Pasha retained control of the Castle, while the dissident *janissaries* had seized control of the city. For nine days the city rocked to the pounding of the Castle by the Admiral's cannon. It was during this period of the fighting that Poulard learned that about four hundred Christian slaves, locked in the dungeons of the Castle and neglected by its defenders, were dying of hunger and thirst. With some courage, he left the sanctuary of his consulate with a load of food supplies, forced his way through the opposing forces and succeeded in getting into the Castle. He saved many lives, but the supplies of the defenders, which were always dependent on the gardens of the *menshia*, dried up completely and they were forced to capitulate. The Castle fell and Khalil Pasha, after an abortive attempt to recapture the city with the aid of the *Kuloghlis* from the *menshia*, fled to Egypt.

His flight was followed by a period of complete anarchy, as divisions broke out again between the *janissaries* themselves. In as many weeks, three Deys[1] were elected by one section of the troops, murdered by others, and replaced. By the Spring of 1711, there had been such a suppression of *janissary* opposition by murder, flight or exile, that, when a particularly ruthless Dey, called Mahmoud, was elected, he was able to retain the throne for a period sufficient to cow all adversaries.

Poulard described the scenes in the city, in a terse letter, undated, but written in April:

> The Dey, having tricked the Turks who raised him by fair words, now cheats them. Every day, he drowns, strangles or exiles them. The Moors also are torturing each other. One hears nothing in this desolate city but cries, as they rob and cut each other's throats. Now, all the people regret the passing of Khalil Pasha.

[1] Dey. The word means 'uncle' in Turkish, and was a term of respect used by the *janissaries* for their own elected leaders.

With the *janissaries* subdued, and the city under his control, Mahmoud Dey seems to have felt that there now only remained one other possible threat to his authority. This was that force, always feared by the *janissaries*, which had so far kept itself clear of all political entanglements, but nevertheless was a coherent, if silent, opposition—the *Kuloghlis* of the *menshia*.[1]

As it was customary, on the arrival of a new ruler in Tripoli, to send *Kuloghli* messengers to the outlying districts, carrying documents of accession, Mahmoud Dey prepared a strategem of almost Byzantine subtlety to destroy the leader of the *Kuloghlis*, the young Ahmed Karamanli. Letters were handed to him to take to the Berber sheikhs in Gharian. These were not documents of accession, but orders to the sheikhs to execute Karamanli, for which they would be suitably rewarded.

The plot was simple, and would have been effective. If Ahmed Karamanli were killed by the tribesmen of Gharian, there could be no grounds for trouble between the *janissaries* and the *Kuloghlis* round Tripoli. In fact, it should lead to a feud between the *Kuloghlis* and the Berbers, and reduce the threats from both to Mahmoud Dey's future authority.

But if Mahmoud Dey was subtle, he was dealing with a young man of equal subtlety and resource. Ahmed Karamanli could not read but he had taken the usual scribe with him, and during the journey he made this man open the letters and read them to him. He destroyed the letters and ordered the scribe to write a new letter informing the Gharian sheikhs that they were under arrest and must return with Karamanli to Tripoli.

Six days later the sentries on the town walls saw a column of horsemen sweeping across the *jefara* plain. They were a joint force of *Kuloghlis* and Berbers, combining to overthrow the new Dey. A messenger, carrying a note from Karamanli to Mahmoud preceded them. When it was opened, the message consisted of only a few words. 'What you would have done to me, that will I now

[1] Fear of the *Kuloghlis* was endemic in the *janissaries*. In Algiers in 1690, the latter had massacred all the *Kuloghlis*.

do to you'.[1] At this grim warning, the few remaining members of Mahmoud Dey's Divan deserted him. He lost his nerve and hanged himself. The announcement of his death led to more rioting in the city. In a letter, dated August 1st, Poulard wrote: 'The Moors continue to torture each other. After Mahmoud Dey hanged himself, the same day saw three new Deys elected and then overturned by the janissaries.'

Meanwhile Ahmed Karamanli, with his mixed troops of horsemen, had reached the city gates. The gates remained shut and prudently, after marching his troops once round the walls, he withdrew to the safety of the *menshia*, where he set up a camp for reception on the edge of the oasis.

Within the city, the few remaining members of the Divan, including the *Qadi* and *Mufti*, held a short but vital discussion and then, accompanied by the *bash agha* or senior officer of the *janissaries*, the *taiffa*, the city elders and the sheikhs of the city Quarters, they opened the south gate and, advancing across the intervening sands, made their submission to their new leader. They were followed by the French and British consuls. Poulard reported himself as pleased with his reception: 'Karamanli Bey,' he wrote, and it is the first account we have of the founder of the new dynasty, 'is now reigning Bey, placed on the throne by the mountain Arabs. He is a *Kuloghli* and a very pleasant man'.

Pleasant, but what more? Whether ambition to rule sprang from this moment of chance victory, or had always been a latent force, tradition—which at this stage of his career is almost the only source—does not relate. There is no record of what he said or thought as he took up the burden of rule, amidst a multitude of dangers to his life, an exhausted treasury, an economic standstill, and a kingdom in almost complete collapse and anarchy.

His first concern must of necessity have been security—security of his own person; security of the Castle which must eventually

[1] The only source for this account of Karamanli's strategem at Gharian is the contemporary local historian, Ibn Ghalboun, whose account, quoted by Féraud, remains in the original Arabic MS. in Paris.

be his only safe base; security of the city of Tripoli itself. Without this firmly established, his reign would be short.

In those hot August nights, in the shadow of the palm trees on the edge of his own territory, the *menshia*, he must have sat brooding many hours on the carpets spread on the sand, with the close intimates of his clan around him and, beyond, a circle of watchful black slaves keeping guard. Carefully, he must have laid the plans for what was to follow. He knew his principal enemies were the remaining *janissary* Aghas, who once recovered from their surprise, would soon be poised to strike him from his place on the throne. Their removal must be his first concern.

But on the morning of the second day, after the submission of the Divan, whatever had been plotted under the stars by the *Kuloghlis* had to remain in abeyance. A new and more pressing danger had appeared. That morning a party of *Kuloghli* horsemen galloped in from the east, with the news of the appearance off the coast, near Leptis, of a flotilla of warships flying the Ottoman flag. Fishing boats making contact with the fleet as it moved slowly westwards towards Tripoli harbour, confirmed that the Turkish flotilla was under the command of a Turkish admiral and included troop transports. On board the admiral's flagship was Khalil Pasha, the deposed ruler, returning to take his place on the throne.

Captains of a different mettle than Karamanli might now have given up, retired to the *menshia* and made their submission to the Sultan's commands. But Ahmed Karamanli must have made some quick calculations. Dangerous though this threat to him appeared it had one asset. The dissident *janissary* Aghas in Tripoli who threatened his life must be even more opposed to Khalil Pasha, whom they had driven from the country. Temporarily at least, he could therefore count on their support against the invader.

By the afternoon of August 6th 1711, the Turkish flotilla had entered Tripoli bay and come to anchor in the harbour, saluted by the intermittent fire of cannon controlled by *janissaries* still loyal to the Sultan. Poulard, from the roof of his consulate, saw messengers riding with the news to the *menshia* where Karamanli and his adherents still maintained their headquarters. The Turks may rightly have been dubious of their reception, for they first sent a boat ashore carrying a herald and a scribe from the flagship. The herald landed at the Marine gate where he was met by a few officials and a crowd of hastily assembled children, dutifully crying 'Shaar Ullah—God's justice', the usual cry of welcome made for envoys of the Sultan. At the Marine gate, the herald and scribe mounted horses and rode slowly through the City, watched virtually in silence by the crowds, and then across the sands to the edge of the *menshia*, where Karamanli received them with courtesy and the traditional coffee. Here before the assembly who listened in silence, the scribe solemnly read out the Sultan's *firman* confirming Khalil Pasha once more as the appointed ruler of Tripoli.

Two days later a full meeting was held in the audience chamber of the Castle. For this the Turkish admiral, but not Khalil Pasha, came ashore with some of his staff and a *janissary* guard. Karamanli wisely did not attend, fearing a possible attempt by either the Turks or the *janissary* Aghas to seize or assassinate him. Instead he sent one of his own adherents, also a Turk.

At this meeting, to the surprise of the Turks, both the Divan and the *taiffa* refused to accept Khalil Pasha as their ruler. At one point tempers rose so high that the Turkish admiral drew his sword and threatened the officer representing Karamanli. But he thought better of this and eventually withdrew in some haste to the flagship. While he was being rowed back to the flotilla desultory firing broke out between small parties of *Kuloghlis* and some of the loyal *janissaries*, but Poulard thought this was just an attempt to show the admiral the strength of feeling in the City against Khalil Pasha.

It would now have been expected that the Turkish admiral would land his troops and impose Khalil Pasha's enthronement by force, and doubtless these had been his instructions. Instead, during the succeeding night, a number of secret messengers shuttled between the Turkish flagship in the harbour and Karamanli's encampment. Next morning to the surprise of the city, the flotilla was seen to raise anchor, tack out of the bay, and move off westwards along the coast.

At the same time Karamanli caused a report to be circulated that the refusal of the Divan and *taiffa* to accept Khalil Pasha was based on the fact that the Sultan's *firman* of appointment, drawn up in Constantinople, had been signed, not by the Sultan, but only by the Grand Vizier and was therefore invalid.

The Turkish flotilla moved slowly further westwards, within sight of the coast, tracked by parties of *Kuloghlis* and a small scout vessel from the *taiffa*. It passed close to the port of Old Tripoli, the site of the Roman town of Sabratha and on the 12th of August, came to anchor in the small harbour of Zuara among the salt boats from Venice.[1] Here, Khalil Pasha with 200 of his own adherents accompanied by 800 of the admiral's *janissaries* were set ashore. Carefully followed by *Kuloghli* pickets, these small forces advanced a few miles eastwards from Zuara and dug themselves into entrenchments among the sand covered ruins of Sabratha. For ten days they awaited battle, while the Turkish flotilla cruised apparently aimlessly up and down the adjoining coast, firing occasional shots at the rapidly increasing horsed-troops arriving from Tripoli.

By August 30th Karamanli's main body of troops had arrived, and almost immediately a mixed body of his *Kuloghlis* and Tripoli *janissaries* advanced in force on the Turkish entrenchments. As if at a pre-arranged signal, the admiral's troops deserted the entrenchments and fled to the shore, where boats from the transports were waiting to pick them up. Khalil Pasha's few remaining adherents could do nothing but fight for their lives against the overwhelming force against them. They were killed to a man. Khalil Pasha's head was cut off and sent to Tripoli, where it was exposed to view. As for the Turkish flotilla, it turned without further ado and sailed for home. It seemed clear that Ahmed Karamanli had come to some agreed piece of treachery with the Turkish admiral.

[1] Venice had a contract for a supply of salt from the salt pans at Zuara.

Poulard, the consul, was in no doubt. In a short despatch on the event he wrote: 'African gold has played a part in this. Khalil was sold to the highest bidder'.

But of the future, he was full of foreboding and wrote gloomily to Marseilles, 'The Turkish government should have been re-established, without it Tripoli is a lost country.'

Poulard, to whose alert ears in the succeeding days came many reports of plots and counter-plots among the *janissary* Aghas in their barracks, and who feared another bloody *coup* and a recrudescence of anarchy in the City, might more carefully have considered the character of the man who was now in temporary power. Ahmed Karamanli, by two skilful stratagems, had already disposed of his enemies; he must now, with equal care, have been considering how to dispose of the last major obstacle to his control of the throne.

He had returned to his house in the *menshia* where he was closely guarded by his clansmen. Daily he went to the Castle with a strong guard, including his negro slaves, the so-called *hampas*,[1] to conduct the business of state. Here, he met the *janissary* Aghas in an open and friendly manner betraying nothing of his suspicions. In a winning speech to them in September he thanked them for their help in driving away the Turks, and then invited them to a banquet at his house in the *menshia* to celebrate their victory. The invitation was accepted without fear, since the Aghas numbered about 300 and were well armed and supported.

The site of this house, long deserted,[2] could until recently still be seen, placed on a hillock, from which one could look across the green carpet of palm trees below to the seashore and the desert. The house was built in the north African style, with high windowless walls surrounding an inner courtyard from which the dwelling rooms opened. Double doors led through a narrow

[1] *Hampas* (Turkish). Black slaves attached to the persons of the Pashas, and trusted for their loyalty and obedience.

[2] The Arabs of the area have always believed it to be haunted.

passage, called the *saquiffa*, to the inner doors, and on either side of this passage were small storerooms with inner doors.

In the courtyard Karamanli awaited his guests, and as they rode up they could hear the loud shrilling of the pipes and beating of the drums of the musicians, covering all other sounds. As each Agha arrived, he dismounted and entered the double doors of the *saquiffa*. These clapped to behind him, and in the darkness of the passage, Karamanli's black *hampas*, lurking in the storerooms, seized and quickly strangled him. Thus, to quote the chronicler:[1] 'These guards assassinated the Turks, as they passed, quickly conveying the bodies into those recesses out of sight, so that the next Turk saw nothing extraordinary going on when he entered the fatal skiffer, but, quitting his horse and servants, met his fate unsuspectingly . . .'

It was thus, in the short space of an hour, that Ahmed Karamanli rid himself of some 300 of his most dangerous opponents.[2] The next day, according to the tradition, his troops ransacked the houses of the murdered Aghas and collected a large quantity of booty. Of this, a fair proportion was immediately shipped off to Constantinople for the Sultan, with a request for official recognition of his enthronement. And, as if now feeling comparatively safe, he took the decisive but necessary step of leaving the *menshia*, so long the refuge of his clan, and entering the City, took up his quarters in the Castle.

'*Un astucieux qui favorisa la Fortune*', thus Ahmed Karamanli's French biographer dismisses him.[3] But he was more than this. In the long struggle, now to begin, for the maintenance of his seat on the throne and the furtherance of his dynasty, he was to show a wider range of qualities. In war resolute and energetic, in diplomacy, crafty, patient and persuasive, with an intuitive judgment

[1] There is no reason to doubt this account, given orally to Miss Tully sixty years after the event, and accepted by all later historians.

[2] The secrecy with which this coup was carried out is probably the reason why it is not mentioned in any contemporary consular account.

[3] Charles Féraud, *Annales Tripolitaines*.

of the character of his fellow countrymen, perhaps deriving from his mixed Turkish and Arab blood, his character has, indeed, some analogy with the qualities shown by the English barons of the 13th century and the Medicis of Italy. Certainly fortune seemed to favour him, but he had the faculty of perceiving it and using it to his advantage—a quality he shared with many greater captains.

All these qualities were to be required as he took his seat for the first time as Bashaw[1] of Tripoli and faced his assembled Divan and *taiffa*. He was aware that his internal enemies were still numerous. There were the few remaining *janissary* Aghas who had escaped his net and might still be capable of mounting a revolt against him, perhaps with the support of those citizens of purely Turkish origin who would naturally resent a ruler of mixed and therefore inferior blood. There were also a large number of strictly orthodox notables who, from religious scruples, regarded his flouting of the Sultan's commands as a heresy against the hereditary Caliph of Islam. Lastly, there were the uncommitted citizens who stood aside in trepidation, fearing to favour the losing party and without any confidence in the next turn of events.

His first task was to secure the Castle. He expelled the customary *janissary* garrison to barracks in the City. In their place he put a few selected *janissaries*, known to be faithful, his *Kuloghli* clansmen, and a strong personal guard of black *hampas*. As Bey du Camp, he appointed his half-brother,[2] while the Navy, the Customs and other posts were given either to *Kuloghlis* related to his own family, or, where a standard of literacy was required, to those phenomena of the Barbary States, the Christian renegades who had neither racial ties nor family loyalties to affect their obedience to the master who paid them.

With the security of the Castle assured, the next most pressing

[1] 'Bashaw', an English variant of the Turkish 'Pasha', used by all consuls and historians to describe the rulers of the Karamanli family.

[2] The Bashaw later appointed his eldest son as Bey, and this system was continued by his successors.

need was to restore confidence by stamping out the anarchy in the City and getting the mercantile life of the Regency started again.

In Tripoli robberies and murders were a daily occurrence as gangs of thieves took their toll, and family feuds and street and racial quarrels were freely vented. Every man's house had become a fortress, and to move in the streets a dangerous hazard. In the closed bazaars and shuttered streets, the idle and frequently drunken *janissary* roamed unchecked, menacing the passers-by. To offend him, according to Turkish law, was a punishable crime; to strike him could carry a death sentence.[1] Immune from the civil law and unchecked by his superior officers, he could wander at will. Even more threatening to the Christian or Jew upon the streets could be the wandering *marabout*, or holy man, of whom there was a considerable number. This product of Islamic superstition was frequently either a lunatic or an impostor. His behaviour was erratic and frequently fanatic, and his influence for good or bad could be felt, not only by the poor and ignorant, but equally at times by the Bashaw and his ministers. Everyone, from the Bashaw to his humblest subject, believed that the scraps of paper he handed out containing some Qur'anic gibberish contained advice on matters of state, protection from bullets, enabled barren wives to become fruitful, the diseased to be cured, the enemy to fall sick and die, and the love-sick to be gratified. Thus in one day, the *marabout* might be called to advise on a high matter of state and write a paper for the cure of a common cold. Dirty, avaricious, often completely mad, he moved at will, followed always by a crowd eager to see him threaten or abuse the passer-by. Thus, to a passing Christian or Jew, the *marabout* could bring disaster. He would often throw himself into a frenzy and scream abuse or even attack the heretic. The mob would soon join in, and without any town guard to protect the victim, the result might be serious injury or death.[2]

[1] To remove a drunken *janissary* from a tavern, the Christian keeper used a ladder which, placed over the *janissary*'s head, could manipulate him into the street without anyone committing the capital offence of touching him.

[2] In Tripoli, no Christians—consuls, merchants or travellers—ever moved in

Robbery and murder were completely unchecked and the City's commercial life paralysed.

Many of the principal dangers to security were swept from the streets of Tripoli during the early months of Ahmed Karamanli's rule. An Agha, appointed to supervise security in the City, was chosen for his reputation for severity. A central *sandanar*, or guard-house, was opened, and guards with full powers of arrest ranged the streets. The swaggering and importunate *janissary*, brusquely treated, was returned sulking to his barracks; the *marabout* collected and carefully conducted to where he could do the least harm. Murder was punished by arrest and almost immediate execution,[1] robbery by the severing of a hand or foot.

The result of this was that the bazaars of the City began to reopen, the caravan loads of food supplies from the *menshia* so necessary for daily life in the City, began to flow in; and slowly a trickle from other towns made its way across routes formerly haunted by marauding tribesmen. The magazines of the City merchants, long empty since shipping had ceased to call in the embattled Regency, began to fill up again and to open their doors. Trade, the life-blood of the country, slowly revived.

---

the streets without dragomen or guards. No such protection was available for the large Jewish colony, who, though financially in control of much of the City's economy, were subject to the most humiliating regulations laid down by Islamic convention. Confined behind locked gates to a Quarter of the City of their own, from which they could only emerge during the day, they were obliged to wear black clothes, were not allowed to ride through the City, and if outside must dismount if a Moslem passed them. The most menial tasks—public executioners, scavengers etc. were allotted to them. But though their menfolk could be maltreated, insulted and cheated with impunity by any Moslem, their womenfolk, esteemed for their vivacity and sexual skill, were taken as concubines into the *harims* of leading Moslems, where they were frequently able to obtain positions of great influence. Jewesses were to play a not unimportant part in the history of the Karamanlis.

[1] Though Jews were employed as public executioners, it would have been regarded as unclean to let them touch or see their prisoners. Moslem criminals were hanged by a rope passed over a wall or through a hole in it to the executioners on the other side. Thus, the *convenances* were observed.

Though the Treasury was virtually empty Ahmed Karamanli, realising that at all costs he must keep his small standing army in being to deal with any danger to security from within the City, or to the trade routes, managed to collect enough money to pay it.[1]

With this small force, which he frequently led himself, he managed within a year to secure the areas adjoining Tripoli, drive the raiding nomads back to the desert and subdue the towns of Tagiura, Tarhuna and Misellata, where revolts against him had arisen. But it was too early for him to venture far from the capital. So long as the Sultan did not recognise him, there was always the possibility of a Turkish attempt to dethrone him by warships from Constantinople. It was well he had taken these precautions for on July 28th 1712, another attempt was made by the Sultan to send a nominee Pasha to Tripoli, named Janem Khoja.

Nevertheless, despite his continued success against his enemies, his situation towards the end of 1712 was desperate. His treasury was empty, the payment of the troops who gave him and the country its only real security, was long in arrears, and it was only by a great effort of personality that he had succeeded in raising enough adherents to defeat the *janissaries* who had risen to aid Janem Khoja, the Sultan's nominee. Virtually the only money in the Treasury was the proceeds of a sudden extra tax put upon the Jews.

It was at this juncture, when he was looking desperately around for money to support him, that 'Fortune' came to his aid. Within the space of four weeks in August and September 1712, ships from both the Genoese and Dutch governments appeared in Tripoli harbour, bringing from the Genoese a proposal for a treaty of peace and commerce, with gifts of money and gunpowder, and from the Dutch government an offer for a renewal

[1] It is probable that Karamanli received some assistance from the merchants in the town to help pay his troops. The French consul estimated that he was supporting a standing army of about 5000 *janissaries* and 3500 mounted *Kuloghlis* at this time.

of the former treaty of 1683, with presents including bronze cannon and more gunpowder. The Genoese offer also included the gift of a vessel of 56 guns, and a proposal to pay the Bashaw of Tripoli an annual subsidy of 4000 zecchini, or about £2000.

The treaties arriving so opportunely were eagerly approved, drawn up and signed, and the representatives of the two governments left with the merchant shipping of their friends, assured for a year from attacks by Tripoli corsairs.

This opportune arrival of money and warlike stores gave Ahmed Karamanli the two elements necessary to consolidate himself firmly in Tripoli and its hinterland, and during the following year, the rest of the country, with the exception of the distant province of the Fezzan, was gradually subdued. Arrears of taxes were extracted, and Karamanli's finances correspondingly improved. With peace, and the tribesmen driven back to their *diras*, the caravan routes began to open to merchandise and the economy of the country to recover.

But, while the Sultan withheld his recognition, there were constant uprisings among those who continued to regard the Bashaw as an usurper. Indeed, revolt against the Bashaw was, like poverty, famine and disease to be endemic in the country with such far-flung provinces. Karamanli was never tardy in taking up any challenge. He led his now well paid and trained troops quickly to any threatened area. Against the forces who opposed him—the crowds of advancing and retreating horsemen who still fought in the traditional way of their ancestors, galloping at the enemy with lance and musket, then as swiftly retreating—he opposed his well-disciplined *janissaries*, fighting with dogged Turkish courage in phalanxes, and by fire power steadily held off the attackers, while the horsed *Kuloghli* levies waited to complete the rout when the enemy at length was driven off.

There are few contemporary accounts of these engagements, which ranged as far east as Benghazi, as far south as the oases of the Jofra, and as far west as the Tunisian frontier. In all cases where the revolt was started by tribesmen, Karamanli drove the men into the mountains, where they could be cornered and slaughtered. Then, the characteristic Karamanli signature was added to the affair: the villages of tents were burned to the ground and the women and children driven off into the desert to wander or die.

In 1721, there was a final and abortive attempt by Janem Khoja to regain his throne. He landed in Cyrenaica, where he collected some few adherents and raised his standard. Karamanli immediately launched a force of some 1000 *janissaries* and 1500 *Kuloghlis*, led this time by a Greek renegade Captain, in a swift march eastwards. But the memories of Karamanli's signature the last time he had attacked the area, was still strong in the minds of the Cyrenaican tribesmen. As the forces of the Bashaw advanced swiftly, the opposition melted away. Janem Khoja, once again deserted, re-embarked on a galley at Derna and fled, giving up all hope of retrieving his throne.

This final failure in the various attempts to regain the Pashalik of Tripoli, seems at last to have been understood in Constantinople. A year later, in 1722, two Turkish ships arrived off Tripoli, carrying the long-awaited *firman* from the Sultan, confirming Ahmed Karamanli as Bashaw of Tripoli. He was solemnly invested according to ritual, with the ceremonial *caftan*, or embroidered cloak, by the Turkish admiral. As a gift, the Sultan sent him two war vessels, recently taken by the Turks from the Knights of Malta and the Venetians, for use by his corsairs. They were very welcome gifts to a man who had already begun to recoup his finances further by equipping his corsairs to raid the shipping lanes.

War with France

It was inevitable that Karamanli's policy of turning to piracy as a means of replenishing his Treasury would soon bring him into conflict with the one Power who, for a long period, had maintained an unassailed influence in these seas. Louis XIV had not only dominated the western Mediterranean with his Toulon fleet, but had assumed the mantle of the Most Christian King and thus protector of all those small maritime European states, formerly considered the legitimate prey of the Barbary Regencies.

Ahmed Karamanli's accession, however, coincided with changes in the balance of power in the Mediterranean which made a direct confrontation with France less perilous than previously. The war of the Spanish Succession, in which the navies of Britain, Holland and Sweden had combined to sweep French commerce from the Mediterranean, had led to the occupation of Gibraltar by Britain in 1704 and of Minorca in 1708. This put into effect a far-sighted decision of Britain to maintain a permanent fleet based in the Mediterranean and so weaken France further by putting a barrier between her Atlantic and Mediterranean fleets.

This decision by Britain to maintain garrisons and a fleet in the western Mediterranean, close to the shores of Barbary, brought the Regencies a new and important role. They were no longer tolerated merely as a useful brake on Britain's commercial rivals in the area, they became increasingly necessary bases for supplies of foodstuffs for the British garrisons and fleet at Gibraltar and Port Mahon.

The Barbary rulers were not slow to note these changes in the power and influence of the maritime states. Those solitary pirate vessels, lying close offshore to the Mediterranean coast, must have noticed on the horizon the passage of the great warships of the contending Powers; and probably the captains of the Tripoli *taiffa* could report having heard Rooke's guns at Gibraltar and Leake's at Port Mahon. They must have learned soon of the destruction of the Spanish fleet by Byng in 1718.

Quick to sense the new balance of forces, they must have felt a release from the irking shackles of French control which had galled them for years. With this feeling grew a corresponding resentment at the arrogance with which the French had treated them, and which was never more in evidence than in the way the French interpreted the peace treaties between them. While

Tripoli, Tunis and Algiers had as far as possible scrupulously obeyed those articles in the treaties regarding maritime captures and the release of prisoners, the French had long ceased to do so. While French shipping went unmolested and Frenchmen captured on other vessels were released, Turks and Moors from the ships of the Regencies when captured by French vessels were not released but were sent to the galleys as slaves, while French agents even went to the slave markets in Leghorn and Malta to purchase Moslems for slavery.

Reports on all these matters began to affect the Bashaw and his Divan and *taiffa* shortly after his accession. A growing anti-French feeling was doubtless fanned by the arrogant behaviour of Expilly, the new French consul in Tripoli, who was an outstanding example of what Macaulay called 'the insolence with which Lewis had during many years treated every Court in Europe'. He was not above treating the Bashaw with contempt in front of his Ministers.

For some or all of these reasons, during 1713, the *taiffa* in Tripoli, under instruction from the Bashaw, gave orders to their captains to take French protected prizes. The first capture was a French ship carrying olive oil, which was brought into Tripoli harbour and quickly sold, its crew being made slaves. To the protests of the infuriated Expilly, the Bashaw replied that the vessel could not be restored as it had already been sold, and the state of his finances did not permit his making any payment of indemnity. Expilly, after many efforts to obtain redress, sent off an angry despatch to Marseilles demanding what he called an '*action éclatant*' against Tripoli.

On July 21st 1714, a French warship *Diamant*, under the command of Captain Duquesne Monnier, arrived in Tripoli harbour, apparently to enforce the Consul's demands for an indemnity. There followed a situation that was often to be repeated in the relations between the Bashaw and France. The Bashaw was at his blandest. He pointedly ignored Expilly's attempts to act as a mediator, and sent with his compliments a supply of fresh vegetables and meat aboard the warship, and invited the Captain ashore. According to custom, hostages between shore and ship were exchanged, and Duquesne Monnier and some of his officers came ashore.

On landing at the Marine, they were met by a reception committee and escorted to the Castle where the Bashaw received them in state in full Divan. In a discussion, from which Expilly was pointedly excluded, the Bashaw declared his delight in at last meeting an official representative of His Most Christian Majesty—explaining that he only recognised Expilly as a representative of the Marseilles Chamber of Commerce. Exerting to the full his undeniable affability and charm, the Bashaw then went on to plead his present poverty of circumstance and consequent inability to pay the indemnity immediately. He then arranged for a stage-managed tour of the poorer parts of the City for the French, as an indication of the poverty of the Regency.

So cleverly did Karamanli play on the susceptibilities of the somewhat gullible French captain that he not only obtained a long delay in the repayment of the indemnity, but extracted an agreement, to the intense chagrin of Expilly, that the amount of the indemnity should not according to custom be assessed by the Marseilles Chamber of Commerce, where it might be grossly inflated, but by some other independent body. Duquesne Monnier also agreed to pass a request to Versailles that an envoy from Tripoli might be sent to pay the Bashaw's respects to the French court.

With further mutual compliments, *Diamant* left Tripoli after a stay of only ten days, having extracted nothing but a vague promise of repayment. It is not on record that this indemnity was ever paid.

A year later, the court of Tripoli did send an envoy to Versailles. He took with him presents of blood mares, ostriches and gazelles. He was well received by Louis XV and returned with presents for the Bashaw. Relations between the two countries temporarily improved when the arrogant Expilly was transferred in 1722, and a newly ratified Treaty of Peace and Commerce was brought by a French naval squadron, with a welcome gift of gunpowder. In return, the Bashaw sent what was to be the first of many such gifts to France and Britain—some Roman columns from the half buried ruins at Leptis Magna.[1]

Ahmed Karamanli was wisely anxious to avoid further confrontation with France, but the changing nature of Mediterranean politics made this almost inevitable, so long as France pursued her policy of considering all Catholic states as under her protection.

At the Treaty of Passarowitz in 1718, the Sultan had agreed to order the Barbary States to cease their attacks on the shipping of Austria and Venice. He could of course do no more than issue the usual *firmans*, but even these could not be entirely ignored, and though some corsair activity on the part of Tripoli continued against these states, the loss to the Bashaw's Treasury was considerable. When, in 1723, the Sultan's envoy arrived in Tripoli with the periodic *firman* confirming Karamanli's appointment, the Bashaw frankly told the envoy that the peace with Austria and Venice, coupled with French protection of all Catholic countries, meant virtually the end of any corsair activity for Tripoli. This would only be possible if the Sultan agreed to meet the costs of the *janissary* troops, whose pay came entirely from this source. Needless to say, nothing came from this request.

In the circumstances, Tripoli could only turn once more to attacks on French protected shipping to supplement a dwindling income. This was a policy much against the Bashaw's natural instincts of caution, but he was encouraged to pursue it by a general wave of anti-French feeling among his Divan and *taiffa*, and the population of Tripoli, the result probably of many past humiliations, not unconnected with the appearance in the Mediterranean of France's traditional enemy, Britain.

Lodington, the British consul who, while France had remained mistress of the western sea during the many years of his work in Tripoli, had tried in his small way to counter French arrogance and presumption, wrote one of his rare despatches to London in June 1728 on the change of tone in Tripoli: 'This Government

[1] They are in the church of St. Germain de Pré in Paris.

desires nothing more than war with them, and I believe it would break out tomorrow, were it not for fear of the Grand Signior's lash[1] that they lie under . . .'

While the merchant shipping of Genoa, Sicily, Malta, the Papal States and other Catholic countries came in one by one as prizes to Tripoli, the French decided to act, and news began to come into Tripoli of a gathering of French warships at Toulon, with preparations for an attack on Tripoli. Several meetings of the Divan were held, in which the experienced European renegades[2] took an active part. It was decided to put the City and Marine into a state of preparedness. As a token of this, Catholic slaves from the recent captures were put to labour in repairing the City's defences.

There can be little doubt that experienced gunners among the renegades had pointed out that Tripoli had strong natural advantages for defence from the sea which, if properly used, could be very formidable to attackers. Across the northern entrance to the harbour lay a series of rocky reefs, which extended partly along the harbour bar, cutting off a close approach to all but ships of a shallow draft. The 16th-century Spanish builders of the City's defences had increased these natural defences by erecting a series of forts along this rocky promontory. At the eastern end of the reef stood a formidable fort with a battery of 18 guns, called *el Mandrik* which, in concert with a fort on the eastern side of the bay called the *English battery*, of 12 guns, could by cross fire seriously gall any shipping trying to navigate the entrance. From *el Mandrik*, extending westwards to the City walls at intervals were a series of small batteries, totalling 22 guns. From the walls, facing the sea from east and north were further batteries of 62 guns, and the high bastions of the Castle had each a battery of guns, of which two faced the sea and the third could cover a sea landing aimed at the *menshia*.

[1] The Sultan of Turkey.

[2] Italian historians account for the sudden influx of renegades to the Barbary States as owing to the depressed conditions in Calabria under repressive landlords.

In theory this was a very strong defensive position, since, while the line of reefs across the harbour mouth kept attackers at a distance, from the west, both *el Mandrik* and the *English battery* could cover the deeper draught entrance to the east, preventing bigger ships from getting closer into the bay. The Bashaw, however, through lack of money, had been forced to neglect these defences, which so far had been less necessary than those prepared for the defence of his throne from forces within the country. Trained gunners were probably available in small numbers among the renegades, but both powder and shot were in very short supply, and the sea batteries were sited on rotting gun-carriages and rusted equipment and so inefficient as to be almost useless. In fact, the situation of the sea defences was altogether deplorable.[1]

Nevertheless, feverish attempts were made to put this poor material into some posture of defence. Catholic slaves were driven daily from the *bagnios* in the Castle and set to work building a new fort, to be called the *French fort*, on the rock below the City walls. It was designed to be an efficient counter to the shallow draught French bomb vessels[2] which could be expected to attack from close in under the Castle; but with the shortage of gunpowder, shot or cannon the battery could not be properly manned.

In any case, this was all that the energies and the skill of Tripoli could do, and the Bashaw sat down anxiously to await events.

On July 16th 1728 the lookouts on the Castle bastions sighted the topsails of a French squadron, tacking in from the west. Immediately a warning gun was fired from the Castle battery, and preparations were made in the City to evade the attack

[1] When news of the French preparations reached the Bashaw, he had sent an urgent message to the Sultan, asking for supplies of cannon and shot; but the French consul in Tripoli, Martin, had already forestalled him, by telling his consular colleague in Constantinople to put an embargo on any French protected shipping from carrying the goods.

[2] The French navy had recently brought into use a mortar bomb, with a flying fuse, which could be fired a considerable distance.

should one take place. While the crumbling batteries and antique iron guns of the outer forts were manned by the few trained gunners, and the very meagre supplies of powder were served out, a great exodus began from the City through the *menshia* gate.

An endless stream of townsfolk, carrying their personal possessions, and followed by their animals carrying the wooden frames of doors and windows—a vital precaution in a land where wood is scarce—now filed through the *menshia* gate, crossed the intervening sands, and trekked into the concealment of the oasis, where they set up tents and temporary shelters. The notables followed to their country villas. There were long files of Christian slaves in chains, other Christians and Jews guarded by the Bashaw's *janissaries*, and finally, carrying as much of their personal effects as they could, the consuls and their families, the Catholic missionary Fathers and any other Christians of rank. The latter were taken to a large house belonging to the Bashaw, where they were kept under careful supervision. Here, a mile or so from the City walls, the population of Tripoli settled in comparative safety to await events.

By the morning of the following day, July 17th, the French squadron, which was now seen to consist of two large warships from the Brest fleet, four frigates, three shallow-draught bomb vessels, two small galleys and two pinnaces, had taken up positions off the bay of Tripoli.[1]

The French consul Martin, who had replaced Expilly in 1723, now paid a ceremonious visit to the flagship of the squadron, which he found commanded by Admiral Nicola de Grandpré, who was accompanied by a political Commissar from Versailles named d'Héricourt, who carried the instructions from the French government, and was empowered to negotiate and sign a Treaty of Peace. d'Héricourt himself did not go ashore to negotiate, but sent Martin, who demanded and was immediately granted, an audience with the Bashaw.

Martin spelled out the contents of the French Note, in which

[1] Lodington reported the squadron to consist of 6 men of war, 2 galleys, 3 bomb ketches and some tenders.

it was stated that the French squadron had come with a primary objective of renewing the former peace treaty between France and Tripoli, last signed in 1720. But before this could be done, there were certain conditions which must be complied with by the Bashaw's government: the immediate payment by the Bashaw of a sum of 50,000 Seville piastres for the loss of the French protected ships which had been sold by the Bashaw as prizes; the immediate release of any French protected ships at present held by Tripoli and the enlargement of their crews from slavery; a new peace treaty to contain the same terms, favourable to France and giving her precedence over other countries, as in former treaties.

On receipt of this note, the Bashaw, already displeased that Martin, rather than the official Commissary, had presented it, called a full meeting of Divan and *taiffa* to discuss the situation. At the same time, in accordance with Arab courtesy, he sent his chief minister, the Grand Kehya, to pay a visit as his own representative on the French admiral. The minister was very coldly received and no attempt was made to return the courtesy visit. Indeed, M. Martin brought another message saying that M. d'Héricourt would only come ashore if hostages were sent aboard the flagship. Although angered by this lack of traditional courtesy, the Bashaw agreed to send his own son Ali, and a nephew as hostages. His anger increased when this offer was refused, and instead the French demanded that five of the leading Tripoli citizens should be held. This the Bashaw refused, and he now added that he would not regard negotiations carried out by a mere consul as adequate.

It seems probable that, under pressure from the British and Dutch consuls whose advice he had asked, he decided to make an offer to the French. On the morning of July 19th in full Divan, he informed the French consul that he would pay an indemnity of 7000 piastres, which was all that his treasury could raise. At contemporary values the French demand had been for the equivalent of nearly £4000; the offer from the Bashaw was a mere £500.

With this offer, which may indeed have been the best a

depleted treasury could afford, Martin went aboard the flagship once more, where, of course, the offer was rejected. Martin did not return ashore with the Note of rejection as, with the possibility of hostilities, it was considered dangerous to leave him in the hands of the Bashaw's men. Instead, Martin's chancellor, or vice-consul Broche, who from the evidence seems to have been popular in Tripoli, carried the reply from the Commissar. This was a renewal of the original demands, with an ultimatum for a satisfactory reply set at midday the following day, July 20th.

Early next morning, Karamanli summoned his Divan, and before the great circle of Consuls, Aghas, sea captains, townsmen and religious heads, his scribe read out his suggested ultimatum to the French. He asked for their views, and, according to their Arab historian,[1] they all rose to their feet and demanded that no further offer should be made to the French. They were they said, prepared to risk any loss of life or property rather than yield to such demands. The scribe was called forward and set to draft formally Karamanli's reply.

If the tone of this letter from a largely illiterate Prince was undiplomatically abrupt, its meaning was clear:

I have called my Divan and unanimously my officers and leading citizens have replied that if my friend, the Emperor of the French sends these people to make war, it is well. If they are sent to make peace, they should send a proper representative ashore to communicate with us and hear our reply. As to payment, no-one consents to make it, and no one will give it. As for your bombs, we do not fear them; you can throw them if you wish. I know that if this takes place, there will be no peace between France and Tripoli for centuries.

The reply was sent, but Broche was retained ashore under the Bashaw's personal protection, and eventually taken to the *menshia*, to join the rest of the diplomatic corps.

The receipt of Karamanli's reply was followed by a council of war aboard the Admiral's flagship *St. Esprit*, attended by all the ships' captains. Under the supervision of the Commissar, a

[1] Ibn Ghalboun.

formal document was drawn up declaring a state of war with Tripoli, and, armed with copies, the captains returned to their ships. Guns were run out, decks cleared, and the bomb vessels lowered their masts and were warped in closer to the shore. The deserted city awaited the attack. The Bashaw remained with his men among the gun batteries on the bastions of the Castle.

At 8 p.m. on the 20th July the bombardment began. While the warships and frigates engaged the shore batteries, the bomb vessels, drawing close inshore, opened fire with their variable fuse bombs, which had been recently issued to French gunners, and were reasonably accurate and destructive. From the roof-top of their communal house in the *menshia*, the diplomats could see a great rain of bombs ascending in smoking parabolas and falling on the city. Some exploded in the air and others with slow fuses burst at intervals among the buildings. A primary target was the Castle, and the first bombs thrown fell on this though they caused no casualties. But they served their purpose in driving the Bashaw and his suite out beyond the city walls to a spot from whence the movements of the warships could be observed, and any attempt to land troops on shore be repelled. Another early casualty was the French consulate itself. The bomb gunners observed a party of Moors on the balcony tearing down the French flag, and fired on them. After several hits the building collapsed in ruins.

At intervals for the next five days the bombing continued with no reply from the Tripoli gunners who had run out of ammunition. Surrounded by his experienced European renegades and his sea captains, Karamanli watched the destruction from his vantage point on the shore. It had been calculated that, in that scalding midsummer month, unable to land for water or supplies, and under the constant threat of a change of wind which would put him on a dangerous lee shore, the French admiral would at length be forced to leave.

It seemed these calculations were correct. On July 26th firing ceased, and a boat was observed leaving the French flagship with a message which was laid on a reef of rock near the shore. This was brought by a shore boat to the Bashaw. It contained a request from the French for peace.

The Bashaw summoned the Divan and read the message to them. It is recorded that only the Agha of the *janissaries* rose and suggested an acceptance of the offer, in case later conditions proved harder. But the remainder of the Divan and *taiffa*, for whom continuation of the war with France meant rich pickings in piracy, declared in unison that they would never make peace with people who had come to bomb their city in this manner, and that it were better to perish than surrender. The Bashaw, therefore, drew up a reply in which he taunted the French admiral to continue the bombardment. He, Karamanli, would refuse any treaty with them. And he added once more that he would only treat with the King of France direct. 'They declared,' wrote Lodington, in a despatch of July 24th to the Secretary of State, 'it was very indifferent to them whether they had peace or warr . . . and that his Excellency would give an account of their proceedings against him to their King. . . .'

The receipt of this message was followed by no further action by the French ships, and it seems that Karamanli's calculations were correct, and that the Admiral was only suing for peace because he had run out of supplies and was worried about the wind. The bomb vessels, in any case, had now fired off, according to Lodington, about 2800 bombs which was possibly their full carrying capacity. Equally, the toll on the water supplies of the fleet, after several weeks at sea in a very hot season must have had its effect. For two further days the squadron lay off Tripoli bay, closely watched from the shore. But no further attempt was made to attack the city or send any messages ashore. On July 29th it set sail and was soon out of sight.

The population now began a slow and painful return and found the city to be one third in ruins. Forty mortar bombs had fallen on the Castle, the French consulate was practically demolished, and seven bombs had fallen on the roof of the British consulate. To a country with a large and expendable slave population, the repair of a partly destroyed city did not present insuperable problems, and was soon achieved. The casualties from the bombardment were also very low, owing to the population prudently having taken shelter in the *menshia*. The only certified casualties were those of the seven looters who had been buried in the collapse of the French consulate. There was, however, considerable rage against the French among the population, though the Bashaw gave strict orders that Chancellor Broche and any other French subjects, were to be well protected.

The Bashaw was meanwhile profiting from the state of war with France to send his corsairs out in raids on French shipping. Lodington reported:

He has already sent out several of his Corsairs to cruise upon their bandiera [French protected flags] and others are also preparing to get away with all manner of expedition, and, as I understand there are a great many French vessels up in the Levant, its my opinion they will do considerable damage among them, and have already seized upon 4 of their vessels in this and other adjacent Ports. . . .

The Bashaw's proverbial luck now appeared to help him. While in desperate straits to furnish his corsairs with powder, shot and warlike stores, largely expended in defending the city, a Dutch squadron suddenly appeared in port charged with the renewal of the peace treaty between Tripoli and the Netherlands. As gifts, it brought the usual large quantites of powder, shot and cannon.

The consequence of this was that by the end of November, when normal shipping movement in the Mediterranean ceased for the winter, 21 French vessels had been captured, their hulls and goods sold, and their crews thrown into slavery. It was now impossible for French merchant vessels to move south of Malta without an armed convoy. Correspondingly the Bashaw's treasury improved.

During the winter months, urgent discussions went on between the French Chamber of Commerce in Marseilles and the Comte de Maurepas, French Minister of the Marine. By January it had been decided that nothing short of a decisive and conclusive action by the French could destroy the nest of pirates in Tripoli, and drive Karamanli off the throne. To carry this into effect, it would be necessary to bombard the city of Tripoli once more, and then land troops, defeat the *janissaries* in the field, and capture the city. The collapse of the regime would automatically follow.

To command this major enterprise, a well known and audacious French sea captain, called Du Guay Trouin, was summoned to the French Ministry of the Marine, and ordered to draw up a plan to be put into effect when the Mediterranean sailing season began in the Spring. This was done quickly by this energetic Frenchman, and it was agreed that a force of 11,000 troops in forty ships should carry it out. It was also believed that the capture and occupation of Tripoli would result in arresting the depredations against French shipping from the pirates in Tunis and Algiers.

Orders had already been given for the troops and transports to assemble at Toulon, when one of those imponderable political pressures, which so often came to the rescue of the Barbary rulers, began to operate. Reports of the projected enterprise reached Constantinople where the Sultan, fearing the results of a French foothold in North Africa, acted immediately.

The Capudan Pasha, the Turkish admiral of the fleet, summoned the French ambassador and demanded an explanation of the reports. The latter explained that the continued depredations of the Tripoli pirates on French shipping obliged the French government to order a severe chastisement, and this was within the rights of all the great powers.

The Capudan Pasha listened politely, and then pointed out that though the right to chastise piracy was internationally recognised, this right did not extend to the occupation by the French of any of the Sultan's dominions. If such an occupation took place, the Sultan would not hold himself responsible for the reaction of the Turkish population against French persons and interests in Turkey.

The hint was sufficient. The French had large commercial interests in Turkey and the Turkish provinces, and there was a considerable number of French nationals living there. The French ambassador hastened to inform the Capudan Pasha that, on reflection, it was no intention of the French government to occupy any part of the Regency of Tripoli. The main enterprise was not called off. In its place, it was decided to send Du Guay Trouin with a strong enough force of warships to blockade the port of Tripoli, while at the same time, a small force of fast and well-armed frigates would sweep the seas round Malta and either capture or destroy any Tripoline corsairs. In January 1729 a strong force of seven frigates from Brest and Toulon arrived off Tripoli and began a close blockade, which soon had the required effect of strangling the city's sea trade. The Turkish elements in the Bashaw's *taiffa* were in favour of opposing this with whatever forces were available, since at that time of year, with the winter gales, such a blockade would be difficult to maintain for long. But Karamanli was now thinking of peace, the more so since a new pretender to his throne had risen among the Berber tribes in the Gharian region and was rallying supporters.

The Bashaw moved energetically and successfully against the usurper, but it was clear that he could not continue a possible fight on two fronts and, so long as he was engaged with the French, encouragement would be given to the dissidents in the countryside to rise against him. He therefore set in motion peace discussions, via Chancellor Broche, and the French consul in Tunis, M. Pignon. Peace was eventually agreed when two ambassadors from Tripoli presented themselves at the French court, and made a profound apology to Louis XV and a promise to respect the peace in the future. An indemnity of 20,000 piastres was demanded by the French, and paid. French slaves were released from the *bagnios* of Tripoli, and an exchange of prisoners was made—those which Du Guay Trouin's frigates had captured being returned to Tripoli. In a personal bargain between the Bashaw and Du Guay Trouin, the latter released two French master gunners, on loan to the *janissary* army, which was then preparing to march on the Fezzan, where the local Governor had refused to pay any further tribute.

Led by the Bashaw's eldest son, the Bey Mohammed, the *janissaries*, accompanied by the two French gunners, made a swift march on the Fezzan, captured its capital Murzuk, razed the walls to prevent further defiance, and brought both the Governor and his son back to Tripoli as captives. The Bashaw, who would normally have publicly executed these two rebels, showed here his subtle knowledge of Arab psychology. He had the two captives led in chains to the slave market, and there put on sale publicly. The Bashaw then purchased them for the humiliating sum of two copper coins. Following this, they were released, the Governor was returned to office, and left for Murzuk with a force of *janissaries*. Nothing further was heard of him or his family during the present Bashaw's reign.

From about the year 1722, Ahmed Karamanli may be said to have entered on a period of relative prosperity in which both he and the country benefited considerably. Fat yearly subsidies came in to his treasury from his treaties with Britain, France, Holland, Sweden and Denmark, the taxes of his subjects came in with regularity, the trade routes to central Africa were open once again, and the long caravans of black slaves, ivory, ostrich feathers, spices and gold dust arrived along the three caravan routes from central Africa. Prizes from the corsairs came in with Christian slaves from Genoa and Spain, and the sale of these vessels brought in revenue from both Tripoline and European purchasers. An additional source of income was the regular supply of beef and grain to the British garrisons in the newly-opened ports at Gibraltar and Port Mahon.

With this prosperity, the Bashaw developed a taste for building. He imported builders and masons from Italy, fresco carvers from Egypt, and, just beyond the Castle entrance, erected the still magnificent Karamanli mosque, a burying place for his newly created dynasty; a building bright with marble, Chinese tiles, and great carved frescoes of Qur'anic sayings. He also carried out some ambitious building in the western area of the Castle itself, creating the still handsome *cortile Caramanli* as a dwelling place for himself and his extensive *harim* of Albanian, Turkish, Libyan and negro women.

But the prosperity and life of luxury, to which all his heirs were to be addicted, did not lessen his watchfulness. Behind a smooth and courteous countenance, he could be utterly without pity or emotion. From his newly built marble and tiled courtyards and his bright audience chamber, his spies went everywhere. Treachery in the Castle had been made almost impossible by shutting iron-covered doors between the various apartments at night, a black slave with a pair of loaded pistols always stood by the Bashaw during audience, and a scimitar lay beside the cushions of his throne. Those who came to pay their respects were never certain whether the strangler's cord or the dungeon awaited them. He could still pounce, with tigerish ferocity, upon known or suspected enemies. In 1722 he had not hesitated to have his half-brother strangled, fearing a plot; and he never hesitated to kill rather than to question. But to the outer world he turned a face of benevolence and punctilious courtesy. He devoted much energy towards raising his prestige and that of the Regency at the courts of Europe. To this end he recruited intelligent and trustworthy men to his secretariat, most of them renegades, and linked them to his family by marriage. He also sent ambassadors to Britain, France, Holland and Sweden, the major maritime powers. Nearer home, he tried to enter into amicable relations with the foreign consuls.

The consuls

Ahmed Karamanli was fortunate in having throughout his reign an unusually patient and understanding British consul, Benjamin Lodington, who was consul when Ahmed Karamanli assumed power in 1711, and remained consul in Tripoli altogether for nearly forty years. Very little is known of him,[1] as his reports to London were always short and frequently only concerned with shipping intelligence, for which he was a good news gatherer as he himself ran a small freighting business. But that

[1] Lodington had a brother, who had been a consul in Tripoli before him.

he was a wise, cautious and friendly man, with shrewd understanding of the Turkish temperament—which he once describes as 'ye dogged humour of ye Turk'—seems evident from the fact that through his long stay in the unenviable climate and deplorable conditions of life in Tripoli, he rarely makes a complaint, though he lived through a series of political upheavals, plagues, famines and wars. 'Our affairs,' he tells the Secretary of State in a despatch of January 1726, and it is an epitome of his long years in office, 'still continue in the same good order.'

His only complaints were to be those of many consuls who followed him: lack of money to carry out his official duties, salary often months in arrears, answers to his few requests often ignored.

> How much I am disabled to maintain ye honour of my post [(for her Majesty's service), he wrote in one complaint,] amongst these people for want of due payment of my Sallary and Extraordinaries, which have been usual and constantly Expected by the Turks, and much more so since ye French are so liberal amongst them,

and in another pertinent paragraph asking for gifts for the Bashaw:

> of which I have given them hopes for a long time, Your Grace may see an Amicable correspondence is desired with these people, for tho' they cannot do us any good, they may do us a great deal of harm in Interrupting our Turkey and Levant trade.

It was probably Benjamin Lodington who drafted a memorandum[1] for consuls in Tripoli, which gives a glimpse of protocol at the court of Tripoli, and how consuls should conduct themselves on arrival.

> All ye consuls will visit me without observing any order, upon my arrival. . . . I can return none of these visits till I have presented my Credentials to ye Bashaw. When I visit ye Bashaw by his appointment, that part of ye presents intended for him must be carried by me. . . . I shall find ye Bashaw sitting. The form of salutation is to advance and kiss his right and left cheek and make him a bow. I sit on his left side,

[1] Unsigned, but in both Lodington's style and spelling.

being the place of honour in Tripoli. I make my first visit alone. To take care I am saluted with 7 guns, being my privilege . . . This salute is made by Treaty and must not be paid for. [On the question of consular precedence he adds,] It can never be necessary for him to put himself on a footing of having a scramble . . .

Lodington retired from the Service in 1729 and returned to London, where he shortly afterwards died, worn out after forty years in an unhealthy climate. Before leaving Tripoli, he had chosen another British merchant named Beswick to act as consul *ad interim* until the Secretary of State had decided on a replacement. Beswick seems to have learned from Lodington how to conduct consular work, and from his correspondence seems to have been a conscientious and zealous official. He probably had hopes that his tenure of the post might be eventually confirmed from London.

Whatever Beswick's hopes may have been, however useful his services were, his post was at the disposal of the Secretary of State at the Home Office, upon whom those pressures of 'interest', by which the Government of George II maintained its influence and kept in office, were operating. Only thus can be explained the news of the appointment to such a difficult post in Barbary of a retired naval officer named Reed. It is doubtful if Reed were chosen for any qualities of temperament; he had certainly none of experience.

Reed's appointment was gazetted in 1730, and the moment he received notification of it, he obtained in London the whole of the salary and allowances of the Tripoli post, of which he remitted nothing to Beswick who, one can only suppose, kept the consulate running out of his private means. By a series of procrastinations, which seem incredible, Reed succeeded in keeping himself in London for a further three years, while not a penny went to Tripoli from his salary. How Beswick managed is not recorded but he sent home constant pleas for financial help. In 1733, Reed finally sailed, taking a vessel to Port Mahon, and from thence he made a leisurely transhipment on to a smaller vessel bound for Tripoli.

In May of that year, Reed's vessel arrived off Tripoli harbour, and dropped anchor at the entrance, while firing a signal gun. A strange silence greeted it from the shore. There was no sign of movement along the harbour, and no signal gun from the Castle acknowledging the salute. The ships riding at anchor along the mole also seemed deserted. After lying for some time offshore awaiting the appearance of the customs and quarantine officials, the ship put a boat ashore to find the authorities and inform the Castle of the arrival of the new British consul.

It hastily returned with the news that Tripoli was in the grip of the plague, and that every person of consequence was shut up in his house under close quarantine, and that as many as a hundred people daily were dying in the streets.

While this news was being received, another boat was seen putting out from the shore. In it was Beswick who had, at some risk to himself, emerged from his closely confined house to report to the consul. He did not come aboard the Port Mahon vessel but shouted his news from a safe distance. What he had to report was that the plague had decimated the town: of the consular corps, both the French and Dutch consuls were dead—only the French consul's wife surviving out of a staff of 19 persons, 142 Christian slaves had perished in the Castle *bagnios*, and the toll in the city itself included 464 Jews and a total of nearly 17,000 Turks, Moors and Arabs.

Reed naturally decided not to land, and the Port Mahon vessel hastily sailed, Reed having first instructed Beswick to continue running the consulate. Back at Port Mahon, where he remained a further ten months, Reed received regular letters from Beswick on consular matters, which he forwarded as his own to London. But he sent Beswick no money. At length in March 1734, when the epidemic had died down, he arrived to take up his post. His first act, on arrival, was to throw Beswick out of the consular house; and when Beswick's brother protested, he was struck by Reed in a very unseemly brawl. He also refused to pay Beswick one penny for all the expenses he had undertaken, during a four-year tenure in the consulate.

Beswick's constant letters of protest to London remained unanswered and, unable to get any assistance from Reed, he decided to go to Tunis to apply to the British consul there for redress. Reed, however, refused him a passport to travel without which he would have been liable to capture at sea and possible sale as a slave.

Beswick, however, was highly regarded by the Bashaw, and with help from the Divan, he eventually sailed for Tunis without a passport. Here, with the consul, he drew up an affidavit for despatch to London, claiming money for his four-year tenure of the Tripoli post during Reed's absence. Reed meanwhile, to forestall this, drew up an affidavit of his own accusing Beswick of a number of crimes, which included fraud and, more dangerous still, accusation of insult to the name of George II, in the presence of other persons. In spite of the fact that Reed's only witness to his affidavit was his illiterate servant, nothing seems to have been done about it in London. Poor Beswick at this point disappears from official correspondence.

Reed as the newly accredited consul was received with full honours by the Bashaw. He brought with him a gift of £500, the sum agreed by the Treaty on the arrival of a new consul, and numerous gifts, from George II, including gold and silver watches, clocks, diamond rings, a pair of richly-chased guns, and two pairs of pistols. There was also a quantity of silks and brocades for the Bashaw's *harim*. (Lodington's hand may perhaps be seen here.) These were handed over in full audience at the Castle, when Reed, dressed in his naval uniform, read his letter of appointment.

But these pleasant auguries of stewardship were soon forgotten. Reed had already shown something of his character in his behaviour to Beswick. Ignorant, abusive, and a liar, in three months his relations with the Castle had become so strained that the Bashaw refused to deal with him direct, and transactions were carried out by Reed's consular assistant. By 1738, the Bashaw had had enough of him and was writing direct to the Secretary of State, the Duke of Newcastle, to have him recalled. Two further letters from the Chancery in the Castle were sent during the succeeding years, complaining of Reed's 'outrageous behaviour', but the support of the Duke still kept him in office. Finally in 1743 the Bashaw took the extreme step of sending a special messenger to London, with a letter addressed directly to the King. In this he requested the recall of Mr. Reed, the present consul, 'on account of the great and extraordinary ill-conduct of him'. The letter ended with a suggestion that John Beswick should be reappointed, since he had 'as consul five years in the absence of Consul Lodington, behaved with great integrity and to the entire satisfaction of everybody.'

This letter was also ignored. On a new dispute breaking out between Reed and some of the Bashaw's ministers, Karamanli took a final step in ordering the Consul to be confined to his house, thus completely cutting down his activities. This was at length effective. In 1744, a British trader from Tunis named Robert White was appointed consul in Tripoli. Reed was lucky that he had not been sent to Tunis or Algiers, where, with his behaviour, a much more unpleasant fate might have overtaken him.

In 1728, the Bashaw had despatched his first ambassador to London.[1] This was his nephew, Qasim Chelebi, a man who had already had experience of the courts at Paris and Rome. His visit lasted one year and, under the rules governing diplomacy at that time at the Courts of Britain and France, he was granted a sum of £700 for his stay, and a house in Suffolk Street.

The Court of George II found him a man of 'agreeable, courteous temper', and his visit, even by the colourful standards of Boswell's London, sufficiently impressive. He appeared richly dressed in silks with gold and silver brocade, and was followed by a suite of twenty-three servants, of almost mediæval diversity. They included a court jester, a dwarf mute, his tailor, a barber and wardrobe servants, cooks and coffee makers, and several negro slaves, all dressed richly in the different costumes of their

[1] The consular correspondence is full of requests to the consuls to prevent these expensive visits, since their charge fell on the King.

service. This assorted party was housed in Suffolk Street and looked after by a London housekeeper, Mrs. King, whose catalogue of adventures is, alas, lost to us. They did include the mysterious disappearance of one of her English cookmaids, who had apparently been disposed of by one of the Ambassador's suite, and buried in his garden.

Chelebi returned to Tripoli in 1729, bringing the Bashaw messages of goodwill and presents which included a hundred barrels of English gunpowder.

Last years of Ahmed

By 1741, Ahmed Karamanli, after thirty years on the throne of Tripoli, had reached a relatively serene old age. He had now become the great figure in the history of Tripoli, an eminence which he has never lost. Whatever the failures and weaknesses of his successors, the mystique of personality which he bequeathed to them was always retained. By the literate Arabs, he was to be remembered and admired for his boldness in adversity, his skill in intrigue, his ruthlessness in action. It was with these qualities that he had subdued his many opponents, faced up to the European powers, crushed the usurpers who sought his throne, and reduced the power of the Arab tribes. His diplomacy was simple and effective. It was based on a careful study of his opponents and their weaknesses and divisions, which he then played upon with great subtlety. Thus he divided the European consuls, taking care to be informed of their personalities, their rivalries, and their susceptibility to flattery or persuasion. He had a gift—a sort of intuition—for this which enabled him to circumvent treaties and break obligations. To the constant consular protests about acts of piracy carried out by his corsairs, he would, according to his Italian historian:[1]

> Oppose various arguments of interpretation, drawing out the question as long as possible by promising the future punishment of the offenders,

[1] Rodolfo Micacchi, *La Tripolitania sotto il dominio dei Caramanli.*

or by long drawn out, subtle arguments in the Divan. He was clever at giving each consul the opinion that he was specially favoured. In reality, he only favoured those who served his own ends.

To the less literate Arabs of the *Sahel* and the *menshia*, and to the tribesmen of the interior, his memory remains green as someone almost semi-divine, a dispenser of true *baraka*, that mysterious afflatus of kings and holy men. Even his bloody exploits became legends, and his reign, the 'good old days'.

During the latter years of his life, he was able to indulge in his passion for building. He improved many of the town mosques, and further beautified the fine mosque near the Castle which bears his name, and in which his dynasty were intended to be buried.

But though, in these last years, he may have begun to think piously of a celestial future, this did not prevent him from carrying out what some of his biographers think was the most callous massacre of his whole career.

In June 1742, the annual caravan which had taken the Meccan pilgrims to the Holy Places, was returning from Cairo. Travelling with it, with a magnificent retinue, was the brother-in-law of the Dey of Algiers. This young man had been exiled to Cairo as a possible Pretender to the throne of Algiers. While in Cairo, he had raised a large sum of money, recruited an army of about 700 men, and was returning to Algiers to overturn the Dey. In this plan, he had the secret connivance of the Bey of Tunis, who had agreed to supply him with more troops and money on his arrival there.

The Bashaw's spies had already informed him of this plot, and he had been in contact with the Dey of Algiers, and the result was a friendly message to the young man, Hajj Mohammed, to make the usual halt of the caravan at the gates of Tripoli, where he would be the personal guest of the Bashaw. As an earnest of his good intentions, the Bashaw sent one of his sons and the Grand Kehya from the Divan to meet the party and escort Hajj Mohammed to the Castle.

Did Hajj Mohammed know nothing of the massacre of the

janissaries when they were the Bashaw's guests thirty years earlier? It seems not for, leaving his armed escorts at the city gates, and only accompanied by a few personal followers, he entered the Castle. Here, in one of the rooms near the entrance, a party of soldiers rushed in suddenly, and after a brief struggle strangled the lot. It is probable that renegades were used for this murder, as the superstitious negro *hampas* of the Bashaw might have bungled, or even refused, to murder someone who had come from Mecca.

Simultaneously with this murder, the Algerian escort to the young man was surrounded by *janissaries* and massacred, and the booty of the caravan, doubtless Karamanli's share of the bargain with the Dey of Algiers, was brought into the Castle. It totalled 500,000 sequins, 200 Arab blood horses and 250 camels.

Perhaps this was the last flicker of his old spirit, for by now the old man was growing sick and failing. For a long period he had been slowly going blind, but had been so successful in concealing it that even his concubines were unaware of it.

His mind now turned to the continuation of his family on the throne of Tripoli. Of his two sons, the elder, Mahmoud, was by a Turkish mother, and Karamanli feared that this might give the Turkish elements in his government a hold over the throne which could alienate the populace, upon whose goodwill the Karamanlis finally depended. In 1745, therefore, he summoned the Divan, and publicly handed over the throne to his younger son Mohammed, who was by an Arab mother.

Having done this, and set his seal to the documents of accession, he left the Divan, and ordered two of his most faithful pages to accompany him to his *ghurfa*, or privy chamber. Here he carefully loaded two pistols, with three balls in each, and handed one to the senior page with strict orders to pass him the pistol, should the first misfire. Then, crying out the first sentence of the first chapter of the *Qur'an*,[1] and before either of the pages could prevent him, discharged the pistol into his own stomach and fell dead.

Thus died certainly the greatest of the Karamanli family, whose

[1] A traditional prayer before the start of a journey.

name for some two hundred years was to be regarded by the people of Tripoli, as signifying a sort of golden age, an almost legendary time, when a Prince of their own blood overthrew the invading Turks and led them to unity and a sort of independence.

'*Sultan rasu*' he was called which might be interpreted as 'Sultan through his own endeavour'.

2

MOHAMMED KARAMANLI

1745–1754

The weak Bashaw

On November 4th 1745 the firing of cannon from the Castle, and the shrill ululations of lamenting women on the city roof-tops, announced the death of the founder of the Karamanli dynasty.

Having selected his second son Mohammed as his successor, rather than his firstborn, Mahmoud, he had wisely chosen a moment to die when the latter was absent from Tripoli, thus making certain the enthronement of Mohammed would take place without any interference from the pro-Turkish partisans of Mahmoud. In fact, the messenger who carried the news of the Bashaw's death to the absent son brought also the news of his younger brother's election.

To the Arab population of Tripoli, as the Bashaw had surmised, the election of Mohammed was popular. Not only was he the son of the old Bashaw's wife Zeinab, of pure Libyan descent, but in character he was entirely different from Mahmoud, who spent his time in dissipation with his Turkish *camarilla*. Further, during the period when he was commander of the army, he had shown a mild temperament and a talent for administration. His election was, of course, covertly opposed by many of the Turkish elements in the city, and some also of the old Bashaw's circle, who had hoped to profit by the well-known feebleness of the elder son. The death of the great Bashaw also encouraged some of the tributary tribes into their endemic restlessness, now that the strong hand was withdrawn.

The first act of the newly elected Bashaw, after receiving the oaths of office from his Ministers and the ceremonial visits of the consuls, was to arrange a magnificent funeral for his father. No expense was spared for this entombment of the first of the Karamanli dynasty. As the coffin, clothed in green silk embroidered in gold and silver, and bearing on its surface the dead man's jewelled turban and scimitar, passed through the narrow streets of the city, followed by the *janissary* soldiers and the sumptuously dressed *hampas* of the dead man's personal guard, and the Ministers of the Divan, it was pursued by crowds of wailing women and screaming *marabouts*. The ordinary people pressed close to touch the coffin, and so obtain *baraka* from the grand old man who, concealing from the world his failing powers, had killed himself so that he should remain in public memory a symbol of greatness, and not blindness and senility. He was inhumed in his own great mausoleum, built, 'of the purest white marble . . . filled with an immense quantity of fresh flowers dressed with festoons of Arabian jessamine and large bunches of variegated flowers, consisting of orange, myrtle, red and white roses'.[1] Here, in a tomb surrounded by coloured marbles and majolica tiles, he lies buried.

A few days later, the new Bashaw, surrounded by his court, made his own formal procession through the city.

Mohammed Karamanli had come to the throne at a time of relative peace in the country, both internally and externally. By strong measures, his father had put down all attempts at rebellion from within, and relations with the European powers, and the regular subsidies received from them, had led to an almost complete cessation of corsair activity. Trade and the economy had considerably improved and new industries had been induced to open up in the City. But there were important people who had suffered. These were the renegade officials at the Court who had no stake in the country and relied on corsair activity to give them booty and money, and those commercial interests, both Moslem and Christian who, in the past, had made large profits out of the sale of captured ships and the sale or ransom of Christian slaves. During the final years of Ahmed Karamanli's reign, a firm stop had been put on these activities: corsair vessels had been forbidden to leave port, and ship's captains, renegades, merchants and slave-dealers had suffered accordingly.

The Bashaw's instructions to his heir had contained two car-

[1] Miss Tully.

dinal rules, necessary for successful control of the country. The first was to maintain the peace treaties with the European powers, so that never again should the country be forced to fight on two fronts; the second was to maintain always close and friendly relations with the Mahmid tribe, who inhabited the area of the *menshia*, and whose aid in men and supplies had always been the main support of the Karamanli family.

The new Bashaw's first diplomatic act, after taking office, was to summon the French consular representative, de Gardane, and present him with a letter, addressed to the King of France, affirming the peace treaty of 1723 and stating that he would send an ambassador to Paris. The new Tripoli ambassador to Paris had already been selected. He was the Bashaw's own brother-in-law, Ahmed Hussein, the son of the former Great Kehya Hussein, now in retirement, and arrangements were in hand for his departure.

Suddenly, on November 21st 1745, with one of those tigerish strokes reminiscent of his father, the Bashaw caused Ahmed Hussein and his old father, with several other members of the family, to be seized and strangled, accused of plotting with his elder brother Mahmoud to overthrow him and place Mahmoud on the throne. Whether there was any truth in this accusation will never be known, but it is significant that another of the Bashaw's brothers fled to Tunis, while the indolent Mahmoud was exiled to Derna, where he was appointed Bey.

A few months later, a new and properly accredited French consul named Caullet arrived, and the Bashaw was able to re-affirm with him the peace treaty between France and Tripoli.

Meanwhile, the comedy of the British consul Reed was not yet over. Although he had been declared *persona non grata* by the former Bashaw, and confined to his house, he contrived to hang on to the consulate. Unable to have any contact with the Tripoli government himself, he used a nephew of his, with the romantic name of Valentine Applegath, to carry on the consular work, while he sent a number of money bribes to the government ministers, hoping that after Ahmed Karamanli's death he could get the edict against him revoked. He ignored the fact that he had been officially informed of Robert White's appointment to replace him, and wrote to the Secretary of State saying that he was retained in his consular house by illness, not by the Bashaw's decree, and, so that White could be delayed as long as possible, he reported quite untruthfully that plague had broken out in Tripoli.

White had, in any case, been retained in London by the Secretary of State's office, to help clear up the tangled matters left behind in Suffolk Street by the last Tripoli ambassador. The ambassador had departed heavily in debt to London tradesmen, and there was the still unexplained discovery of the dead body of one of the English cookmaids in the Suffolk Street garden.

These complicated matters delayed White, but meanwhile he despatched two letters to Tripoli. One was to the Bashaw in French informing him of his appointment as consul, and giving a short account of his qualifications, which included many years' residence in Tunis, 'where I was so cognisant of the habits and manners of the government, and the humour of the people that I never gave any reason for dissatisfaction'. He concluded with a request that Reed might be allowed to return to England 'without any molestation from your subjects'. His second letter was to the Dutch consul, asking him to take over the affairs of the British consulate for a few months until his own arrival.

Reed who, if he had few qualities to recommend him, had at least that of persistence, had not shot his last bolt. By means of his bribes to the new Bashaw's ministers he extracted a letter, apparently written by the Bashaw, describing him as 'a worthy, honest and reputable man', who had 'the goodwill and affections of all my subjects'. Armed with this, he left Tripoli for London in 1747, taking with him most of the consular files, so that consular business could not be transacted in his absence. On arrival, he produced a long memorandum for the Secretary of State's office, in which he accused the unlucky White of being 'a person disaffected to His Majesty, George II,' and one who 'favoured the Pretender'. This in 1747, two years after the '45, was a very dangerous accusation, and it obliged the already busy White to seek affidavits of six of his friends of long standing, mostly reputable London merchants, to attest the falseness of the charge. With these affidavits refuting what White described as 'this infamous imputation of Jacobitism', he added his own memorandum:

Mr. Reed received notice, as early as 1744 that he was superseded, notwithstanding which he assumed the character of consul and continued so to act till the years 1747, during the latter part of which time he took great pains by Bribes and other indirect means to bring the new government of Tripoli to refuse Mr. White. . . . In the said year Mr. Reed arrived in London and delivered a letter from the new Bey,[1] and to perfect his scheme and get himself re-placed in the consulship, he represented Mr. White to the government as a person disaffected to His Majesty and consequently unfit for the trust and employment given him. And, having thus foully and individually aspersed and defamed Mr. White's character, he attempted to seduce evidence to prove the said false and infamous charge. . . .

But Reed's protector, the Duke of Newcastle, had left the Southern Department, and his letter purporting to come from the Bashaw of Tripoli, carries a laconic minute from the Secretary of State's office:

'Q. How this letter came?'

It is answered in the hand of another clerk:

'From Mr. Applegath.'

It was the end of possibly the worst British consul to take office in North Africa.

White arrived in Tripoli in August 1751, in a British frigate from the squadron commanded by Commodore Keppel, who landed with the consul and accompanied him to his first audience with the Bashaw, where the peace treaty with Tripoli of 1730 was reaffirmed in full ceremony.

White was a zealous and conscientious trading consul[2] and

[1] White was accustomed to the Tunisian hierarchy, where the Ruler was a Bey.

[2] He trafficked in salt from Zuara with his vice consul, Traill.

rapidly informed himself on the political situation in Tripoli. In a despatch of September 1751, he described the new Bashaw, as, in general:

> a man of mild and gentle disposition, but the attachment to wine and women induce him to seek a retirement that is inconsistent with making any good and reputable figure in the government of the country. The Ministers have their own interests to pursue, and they make use of the ascendance they have over the Prince to serve these interests. Hence Cabals and Parties among them.

It was a prescient reading of Mohammed Karamanli's character and does much to explain the events which now succeeded.

It had probably been an honest determination by the young Bashaw to follow the advice of his father, and stop the pursuit of piracy in the Regency thus maintaining good relations with the European powers. But from the time of his accession he came under pressure, much against his will, to return to the dangerous but lucrative profits from piracy.

The main pressure in the Divan came from the Turkish elements, who gained nothing from State subsidies to the Treasury and much from the divided profits of piracy, and who, with few personal commitments in the City, had the least to lose from any destructive attacks on it from the sea. Their pressure was increased also by the growing number of European renegades who, originally recruited and controlled by Ahmed Karamanli, were now coming in greater numbers to seek a living at the Court of Tripoli. There were also the commercial elements in the City, both Moslem and Christian, who made a profitable investment out of slavery and the sale of plunder.

All these differing interests combined to bring about an eventual capitulation on the part of the weak Mohammed Karamanli. He agreed to a resumption of piracy with all that it entailed, though he insisted that the peace treaties of Britain and France should be strictly respected, for fear of immediate and powerful ripostes. On April 15th 1748 Tripoli, after thirty years of peace, embarked once more on a course of piracy far exceeding anything in Ahmed Karamanli's reign.[1]

The first to suffer were the Neapolitans. On that day of April, Signor Bigani the Neapolitan consul, was summoned to the Castle, and brusquely informed that, from that moment, a state of war existed between Tripoli and the Neapolitan kingdom. The strict rules of piracy were carefully observed. No sooner had the document announcing the decision been handed to the consul than a flag was run up on the Castle battlements, a signal gun was fired, and, to the cheering of waiting crowds on the Marine, four corsair vessels that had been waiting ready geared for war, slipped their cables and sped for the harbour mouth. Bigani, who was now in danger of being seized and put to slavery, fled to the sanctuary of the French consulate, where Caullet protected him until he could be shipped to safety in a French vessel.

In spite of some severe reprimands from the French, when careless corsair captains seized French protected vessels, the next six years were spent in comparative freedom from punitive attacks against the Bashaw, the Divan and *taiffa*, during which their corsair fleet, now under the command of Sicard, a French renegade, swept the eastern approaches of the Mediterranean, the Levant coast, and even the North Sea in their depredations on Neapolitan, German, Dutch and Genoese vessels. The harbour of Tripoli was full of captured ships for sale, the markets of booty, and long strings of Christian slaves in chains, from Naples, Hamburg, Genoa and Amsterdam, trudged the streets.

For the French and British consuls, this was a busy and profitable period, and it was in the interests of neither, nor of their respective countries, that it should cease. Some European powers escaped by paying even heavier subsidies. Austria in 1749, and Denmark in 1752, agreed each to pay an annual sum of 20,000 sequins into the Bashaw's treasury. But unrelenting pursuit and capture continued against all the smaller maritime states.

[1] Micacchi lists the corsair fleet in 1745 as 2 frigates of 26 guns, 2 galleys of 24 guns, and 10 chebeks of 10–15 guns.

Meanwhile White was disturbed at the fact that the French consul, with the connivance of his government, was able to steal a march on him:

The Cruizers bring in a number of prizes annually which they sell at very low Rate to Europeans, and the French being well apprized how beneficial this Branch of Commerce is to their Subjects do lodge in their Consul's hand from time to time a number of Blank Passes to be issued as occasion offers. . . . I most humbly submit to Your Grace whether, as we are at so much greater distance than them, from the usuall Channell of procuring Passes, it would not tend to the advantage of British Subjects trading to this place to have the like Indulgence.

By thus purchasing captured vessels at a very cheap rate, the English and French merchants could issue them with passes to engage freely in the lucrative trade which was, quite frequently, that of transporting the annual quota of black slaves from the Tripoli market to Egypt, Turkey and the Levant.

In spite of the Bashaw's relaxation on the piracy trade and his apparent gradual withdrawal from affairs, there was still a number of dissidents anxious to overturn him. The Castle echoed with rumours of plots, and the *hampas* were busy at night. Suspecting treachery the Bashaw had already felt obliged to order the strangulation of the Rais of Marine and his son, and some time later two of his own cousins met the same fate. In 1752, there was a serious insurrection of Turkish elements in the city who probably resented the growing influence of the renegades.

On the evening of Sunday July 30th, the city, which was resting after a long day of fasting during the rigours of a summer Ramadan, was aroused by shots and the sound of cannon. The streets were full of people eating, drinking and recovering from the heat and exhaustion of the day. Through them dashed parties of Turkish soldiers carrying firearms, and among them several members of the *taiffa*.

White, and his French colleague Caullet, immediately called in their nationals, and shut themselves up in their consulates. The former took up the tale four days later in a despatch of August 4th:

The Raises or Captains of the Cruizers attended with 400 men, all natives of Albania, had taken up arms to cut off the Bashaw, the Sheikh, and some other Great People, that were obnoxious to them, (occasioned by the late renewal of Peace with the French). They began their operations in a coffee house where they usually mett (as is the custom of these people in the moon of Ramadan), by placing the vice Admirall on a Carpett, kissing his hand, and swearing allegiance to him as Bashaw.

When they had finished this Ceremony, it was about 10 o'clock in the Evening, they despatched three parties from the main body. The first to a Coffee house, where they knew the Sheikh (the Bashaw's first minister) and some other Grandees were, who succeeded too well in their Barbarious Design, having assassinated him.

The second party marched to the Guard Room and seized all the arms they found, without any difficulty, as the Guards were, at that time, in a distant quarter of the town taking their accustomed rounds; the third detachment attacked the Captain of the Port, who, by his Office, obliged to sleep in a Lodge adjoining the Marine Gate. Here however they were most Valiantly repulsed, and met with a reception due to their Insolence. The Captain of the Port, with only four Attendants, bravely defended himself against all their Efforts to burst open the door of his Lodge, and after he had killed six of them, they thought proper to retreat.

In the meantime, while the several different parties were thus employed, the vice Admirall, with the rest of the Rebells, went to all the Funduks, or barracks, where the Levant Turks, or soldiers, are quartered, and most streniously solicited them to join him; but neither his Magnificent Promises, nor his artful persuasion had the smallest effect on them. And, having information at the same time, that the Bashaw was alarmed, and had sent a considerable body against them, they plainly perceived their Case was desperate, and began to sett about making a Retreat.

In order to effect this, they got possession of a Castle, situated at the north west end of the town, and some of the Rebells kept playing uppon the Castle where the Bashaw resides, with all the cannon they could bring to bear, while the Rest were breaking open the Marine Gate to make their Escape by Sea. In this Scheme they succeeded, for, as nigh as we can learn, about 200 of them got into Boats, and seized a ship of 200 tons, and a row galley that were both ready to sail, and by the help of a favourable Breeze, got clear off. . . .

Next morning, 47 of the Rebells were discovered lurking in the town, and were immediately executed. . . .

A Turkish *marabout* who had run about the streets, trying to arouse the public to revolt, was also taken, and publicly strangled.

The revolt in fact failed when the rebellious Turks saw that not only the majority of the *janissaries* and townspeople were against them, but that strong forces from the *menshia* and the loyal Mahmid tribe were rapidly approaching the city.

There was no further attempt at revolt in the city during Mohammed Karamanli's brief reign. In 1753 there was an attempt by some of the Berber tribes in the Gharian area to avoid payment of tribute, but the Bashaw had recently increased his ranks of *janissaries*, depleted after the attempted revolt of the previous year, by recruiting several hundred from Smyrna, and was thus able to put a strong force of 5000 men against them. Forty-five of their ringleaders were executed and an even heavier tribute was exacted.

It seems probable that Mohammed Karamanli's gradual withdrawal from public affairs, which began about now, was due to illness, probably helped by the immoderate drinking which seemed endemic in the Karamanli family. During the early part of 1754, his illness became progressively worse, and in a despatch of August 24th 1754, White reported his death 'after a serious and painful illness. He died about 6 in the evening. At 7, his eldest son, Sidi Ali, was installed and set in the chair of State, and the same evening proclaimed through the city.'

The victim of both weakness and dissipation, Mohammed Karamanli's one claim to a mention in the history of his country is that, against all pretenders, by intrigue, assassination, and some luck, he had maintained his family on the throne of Tripoli.

3

ALI KARAMANLI

1754–1795

The British Consulate in Tripoli
as it was in the 18th century

Trouble with the consuls

Consul White had reported, that it was at sunset on July 24th 1754, that the conventional three cannon-shots from the Castle announced to the city and the *menshia* the death of Mohammed Bashaw.

The announcement was only made to the public after a day of preparation in great secrecy, for the immediate and unopposed election of Mohammed Bashaw's son, the twenty-three-year-old Prince Ali; and, while the ululations of the women, mourning from the housetops, began to echo across the sands to the *menshia*, messengers had already galloped off, carrying the news of the election to the outlying towns and villages, and from thence to the tribes in the *jebel*.

The complete secrecy surrounding Ali Bashaw's election was made possible by the unanimity of purpose among the 500 European renegades who now filled the Castle and who, during the final years of Mohammed Karamanli's reign, had gradually usurped the positions of his senior ministers and advisers.

To the Karamanli family, these adventurers from the Mediterranean ports who, by a simple formula of renunciation of their creed and by the rite of circumcision, could attain high position in the government hierarchy, were useful and dependable servants. Though mostly deserters from Christian ships, escaped galley-slaves from France, or Levantine riff-raff from the Spanish, Italian and Greek ports, they had resources and skills not available among the illiterate local population. More important, their loyalty and their ambitions were attached to, and flowed from, their paymasters. The dynastic intrigues of family, the interminable feuds of tribe, the local politics of Turk or *kuloghli* were not for them. From their origins they were never candidates for the usurpation of power. Greed was perhaps their driving force.

Ahmed Karamanli, while appreciating their value, had accepted them only sparingly, and never to the deprivation of his senior ministers, using their skills rather than their advice. As such they became shipwrights, captains of his corsair vessels, interpreters in the Divan, controllers of Christian slaves, but rarely more. Under his son, however, they had gradually increased, not only in numbers, but in power and influence so that, by the time of Ali Karamanli's election, they completely surrounded the throne, nullified the Divan, and set a distance between the Bashaw and his indigenous ministers and advisers.

To the European consuls, the Bashaw's situation soon became increasingly dangerous, not only for his relations with the Regency as a whole, but also for the treaties of non-belligerence with the European powers. The French consul, de Gardane, wrote, in a tone of desperation, after trying in vain to see him on matters affecting French nationals:

> The Bashaw is unable to decide anything. He gives audiences only once every 15 days, and is then so suffocated by the local people and their complaints, that he does not know how to give attention to ours. He is out of contact with everything and so indecisive that he has not the courage to pronounce on anything. His two Kehyas, his General of Troops, Treasurer and Chief of Arsenal, are all renegades, while the Divan remains nothing but a name.

It was under the influence of these renegades that the young Prince now took up the reigns of government. His Grand Kehya, Hussein Giorgio, a Greek renegade, worked assiduously, not only to isolate Ali from his family connections, but also to increase his natural fears of treachery and assassination. The renegades were thus able to use the Bashaw to suppress any of the Tripoli notables whose influence or popularity might be dangerous to them. The result of these suspicions was a series of lightning strokes in the familiar Karamanli manner, against his real or supposed enemies.

The first victim was the Bashaw's uncle, an old and respected man and a former Treasurer to both his father and grandfather, 'Nigh forty years under the government of three successive Bashaws,' as White reported in bewilderment. The next to die by the strangling cords of the *hampas* were his own younger

17th-century view of Tripoli from the sea
The Castle of Tripoli in the 18th century

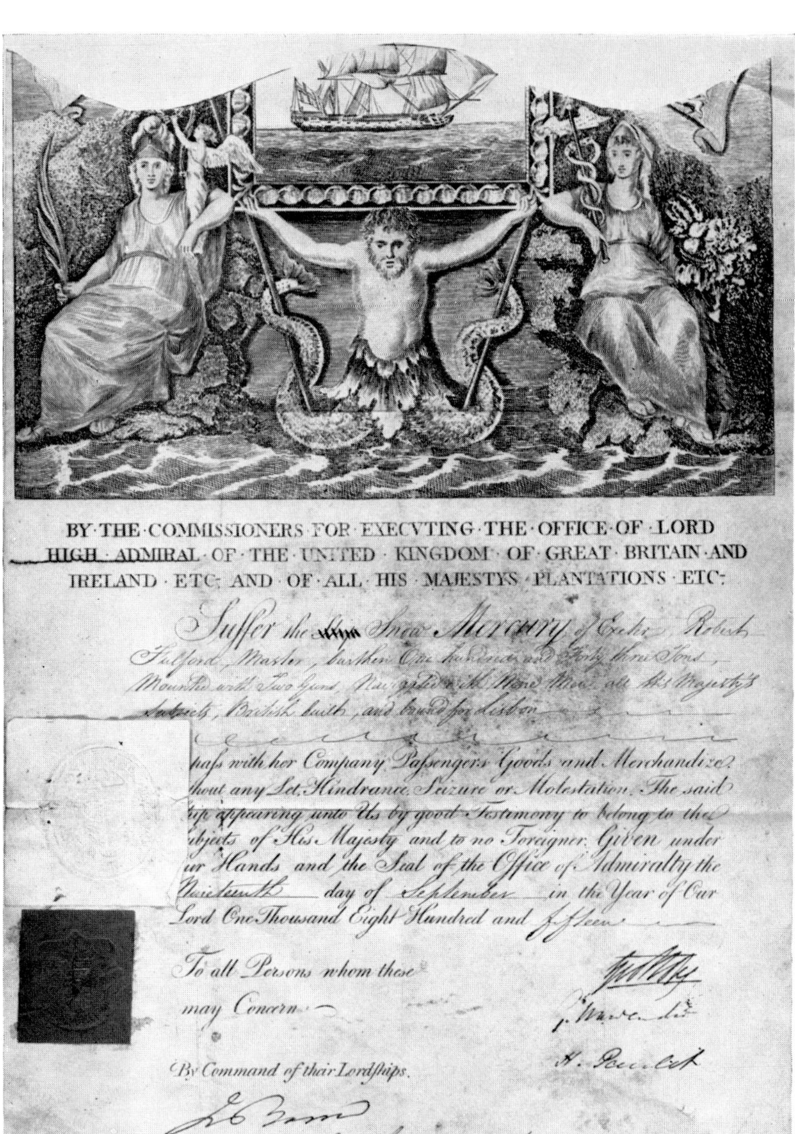

BY THE COMMISSIONERS FOR EXECUTING THE OFFICE OF LORD HIGH ADMIRAL OF THE UNITED KINGDOM OF GREAT BRITAIN AND IRELAND ETC. AND OF ALL HIS MAJESTYS PLANTATIONS ETC.

Suffer the Snow Mercury of Exeter Robert Fulford, Master, burthen One hundred and Forty three Tons, Mounted with Two Guns, Navigated with Nine Men all His Majesty's Subjects, British built, and bound for Lisbon

pass with her Company Passengers Goods and Merchandize thout any Let, Hindrance, Seizure or Molestation. The said ip appearing unto Us by good Testimony to belong to the ubjects of His Majesty and to no Foreigner. Given under ur Hands and the Seal of the Office of Admiralty the Nineteenth day of September in the Year of Our Lord One Thousand Eight Hundred and fifteen

To all Persons whom these may Concern

By Command of their Lordships.

Fifteen Thousand three hundred & Seven

Bottom half of a
Mediterranean ship's passport, 1815

brother and four uncles, as well as an unknown number of leading citizens. Only when these imagined threats to the throne were removed, did the fratricidal slaughter subside.

During the final years of Mohammed Bashaw's reign, Tripoli piracy had declined once more, and a series of new peace treaties had been signed with the smaller maritime powers. With their new-found strength, under a young and pliable Bashaw, the European renegades renewed their pressure on him to break some of the treaties and take up active piracy again. They were successful. To the dismay of the French consul, the notorious French renegade, Sicard from Marseilles was appointed Rais of the pirate fleet, the fleet itself was once more armed and supplied with crews, and in ones and twos, the fast ships left Tripoli to cruise once again off the approaches to the Mediterranean, across the mouth of the Adriatic, and along the coastlines of Italy and France. Sicard himself, in a former English corvette of 36 guns probably sold to him by White, sailed with a merciless crew of specially recruited Arnautis from the Levant.

By the end of the first summer's cruising, the familiar and tragic scenes began to repeat themselves in the audience chamber of the Bashaw and in the slave bazaars, as cargoes of Christian slaves were dragged off to captivity to the *bagnios* of the Castle or to the stone quarries at Gargaresch. England, France, Austria and Holland, who had the power for severe reprisals, alone were spared.

It is a sad commentary on the morals of the times, that Consul White, watching the slaves passing his consulate, could report to London that the Bashaw was now 'putting his marine affairs on a respectable footing'.

Personal relations between White and the Bashaw remained friendly during White's tenure of office. In 1751 he had signed a new Treaty of Peace & Commerce with the Bashaw, and this was renewed, with the usual presents, on the accession of George III in 1760. White however, was primarily a merchant, and like nearly all the British consuls who took up trade in Tripoli, eventually failed and fell into debt. These debts, some of which were incurred with the Bashaw's ministers, led to trouble, but White seems to have been generally popular, and his wife, a vigorous and attractive woman, whose daughter by him was married to the Austrian vice-Consul, was welcomed in the *harims* of the Castle—the first Englishwoman to penetrate those remote fastnesses.

In 1763 White died of apoplexy and, for a while, Mrs. White with the approval of London, ran the consular affairs of England with some effectiveness.

If the Bashaw and his ministers had some small pecuniary troubles with White, they were genuinely to regret his demise when a new British consul arrived to take up his post in 1765.

This was the Hon. Archibald Campbell Fraser, second son of that Lord Lovat, who had been executed in 1747 for his part in the rebellion of 1745. Although the Lovat estates and title were returned to the family subsequently under a general pardon, it was probably estrangement of the family from the government that led to Fraser's appointment to such a minor post as that of Consul of Tripoli. Like his elder brother, who became a distinguished general, he was an army officer, and the reasons for virtual exile to Tripoli must partly be explained by his character, which soon showed itself as haughty, peremptory and sometimes violent. He had some reason to display a fit of temper on his arrival, for he found that Mrs. White, like Consul Reed before her, had carried off to England most of the consular files.

Fraser had scarcely settled down in the new consulate, which, following the destruction of the former consulate in the bombardment of 1728, had been acquired in 1744, than trouble with the Bashaw began. A Spanish sailor appeared at the consulate, claiming to have escaped from the Castle, and reported that three Spanish boys from Port Mahon were being held by the Bashaw who was forcing them to turn Moslem.

There was an agreed procedure in the peace treaties for such a case but, before invoking these, some careful checking of the Spanish sailor's story would have been necessary, to ascertain the exact nationality of the vessel in which these boys had been captured, and an examination of their papers, to see whether in fact the corsair which had captured them had infringed the peace treaties, and also whether the crew of the vessel were nationals of Port Mahon which was now under British protection.

In fact it was afterwards shown that the vessel, according to the rules of the sea, was a legitimate prize, being Genoese and travelling under a false passport, facts which the Rais of the Marine had soon detected.[1] But by then, the precipitate Fraser had already acted.

In a despatch of April 15th 1765 to the Secretary of State he accused the Bashaw, assisted by the Treasurer in the Castle, of having

> in a fit of enthusiasm, bastinadoed the three youngest lads. . . . in the dead of night, in order to try what force might do in making them turn Moslem. They suffered the pain of being bastinadoed with resolution, and persisted in their unwillingness to become Turks expecting that I would come early to the Castle in the morning to their relief. The Treasurer, by the Bashaw's order, and in his presence, repeated the bastinado with his own hand, and a wooden instrument, on their feet, which the lads, unable to sustain, alarmed the Castle with their cries, on which they were threatened with immediate death if they refused to repeat the sentence containing the Mohammedan profession of faith. The three lads, from fear and pain, said they would repeat anything, on which they called in the Priest by break of day, and circumcised them by force, by that means cutting off, as they apprehended, any possibility of my interposition . . .

Two days later, another sailor escaped to the British consulate. Fraser alleged that he himself tried in vain to get an interview with the Bashaw, calling he stated, every day for seven successive days, at the Castle. The Bashaw's only reply was to send a message ordering Fraser to hand over the runaway sailors who were legitimate slaves. Fraser refused whereupon a party of *janissaries* were sent to remove the sailors by force. These delivered an order through their officer, for Fraser to strike his flag and remain

[1] At this period many Genoese living in Gibraltar were running lucrative businesses in forging British papers.

confined to the consulate. According to the diplomatic practice of those days this was a declaration from the Bashaw that Fraser was *persona non grata*. Fraser was undeterred. 'The servants of the other European powers,' he wrote, in a despatch of April 17th, 'tremble at the consequence that this act of violence, unredressed, will have . . .', and he added ominously, 'I shall acquaint Commodore Harrison, now at Malta, who will no doubt take immediate steps to protect His Majesty's trading subjects'.

Fraser having despatched a letter in the same tone to the Commander of the Mediterranean fleet at Malta, kept to his house until the arrival of a British frigate commanded by a Captain Hudson. Hudson came ashore and, possibly impressed by Fraser's social rank, immediately put himself under Fraser's orders.[1] There followed some very undiplomatic behaviour for which Hudson was afterwards reprimanded.

With the frigate's guns trained on the Castle Fraser, accompanied by Hudson, sought and obtained an audience with the Bashaw at which he demanded the release of the crew of the captured vessel. The Bashaw protested with truth that the ship was Genoese and therefore not under British protection, and was travelling under a forged passport which his officer who controlled Marine affairs could confirm. But British consul and frigate's captain were adamant, and with the frigate's guns threatening his weak batteries, the Bashaw was compelled to hand over the Genoese. He stated, however, that he would send a formal protest to King George III.

As if a threat of war without authority was not sufficient, Fraser now proceeded to further folly. Captain Hudson decided to use the visit of his frigate for a reception aboard for the foreign consular corps. While this was being held the Austrian consul was surreptitiously approached by a member of the frigate's crew, an Austrian subject, to ask if his consulate would give him protection if he got ashore as he wished to leave the British service. The Austrian consul correctly informed him that if he could get

[1] In spite of specific Admiralty instruction that naval officers should always rank senior to Consuls.

ashore and present himself at the consulate he would receive the necessary protection. The sailor got ashore, reached the Austrian consulate, and was taken in. The request from Captain Hudson that the sailor should be handed back was of course refused.

Fraser was informed of this by Hudson. He asked Hudson for a file of marines and an officer and with these following him, marched through the city to the Austrian consulate. Upon being denied admittance, they broke in by force, seized the sailor, and dragged him back to the ship. During the scuffle which ensued, Fraser struck both the Austrian consul and his wife, the former Miss White, with his cane.

The action shocked the Castle and the consular corps and protests went to London both from the Bashaw and the Imperial Court in Vienna. 'This consul,' wrote the Bashaw to his ambassador in London, 'seeks embroils more than peace, is a noisy man, without reason; a boisterous, unruly man'.

A further and more menacing message was added that unless the British government removed Fraser the Bashaw would himself expel him.

These complaints, coupled with that from the Imperial Court in Vienna, were at length acted upon in spite of the attempts of Fraser's cousin, the Marquis of Lorne, to prevent his removal. On February 18th a reply to the Bashaw's protest was passed to the Tripoli ambassador at St. James:

I am hereby to acquaint Your Excellency that in consequence of the proofs laid before his Majesty of the irregular behaviour of Mr. Fraser, H.M. Consul in Tripoli, and of the representations made thereon, as well as by the ambassador of His Imperial Majesty, as by Your Excellency, His Majesty has sent orders to the said Mr. Fraser to return immediately to England to give an account of his conduct.

Fraser left Tripoli for London in September 1766, and several attempts to get him reinstated by the Marquis of Lorne are on record. These failed but such was the power of 'interest' at Court in George III's government, that Fraser was granted a pension of £600 a year. He was posted to Algiers, where, apart from falling out with most of his colleagues, he earned a not entirely opprobrious fame by being the first European consul to refuse to kiss the Dey's hand. But by 1773, the Dey also had had enough of him and wrote vigorously to London for his recall.

'He is a bad man,' concluded the letter from the Dey to George III. Perhaps Fraser was happier in his native Highlands. In 1782 he became M.P. for Inverness.[1]

The obnoxious Fraser was succeeded by an English trader from Minorca called Wilkie, but his appointment did not last and, in 1768, a new consul named Barker was properly appointed from London. Barker arrived in 1768, bringing with him, as well as the usual gift of £500 payable according to Treaty on all changes of consul, a considerable quantity of gold watches, clocks, guns and pistols and rolls of English cloth. He carried with him a list of thirty-two members of the Bashaw's staff, each of whom was to be allotted a present according to rank.[2] As vice-consul, he brought with him a young man Richard Tully who, although not officially appointed, was to work as an assistant to him, and generally run the consulate for a salary of £150 a year, to be deducted from Barker's own emoluments.

Probably as a result of Fraser's behaviour towards the Bashaw and his consular colleagues, Barker arrived with explicit instructions as to his diplomatic conduct. The question of precedence in the Bashaw's audience chamber, of the courtesies towards his diplomatic colleagues, when to fly and lower his flag, and the number of signal guns to be fired from ship to shore, etc., were all enlarged upon. Barker also had a firm instruction to use every effort (not excluding bribery, if necessary) to induce the Bashaw to send no more ambassadors to London. The former rule that foreign ambassadors should live while in residence at the charge of the host State, had recently been abolished for all countries

[1] The *D.N.B.* records the subsequent history of Fraser who had a strange tomb erected during his life recording a partly fictitious account of his service as a consul in Africa.

[2] See Appendix for list of the Bashaw's servants in 1768.

except the Barbary States. This had caused heavy charges on the King's purse, as a series of Tripoline ambassadors, usually relatives or friends of the Karamanli Bashaws, had descended on London with large trains of servants, had overstayed the statutory period of six months, and had then departed leaving heavy debts behind them. As they had virtually nothing to do in London, except get into various kinds of mischief and run up large bills, there was pressure on the Southern Department to cut these visits down as much as possible. A sum of money given to the consul to be dispensed in suitable bribes to Ministers proved a more economic way of dealing with this problem.

Politically, Barker's arrival in Tripoli coincided with what might be described as the *nadir* of Ali Bashaw's rule. De Lancey the new French consul, described the situation in a despatch:

The Bashaw is of an appearance and manner generally pleasing, but in character a mixture of feebleness, timidity, generosity, yet with a cruel determination to rule in indolence and inactivity. Indifferent to religion, he remains shut up in his Castle in the midst of 500 or 600 renegades, who abuse his name, change his orders as they wish, and rob him of his money. If one can reach him, he greets one politely, promises all one asks, and does nothing.

The situation of the country was also worsening economically. A series of bad harvests had led to near famine conditions in the outlying areas, causing movements and disturbance among the tribes who, one by one, were throwing off the payment of tribute, which could normally only be exacted by force which did not now exist. Caravans were halted, from difficulty of passing through the disturbed and famine areas, and a renewed fear of plague, which would probably play havoc among the physically weakened Tripolines, was now showing itself both in Egypt and Tunis.

While, as time passed, Ali Bashaw remained more and more sunk in apathy in the Castle, the consuls began to report in 1779 a change in the situation. The Bashaw, by a Georgian wife Lilla Halluma, a fair haired, blue-eyed beauty, had had three sons, Hassan, Ahmed and Yusef. The eldest of these Hassan, according to precedent, on coming of age in 1779, was made Bey or commander of the troops. Intelligent and active, he immediately reorganised the troops and left with them on several forays among the dissident tribes who had refused their tribute. He also reactivated the corsair fleet, which for several years past, under pressure from the European states and lack of funds, had ceased piracy, and sent them out to replenish the depleted Treasury. With his brothers, he rapidly succeeded in reducing the influence of the renegades with the Bashaw. In a very short time he succeeded in becoming a popular figure in the Regency.

Behind the high, dark walls of the Castle, however, where, in their separate quarters, divided by locked iron-bound doors and guarded by watchful *hampas*, the Bashaw and his three sons lived in isolation with their *harims* and their Arab and Jewish concubines, and surrounded by renegades and tale-bearing slaves, intrigue, suspicion and fear were beginning to thrive.

The weak, indolent, but highly suspicious Bashaw, stirred from his lethargy by the innuendoes of his younger sons and the whispers of the renegades, began to suspect the growing influence in the Regency of his eldest son. In following this policy both the younger sons were actuated by a fear, natural in a Karamanli, that when he eventually assumed power Hassan would remove them by murder. Ahmed the second son was, like his father, a weak and amiable creature, much under the influence of the youngest son Yusef. In Yusef, still very young, there was evidence already of a character in which ruthlessness, intrigue, cunning resource, allied to an instinctive knowledge of men, much resembled that of his great-grandfather, Ahmed, founder of the dynasty.

To the watching consuls, tragedy was already brooding over the Castle. The principal figure of that tragedy was the Georgian wife of the Bashaw, the unhappy mother of three much loved sons, Lilla Halluma. It is fortunate for this record that a European spectator now appeared who would lift the story which was to follow out of the sparse, arid consular reports, into a vivid and poignant drama.

Consul Tully

Mr. Consul Barker, who has left no noteworthy record of his service but one of zealousness and good temper, did not long survive the climate and the conditions of Tripoli. He had died in 1772 'in his breeches', as Tully reported, 'of an atrocious throat infection'. During the interim period before the appointment of a new consul, the British consulate was directed efficiently, punctually and industriously, by the vice-consul Richard Tully.

Tully, who since his appointment with Barker, four years earlier, had struggled along on his derisory salary of £150 a year, had been sufficiently encouraged by his personal success in Tripoli to hope, perhaps, that he might be confirmed in the post of consul. From the little we know of his origins, it appears that he was born at Leghorn of Irish parentage, his father having been an exile after the collapse of the exiled James II's abortive Irish adventures. He spoke fluent Italian and therefore found little difficulty in acquiring the *lingua franca* of the Castle and the Bashaw's court, which spoke a bastard mixture of Italian, French and Turkish. He was liked by the Bashaw, for he seems to have had the sort of pliant, friendly nature which orientals find attractive, and he had augmented his contacts, as well as his income, by some small trading ventures with the Bashaw's ministers, as well as with the Bey. Most important of all, his wife and young daughters soon became favourites in the Castle *harims*, bringing a welcome breath of air from the outside world to these incarcerated women. His daughters even learned some Arabic, the language of the *harims*, which was to prove of great importance in later days.

On Barker's death, Tully wrote to the Secretary of State, asking if he might be confirmed in the post of consul. In reply, he was informed that a consul, Bayntun, had already been appointed but that he might stay on as Bayntun's vice-consul, at the same salary as before, if he wished, the salary to come, as before, from

Bayntun's *frais*. Edward Bayntun, a rough and ready sort of man, arrived in 1773, and soon showed his character by upsetting an audience with the Bashaw by physically manhandling the Swedish consul out of the chair of precedence next to the Bashaw.

Another opportunity for making trouble soon presented itself. A drunken British sailor had taken refuge in the Consulate courtyard, from which he was dragged by a group of the *sandanar*, or town guard. Bayntun did not pause to consider the merits of the affair, or how best it might be resolved without trouble. He donned his official uniform, and called for an audience with the Bashaw, from whom he demanded a public bastinadoing of the culprits, on the exact spot where the insult to the British flag had taken place. The Bashaw protested that such a proceeding would be against the tenets of the Moslem faith, and a sign of the weakness of his own authority. He offered instead to have the culprits quietly strangled. To this Bayntun would not agree; a punishment carried out secretly in the Castle would have no effect outside, and no doubt the arrested guards fervently agreed with him. The Bashaw was finally compelled to yield, and a public bastinado of the unfortunate guards, with all the consequent damage to Anglo-Tripoline relations, was carried out under the eyes of the assembled consular corps.

Tully may have been sanguine that such a consul would not last long in Tripoli where an equability of temper and an elasticity of temperament were necessary for success with the local people. In fact, Bayntun lasted only three years, before leaving in disgust for Port Mahon, handing over the responsibilities of the post to Tully. He had avoided, by leaving it to Tully, the disagreeable task of approaching the Bashaw and some of his ministers for the repayment of sums of money, lent to them by English merchants, because of the recent failure of the grain harvests and consequent shortage of funds.

Tully once more tried to obtain the post of consul, and he wrote a careful letter to the Secretary of State, setting out his services so far and his unusual qualifications for the post. He was however, unaware that a local English merchant who coveted the post of consul for himself, had already been in communication with London, and had pointed out a fact unknown apparently, that Richard Tully was a Papist and therefore barred from holding public employment. Tully was however useful, and in a reply to his letter he was informed that a new British consul, Edward Cooke, had been appointed to fill the post, and that Tully, if he wished could continue to work at the consulate as Cooke's secretary on the same terms as before. Now deeply in debt, he could do nothing but comply.

The new Consul arrived in a British frigate in May 1777, with strict instructions to see that the Bashaw and his ministers paid their debts to British merchants, and that good relations were established between the British consulate and the Castle. In fact, Cooke found that far from being able to reimburse the British merchants, the Bashaw and his government were in sad straits themselves. The wheat, for which British merchants had advanced large sums of money, was not forthcoming; Tripoli was short of wheat for its own consumption, and wheat imports were at a standstill from lack of money to pay for them. In a despatch of May 12th 1777 Cooke drew a picture of the Bashaw's situation, blaming the Jews for the parlous position the Castle was in:

The present Bashaw has many able, some great qualities, but is obsessed by a most determined indolence and inactivity. An old Jewish woman, in whose lap he sinks to sleep every evening, after his evening cup of the strongest brandy, and two or three sailors and vagabonds, turned Turks, are his counsellors and lead him as they please.

Later he was to add:

The situation of the country is nearly desperate. The Bashaw grown every day more and more indolent.... The Jews, the leeches of the country, are making large sums out of the Bashaw, and getting it out of the country. He now and again makes his appearance towards evenings, when he is always taken up with the disputes of the inland Moors and the Beduins. He pays little attention to anything else, and the French, Danish, and Venetian consuls have been here two months, soliciting in vain to see him, though they have business with him which he alone can settle. . . . Meanwhile, the scarcity and penury in the country keep increasing. [He begs for] the appearance again of one or two of His Majesty's ships of war in this port.

And, he adds that even after repeated visits by him, in which 'constant unfulfilled promises to pay were given', no money was forthcoming.

By December 1777 Cooke, himself in financial difficulties, complains that the Bashaw is even less to be seen, and that many people are now turning to the Bey, his eldest son. He is very gloomy about the future and thinks that if matters remain as they are, in a few years' time, 'there should not be a European in the country'. As for his own condition, he reports that he is heavily in debt, and complains of the heavy drain on his pocket of what he terms Tully's 'monstrous allowance'.

Depressed and in debt and complaining about his ill health, Cooke obtained permission to go on leave at the end of 1777. He sailed for Port Mahon, and there applied to London for a post in Algiers, leaving the equally penniless Tully to run the consulate on his 'monstrous allowance' of £150 a year.

For the next fourteen years Richard Tully, gentle, friendly, conscientious, was to follow the fortunes of the Regency in a series of neat, carefully written and descriptive despatches which cover the most depressing periods of the history of the Karamanlis. And when in 1783 his sister[1] from England joined him and began her famous letters on which so much of the history of Tripoli is based, it is as if a lens is suddenly put to the eye of the chronicler, so that the Karamanli court springs into sharp focus with all its colour and drama.

Richard Tully certainly merited, though he could scarcely have hoped for, the appointment of consul. The Italian born grandson

[1] Whether Miss Tully was sister or sister-in-law of Tully is not now known. After her departure from Tripoli in 1793, nothing further is heard of her until the publication of her famous letters in 1816. There is some evidence that these letters were published through the influence of Edward Blaquière. But whether Miss Tully was then alive is a matter of conjecture.

of an Irish Papist, without friends or influence in London, he could hardly expect to receive a well-paid post with diplomatic status when the court of George III was filled with place-hunters and sycophants, ready to undertake any post for a respectable means of livelihood. But he lived in hopes, perhaps feeling that with his languages, his popularity at the Bashaw's court, and his industry, he was indispensable to any new appointment. Once more, *faute de mieux*, he resolved to stay on, and continue the running of the consulate on his miserable stipend. To live, he borrowed heavily from various lenders.

Meanwhile, he took up his pen again and surveyed the scene around him. It was growing desperate. The economy of the Regency itself was dependant on the grain harvests. The Libyans believe that the harvests of their country pursue an almost regular cycle of five good years followed by one bad. The bad year can be survived without difficulty under normal circumstances, because the grain stores in the silos are ordinarily sufficient to supply the needs of the people over the bad months. But two successive bad years can quickly lead to much hardship, particularly in the tribal areas where the nomads, unable to store their grain, live by purchasing it through the sale of milk and hides.

In 1779, however, Tripoli had suffered from three successive years of bad harvests. Famine had already appeared in some of the tribal areas whose Arabs were struggling in their hundreds towards the populated areas in the search for food. Food was rapidly disappearing from the city markets, and with it security began to collapse, the dissident political parties recruiting strength by bringing in armed nomads now roaming the country. The situation was reflected in a despatch Tully wrote in November, to the Secretary of State, Lord Weymouth:

The place is in the utmost consternation from about twelve days. A strong party of rebel Arabs, with a man at their head, who calls himself Uncle of this Bashaw, are posted at a few hours ride from this city and threaten to attack at any moment. The Bashaw is calling in people to get together a force to send against them. It is highly to be wished that he may be able to do so, as an irruption of those people would probably prove most fatal to all the Christians, it being the general opinion that they would spare neither life nor property....

The situation was, indeed, one that caused a near panic among the consular corps and some of the consuls were trying to leave:

The French have embarked the best of their effects, and would have embarked all, had not the Bashaw, highly incensed at such a measure, put a stop to it.... Our situation, however, is one of the most disagreeable possible, as, at best, we shall be in a very few days, exposed to a violent famine, no kind of provisions being permitted to come into the town, which was entirely unprepared for such a blockade. Did my circumstances permit me to send my family out of the place, I should be easy. But Your Lordship's humanity will forgive me when I say that the idea of seeing them in a few days starve, or be the prey of the Arabs, tears my heart to pieces....

This threat, the first of many that were to come during Tully's years at the consulate, passed. By the energetic action of the Bey Prince Hassan, the Arabs blockading the town from the *menshia* were defeated and driven off, and the timely arrival of grain ships sent by the Bey of Tunis removed the immediate threat of famine.

But Tully's personal problems only increased. He was living largely on credit, and Cooke, who by now had been absent for a year, was still drawing the full salary of the consulate. He had not been heard of for some time, and clearly had no intention of returning. 'I have,' wrote Tully, 'been left here destitute of almost all kind of resource wherewith to keep up the appearance inseparable from a public charge.' It was a cry for help, to which, as so often before, there came no reply from London.

By April 1780 Tully's financial condition was desperate. It was impossible on his small income to keep the consulate running and support his wife and family. He had formerly augmented his income by a small amount of trading, and by consulage fees from British shipping; but the threat of famine and plague had driven shipping away from Tripoli. He was now living entirely on money borrowed, not only from the Bashaw and the Bey, but also from the local Jews who were asking him an interest rate of 30 per cent. It is a measure of his popularity that the Bashaw could still increase the loans he had already made. It also shows the Bashaw's generosity, when his heart was touched, that he could offer to pay Tully's fare to England, to enable the consul to make personal representations to the Secretary of State's office about his case.

It was at length decided in Tripoli that Tully could not with propriety leave his post without permission from his new Department, the Home Office, from whom he had heard nothing,[1] and that it would be wiser to send Mrs. Tully instead carrying a memorandum from him.

This was done in 1781, but the visit was not successful, though it is evident that some sympathy was felt for him by a minute on one of the files from Lord Mordaunt to Lord Hillsborough inviting the latter 'to give attention to Mr. Tully's case. It is a very compassionate one—with circumstances that render it not only melancholy to the Individual, but meritorious to the Public. . . . Mr. Tully is meritorious of this country.' Alas, on Tully's personal file, were inscribed the fatal words: 'Mr. Tully is a native of Naples, grandson of an Irish papist, brought up in the Romish religion, and has never taken the oaths of government'.

Mrs. Tully returned without success, but the fact that some sympathy had been shown for Tully by Lord Mordaunt, induced this ever optimistic man to try once more in 1782 to take his case himself to London. He was no doubt encouraged in this move by the fact that no new consul had as yet been appointed from London. He once more approached the Bashaw, who again offered, not only to pay his fare to England, but to guarantee his debts to the Jews of Tripoli during his absence.

Tully reached England in 1783 and, perhaps through that gentle, winning personality which had melted the Bashaw and

[1] In 1782, the former Northern and Southern Offices in London had been replaced by the Home & Foreign Offices. Much confusion over the functions of the new offices occurred, and remained for some time. Doubtless Tully's difficulties arose in part from this confusion.

Bey, at last overcame the political and religious objections to his appointment, and was confirmed in the post of consul. This confirmation was, however, subject to several strict reservations. He must give his guarantee that he would pay consul Cooke, in spite of the latter's virtual disappearance, the £150 a year he had himself been drawing, and must allow a certain monthly sum of money to be deducted at source from the rest of his emoluments to be used to pay off his creditors. With these heavy commitments on his salary his financial position could not be regarded as much improved; but the confirmation of his appointment at least gave an added confidence to his creditors, and removed from him the constant fear of being replaced in his post.

Miss Tully arrives

It was on Tully's return from London that an event occurred to which our knowledge of the Barbary State of Tripoli, as it was at the end of the 18th century, owes much. Tully brought back his sister—or sister-in-law—Miss Tully, the only name we have for her. She was a woman uniquely gifted, not only with considerable literary skill, but with an observant and retentive eye, and an unremitting industry in committing facts to paper. From the date of her arrival at the British consulate, in July 1783, she began to keep a diary, which was embodied in a series of letters to a friend in England, somewhat in the style of those of Lady Wortley Montagu. These letters, written often on the same day as the events they describe occurred, are of unique value to the chronicler of the Karamanlis, coming as they do from the pen of one who had constant and easy access to the Castle, who moved on friendly terms among the *harims* of the Bashaw and the Princes, and who set herself with application, to give an account of the history, the manners and the customs of the people of Tripoli. In her first letter she wrote:

> I am induced to believe that I shall be able, during my stay here, to present to you a series of events not unworthy of your perusal. I am

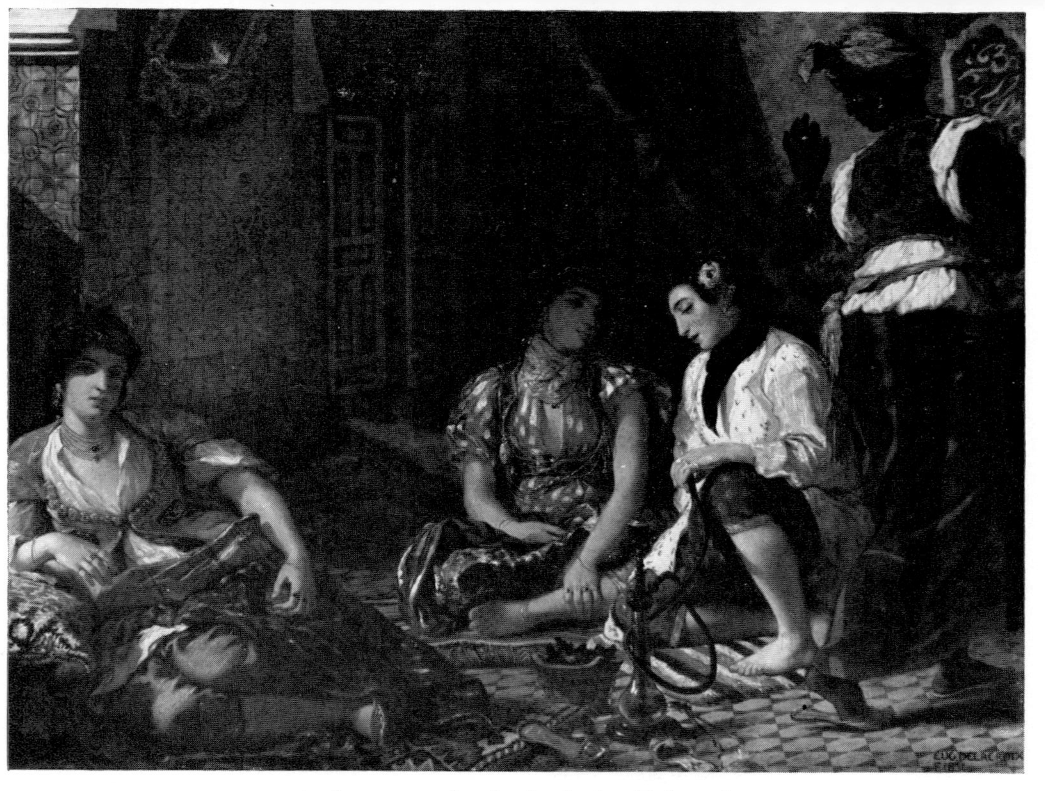

Arab women in the *harim* by Delacroix

Slave market

Janissary officers showing their uniforms

the more confirmed in this belief from the peculiar facilities afforded me by a constant intercourse with the Bashaw and his family. I purpose simply to relate facts as they occur, without the least embellishment, as that, I conceive, would not increase the interest which they may probably inspire.

And so she does, and it is through her eyes, rather than those of the consul, that the dramatic fortunes of the Regency are followed for the next ten years.

By 1783, the situation of the Regency, both politically and economically, had deteriorated still further, and now was reduced to a level of anarchy and stagnation never before reached by the Karamanli regime. Drought during successive years kept the country on the brink of what seemed almost permanent famine, and the threat of bubonic plague, which had once again appeared in Egypt and Tunis, was drawing nearer to Tripoli, brought by the steady stream of starving refugees fleeing towards the towns.

Trade was at a standstill since there was no money available for the purchase of imports, and fear of the plague continued to keep foreign shipping away from north Africa. The Bashaw's treasury was empty and in desperation he was obliged not only to sell his personal silver and plate, but to pawn much of his jewellery to the French consul, in order to make payments to the troops who were his only security. Energetic attempts were made by Prince Hassan, the Bey, to assemble troops and collect tribute from the tribes who were by now in almost open revolt.

In the Castle, that hothouse of intrigue, ambition and dark passions, events were inevitably moving to what many felt must one day be a tragic and bloody climax. The Bashaw, enfeebled by ill-health and brandy, remained shut away in his private quarters, surrounded by a small group of renegades—two of whom had married his daughters—and much influenced by an enormously fat Jewess, ironically called 'Queen Esther', who with great skill had so pandered to his vices and confused his understanding as to be indispensable. With her sinister daughter Mezeltobe, who moved at will about the Castle spreading rumour and intrigue among the *harims* of the three Princes, this woman used her influence to milk what remained in the treasury for the benefit of her family in Tripoli, and to increase the isolation of the Bashaw from all but those who could be of use to her in her schemes. Of weak and kindly Ali wrote the French vice-consul Vallière:

He belongs to all who surround him, even the Jews, who, through a woman called publicly 'Queen Esther', govern through her control over his passions. . . . surrounded by vile renegades who cover him with adulation, distrusted by his children, attacked by a painful malady, the Bashaw of Tripoli is a martyr of sovereigns.

His three sons, shut away in their apartments behind their well-guarded iron doors, watched closely by their black slaves and personal retainers, surrounded by their *harims* and concubines, watched each other and their father with a suspicion and distrust which provided fertile soil for the intrigues of Mezeltobe and others whose profit lay in palace dissension. The characters of these young men, two of whom were later to play small roles in British and American history, were widely different.

All contemporary writers agree that Prince Hassan, the eldest and Bey du Camp, was a person of great charm of character, courage and intelligence. A French commentator, probably Vallière, described him as 'of gracious address, with high personal qualities, and the gift of command'. Miss Tully, who met him frequently in the Autumn of 1783, was even more lavish in her admiration; and a drawing of Hassan Karamanli stands as a frontispiece to her famous Letters, one of the few illustrations in the book.

The Bey . . . is not thirty, a fine, majestic figure, much beloved, being extremely mild and just to his people. His guards and his power are equal to the Bashaw's, a circumstance which raises a jealousy in his two younger brothers, which is cruelly heightened by disaffected persons round them, and renders both of them extremely troublesome to him.

Elsewhere, she remembers him as 'a noble figure and remarkably handsome. . . .'

It was indeed by his energy and intelligence during this bad period that some security was maintained, and the famine, if not abated, at least a little relieved. While his father the Bashaw lay indolent, ineffective and suspicious on his silk cushions, sinking to sleep with his glass of brandy, on the lap of his Jewess, Hassan kept the troops together by sheer force of personality, and by judicious arrangements with Morocco and Tunis, made possible the supplies of grain that kept the population alive. But his activities kept him frequently away from the Castle, and unaware and often uninformed about the intrigues which were directed, first against his influence, then against his life.

The second son, Ahmed (later to become the cause of one of the first epics in American history), the French vice-consul Vallière succinctly described as 'having at best a very weak understanding', was a pleasant but irresolute, suspicious and easily influenced man and an easy tool for the ambitions of the Bashaw's beloved youngest son, Yusef.

Yusef Karamanli, like his great-grandfather Ahmed, is at once the hero and villain of the Karamanli legend. At some time in his youth, he had decided that he and not either of his brothers should be the next ruler of Tripoli. How much this decision was conditioned by the fear with which he infected his elder brother Ahmed, that Hassan, as so often in the lives of his forebears, would kill them on his accession to power, is not known. It is enough that from an early date this bold, active and callous youth, determined on the death of his eldest brother Hassan and the nullification, if not the death also, of his other brother Ahmed.

Suspicious and careful, all three brothers moved closely surrounded by their friends, personal retainers and armed slaves, so that any attempt at murder must be made at close quarters, and alone. Only the sanctuary of the one *harim* where slaves and retainers could not follow, would allow this. This was the *harim* of their mother, Lilla Hallouma, to which all three brothers had unrestricted access.

Prince Yusef must have realised that only in some such manner could he have a chance to kill Hassan, and he laid his plans with great care. To lull any suspicions the Bey might have, he worked ceaselessly to distract attention by stirring up constant small Castle intrigues. In this he was adept, sending hired women such as Mezeltobe and a Tunisian *intriguante* called Sulah, from *harim* to *harim* to stir up enmity between Hassan and Ahmed and their families, and, having easy access to his father whose favourite son he was, he filled the Bashaw's mind with rumour and suspicion about Hassan. At the same time, he worked to convince Ahmed that, as next in succession, he would be Hassan's first victim. He thus kept the Castle in a constant stir of suspicion, fear and intrigue.

But there was another side to Yusef Karamanli's character. He had, like his great-grandfather, that ethereal quality of *bashasha.* He was a great favourite of the poor people of the *menshia*, and careful to cultivate the friendship and attachment of the powerful Mahmid tribe. Bold, energetic, ruthless, yet with a facility for making friends when he pleased, and a charm that worked well among the simple people of Tripoli, he was a dangerous rival for a yet unsuspecting eldest brother.

Yet if Hassan was still unsuspecting, there was one person in the Castle who, closely informed by her women, was an active spectator of the intrigue behind the passions which were being generated. Lilla Hallouma, or Kebira, the Bashaw's only wife (the rest were concubines), the fair-haired Georgian brought from Turkey to marry him when she was little more than a child, lived in almost daily fear. In a letter of November 1783, Miss Tully wrote:

> The countenance of Lilla Kebierra bespoke the character given of her. She is extremely affable and has the most insinuating manner imaginable. She is still very handsome, a fair beauty, with light blue eyes and flaxen hair. Her complexion is perfectly delicate, but has evidently suffered from grief and heavy fasts imposed by herself, owing to the loss of some favourite children, and the present unhappy disputes constantly arising between her three sons, fed by the demon of jealously.

This unhappy woman, whose name remained for many years in Tripoli a byword for tragedy evidently knew and loved her three sons. She guessed their ambitions, admired the grace, courage and zeal of her eldest, Hassan, while fearing the greed, ambition and ruthlessness of her youngest, Yusef. Surrounded by her timid *harim*, who exaggerated every rumour and embroidered every fear, she had no one to turn to among the others for solace, except the kindly Englishwomen, when they penetrated to her *harim* on their occasional visits.

Plague

But all intrigue and ambition were thrust aside in the Castle as, toward the end of 1784, a new danger appeared to threaten the Regency. On January 8th a letter from Miss Tully went off to her correspondent in England, with this ominous sentence: 'We have hardly a hope of escaping from the plague; it increases daily at Tunis; and to add to the misfortune of its reaching us, this kingdom is in so unhealthy a state from famine, that it is thought it will considerably add to its ravages. . . .'

The plague, indeed, was advancing on Tripoli from two directions—the couriers and pilgrims travelling by land from Egypt and Morocco could bring the seeds of it from either. The much needed grain ships from Tunis and Morocco were coming into port with infected crews.

Tripoli had no effective system of quarantine, and Miss Tully describes one ship arriving in Tripoli harbour with half its crew down with the plague. The crew was not allowed ashore, but a cargo of clothing, almost certainly infected with the deadly fleas, that it was carrying for sale by the Tripoli Jews, was landed for the market.

Bubonic plague in the 18th century was still endemic in North Africa, the Levant and southern Europe. It took two forms. In one, the victim would be struck with a sudden rigor in the limbs, followed by a staggering and a difficulty of speech often taken for drunkenness. The body temperature soared as the microbes multiplied with enormous rapidity in the bloodstream. This rise in temperature was accompanied by a splitting headache, a furred tongue and vomiting. At this stage, the victim collapsed while red spots, followed by suppurating swellings, appeared in the groins and neck. The victim rapidly became insensible, and death almost invariably followed, the more quickly if, as now in Tripoli, his constitution was already enfeebled by malnutrition. The final throes, panting breath and a darkening skin, were the almost inevitable precursors of a ghastly end. This was a slow and relatively long drawn out death. The other form of plague, more deadly because more contagious, was the pneumonic microbe, which affected the lungs, and was rapidly spread in a confined space by the mere coughing of the victim.

To the Moslems of Tripolitania, the threat of plague brought out all that was superstitious and fatalistic in their nature. Since the infection was predetermined and came from God, virtually no hygenic precautions were taken. To counteract this supernatural punishment, the only recourse was the holy man, the *marabout,* and most people who could afford to, including the Bashaw, his sons and their families, called on their favourite *marabout* for all the paraphernalia of spiritual protection—the inscribing and wearing of *hijabs*, the swallowing of draughts of liquid in which sacred writings from the *Qur'an* or the *Dalail el Kheirat,* had been pounded and dissolved, the suspension of amulets from the heads of children, the doors of houses, etc., the placing of placatory oil, bread and olives upon the tombs of *marabouts* and saints, and prayers for succour in the town's mosques.

On April 28th Miss Tully, from the rooftop of the British consulate, saw the ladies of the *harims* of the Castle make one of their rare expeditions outside to pray for succour from the scourge. As always, her sharp eye misses nothing of detail or atmosphere:

Last night, a little before midnight, the wife of the Bey, Lilla Aisha, with the three eldest princesses, Lilla Udicia, Lilla Howisha, and Lilla Fatima, walked through the streets by torchlight, from the Castle to the mosque, to make offerings and worship at the shrine of one of their great marabuts. They were completely surrounded by their ladies, who were again encircled by black slaves, round whom proceeded the eunuchs and mamelukes of the Castle, while the hampers, or Bashaw's bodyguards followed. The princesses were accompanied by their brothers, the two youngest princes, Sidy Hamet and Sidy Useph, with their suite. It was one of those fine, calm nights with a clear brilliant sky, peculiar to the Mediterranean. Not a breadth of air disturbed the cloud arising from the aromatic vapour that enveloped this body, as it moved slowly along. Some minutes before it approached, a warning cry was heard from the chaoux [herald], who carried a decisive denunciation of death to all who might attempt to view this sacred procession. Guards hurried through the streets to clear the way, and the loud cheers, or song of Loo, loo, loo, sung by a great number of their best female voices selected for that purpose, was heard at a great distance. The princes, their suite and all the male attendants, waited at the gates of the mosque till the princesses had completed their oblations . . . when they all returned to the castle in the same order in which they had left it.

The present state of the Castle, menacing all its inhabitants in so dreadful a manner, is the cause of this royal, nocturnal visit to the shrine of the marabut.

The Castle, indeed, with its overcrowded passages and courts, its stables, huddled *bagnios* of slaves, airless and dark *harims*, was rightly considered as a dangerous focus for the infection. But no other precautions than those of superstition, were taken. Indeed, Miss Tully was shocked on discussing the dangers of the Castle with one of the Bashaw's senior ministers to be told, 'Sovereignty is the greatest shield, and it is necessary to give the Moors an example not to try and resist the hand of fate.'

More pragmatic were the Christian houses. Tully had spent much of his youth at the port of Leghorn where he had experience of the famous quarantine system, devised by the Grand Duke of Tuscany, which had protected the city from attacks of plague for several years. It was based on a principle of complete isolation from possible sources of infection. If the plague reached Tripoli in epidemic form, he determined to put this into effect, and it seems likely that the other consular houses were induced to follow him.

In January, he advised his family and his colleagues that visits to the Castle should be suspended. The Bashaw was warned that the consular houses might have to close completely. 'The Bashaw,' wrote Miss Tully, 'expresses great regret at the thought of the Christians shutting their houses so soon. . . . for, he says, it will declare a state of infection, and prevent the arrival of grain.'

Three months later, the plague had reached Tripoli, and the British consulate in Zenghet el Yehud made preparations to close. But first, Tully made an attempt to get leave from London to take his wife and family to Europe. He wrote in June:

> The plague continues to make prodigious and unexampled havock in this place. In each of the last three days it has carried off two out of each hundred of these inhabitants, while the little care they take, and more, a number of their customs, both during the progress of the illness and at burying of the dead, seem calculated merely to spread the disease, and leave us no hope of its abating, probably for years.

But no sign came from London and without permission, this punctilious civil servant would not leave. His family stayed with him, probably for lack of means of transport, and on June 28th Miss Tully told her correspondent, 'it is impossible to give you a just description of this place at present; the general horror that prevails cannot be described' and she adds, ominously, 'our house, the last of the Christian houses that remained in part open, on the 14th of this month, commenced a complete quarantine'.

Though the cause of the infection of plague, this deadly and invisible miasma that suddenly struck without warning, was not to be discovered for another 150 years, experience had shown that it could be passed easily from one person to another, not only through direct contact, but also through objects which had been in contact with infected persons. Isolation from the outside world must therefore be as complete as possible, and Tully, obliged to stay and face things out, put into operation the precautions he had learned in Leghorn.

Since the family were to live in complete siege conditions for an unknown length of time, servants were engaged who were willing to accept the hard conditions of seclusion. All animals, dogs, fowls, etc., were sent out of the house. Then, on a pre-arranged day, all doors and windows leading to the street were firmly locked and shuttered, so that no ingress or egress was possible; the keys were then handed to the master of the house who retained them. In cases of extreme necessity, where a servant would have to be sent outside, a small room at the side of the *saquiffa*, or entrance hall, was set aside with a bath in it. Here the returning servant had to live for a fortnight until it was obvious that he was not infected. With the consular house tight shut, a daily fumigation began. Miss Tully with her busy pen followed all these precautions: 'When once the houses are shut their safety will depend greatly on the strictness of the quarantine they keep.' And she lists the precautions: 'Many jars containing several pounds each, are prepared for fumigating the apartments, two-thirds of which are bran, and the rest equal parts of camphire, myrrh and aloes. This perfume, and small quantities of gun-powder are burnt daily throughout the houses.'

Since supplies must at times be brought in from outside, an elaborate system of protection was adopted. On the arrival of the foodstuffs at the outside door, a servant was handed the key by the master of the house. He passed through the *saquiffa*, which was divided into two sections separated by a pile of straw, and unlocked the front door.

Miss Tully noted:

> The servant returns and the person in the street waits till he is desired to enter with the provisions he has been commissioned to buy.... When this person has brought in all the articles he has, he leaves them with the account, and the change out of the money given him, and retiring shuts the door.

The straw in the centre of the *saquiffa* was then lighted and the whole hall fumigated with its smoke, before a servant was sent across to pick up the goods. A similar arrangement was made for any rare visitor to the house. He was obliged to sit near the front door, while a pile of straw mixed with myrrh burned between him and his host. 'Without these precautions,' wrote Miss Tully, 'it would be impossible to escape this dreadful disorder, the rage of which increases every hour.'

On June the 14th 1785 the British consulate in Tripoli closed its doors to the outside world. Here, in the hot, stinking rooms some twelve persons, including at least five women, were to be immured for over a year, with primitive sanitation, lack of water, and no escape from the acrid fumes of gunpowder and bran burning constantly, yet scarcely concealing the stink of the choked privies. Miss Tully, continued calmly to follow in her letters the progress of the plague. From the roof of the house, which overtopped the neighbouring buildings, and where no doubt the ladies fled in the cool of the evening to escape for a while from the stench inside, she could see the streets below and record the full horrors of what she saw.

By mid-June, the contagion had reached its full force in Tripoli city. At first the dead were carried outside the city walls, and with some decency buried in the graveyards near the eastern gate, but soon, as the deaths increased and families were decimated, they lay about in the streets, and were gathered in heaps and taken on camel-back to a common grave. Many of the dying, without relatives to care for them, dragged themselves to the gates of the consulates, hoping that they would get succour, and died there, their bodies rapidly decomposing in the hot sun.

Meanwhile, a repulsive stench began to reach the British and French consulates from the Jewish quarter which they adjoined. The Tripoli Jews had a tax of 20 pataques (about £5) imposed by the head of the Jewish community on every burial outside the city, and to avoid this, were burying their dead secretly in their own courtyards where, unable to be properly interred in the shallow soil, the corpses putrified.

While the streets were full of dead and dying, and the consulates remained cut off from the world, in the noisome depths of the Castle, where hundreds of people were crowded in appalling conditions, the disease raged furiously. At the beginning of the epidemic, the Bashaw had sent his servants to bring the only qualified physician, a Genoese doctor to look after his family, but this man, knowing that to enter the Castle would be almost certain death had fled, and getting aboard a French ship in the harbour, had lain concealed until it sailed. 'His departure,' Miss Tully told her correspondent, when the news reached her, 'is considered a serious misfortune by all the Christians, as the deadly hand of the disease must now, unopposed, seize upon its prey.'

During all this time, the European consulates remained absolutely dependant on the Moslem servants who continued to supply them with food from outside. During the first few months of quarantine, so dangerous was this task, that eight servants bringing supplies to the British consulate had died. But in each case, the task was passed on to another Moslem, who punctually carried it out. 'The Moors,' Miss Tully admitted, 'perform acts of kindness at present, which, if attended by such dreadful circumstances, would be very rarely met with in most parts of Christendom.'

By the end of the year when the plague, by no means over, had begun to abate, some count could be made. The total death toll was about 27,000. Nine-tenths of the Christian inhabitants had died—three French missionaries of the Hospice of St. Louis on successive days, and all but a very few of the 500 Christian slaves in the Castle *bagnios*. The Bashaw lost two daughters and a brother; the Bey, his only two sons, and of the thirty or so ministers of the Divan, only three survived. Half the Jewish community and two-fifths of the Moslem population were calculated to have died.

By October the plague had sensibly diminished, but Tully's experience in these matters would not yet allow the consulate to be opened. In December the deaths still averaged fifteen a day, and Tully's precautions were vindicated at the end of that month, when a fresh attack broke out in the city, and Miss Tully could write 'The plague seems likely to repeat all the horrors of last year.'

As the Spring of 1786 dragged on, as glimpsed from the roof-tops of the consular houses still firmly shut against the world, it must have seemed to the small groups of Europeans as if their imprisonment would never end. By the month of May the disease had once more decreased enough to allow some of the consular houses to open again. On June 16th, the last to do so, Tully threw open the doors of the British consulate. The Tully family and their servants had been immured from the outside world for thirteen months.

Miss Tully, emerging from the rigours of her long quarantine, could now survey the havoc in the town. In a letter of September 10th 1786 she wrote:

> The city of Tripoli, after the plague, exhibited an appearance awfully striking. In some of the houses were found the last victims that had perished in them, who, having died alone, unpitied and unassisted, lay in a state too bad to be removed from the spot, and were obliged to be buried where they were; while others, children, were wandering about deserted without a friend belonging to them. The town was almost entirely depopulated, rarely two people walked together. One solitary being, pacing slowly through the streets, his mind unoccupied by business, lost in painful recollections; if he lifted his eyes, it was with mournful surprise, to gaze on the empty habitations around him; whole streets he passed without a living creature in them.

Richard Tully, though heavily in debt, and burdened with a large family, now strove to do what he could to help the stricken city, and particularly those refugees from the exterior who had no means to sustain themselves. His sister recorded:

> Among those left in this town some have been spared to acknowledge the compassion and attention shewn them by the British consul. In the distresses of the famine, and in the horrors of the plague, many a suffering wretch, whose days have been spun out by his timely assistance, have left his name on record in this place. Persons saved from perishing in the famine, come forward thank him with wild expressions of joy, calling him Boui [father], and praying to Mahomet to bless him.

Tully's kindness was not forgotten. Seven years later, when Tripoli was invaded from the sea, a party of Gharian Berbers came from the mountains to guard the British consulate from sacking by the invading Turks.

Yusef murders his brother

The plague left Tripolitania decimated in population and still in the grip of semi-famine conditions. But its departure only reawakened and deepened the dissensions in the Castle. For a time, the Bashaw was successful in keeping the three brothers apart. The Bey, Hassan, was absent from the city at long intervals, while the second son, Ahmed, was sent as Governor to Zanzur, and Yusef, the youngest, to Zuara. This not only kept them apart, but enabled them to support their families and adherents by imposing local taxes. But the brothers, and particularly Yusef, could not keep long away from the capital, and tension grew with his frequent reappearances among the tribes of the *menshia*.

In Miss Tully's account, there is a graphic picture of the doomed Bey returning from one of his last forays to collect taxes at Misurata. As his *janissaries* approached Tripoli, along the sands of the sea-shore, the European consuls and their escorts rode out to greet him ceremoniously. With Tully must have ridden his ubiquitous and observant sister:

His approach to Tripoli was announced soon after the *adan* by the distant and well known sound of the royal nubar, the band of music that precedes him, and from the voices of all the villagers round, repeating their festive song of loo, loo, loo. As he drew near the town, his horsemen all passed to the front of his troops, and raced backwards and forwards on the sands before him. The Bey and his chief officers were magnificent in their appearance. The Bey was resplendent in gold and jewels: he wore a crescent, chiefly of diamonds of great value in his turban, which was very large and of the finest white muslin, and crossed with a dark purple and gold shawl, the two ends of which were embroidered in gold nearly half a yard deep, and hung over the left shoulder. His upper vest was pale yellow satin, lined with ermine and ornamented with silver, and his under-vest was green and gold tissue. Gold trappings, in the shape of a drop necklace, nearly covered his horse's chest. His saddle, which he received not long since from the Emperor of Morocco, was gilt, highly embossed, and studded with rubies, emeralds, and other precious stones. Two relay horses with very rich housings, one of which was crimson velvet, almost covered with raised gold embroidery, were led by blacks. His two brothers, Sidi Hamet and Sidi Useph went out to meet him, and embraced him with every demonstration of joy, while their suite repeated the song of loo, loo, loo, in shouts that rent the air; but the Bey's friends watched both his brothers' manœuvres with a jealous eye, for, while the Bey declares himself unconscious of danger, his officers seem to tremble when they see him at any time surrounded by either of his brothers' people.

In later years, Miss Tully must often have pondered this final and ominous sentence in her account of what was perhaps her last view of the magnificent Bey.

The Bey's apparent indifference to the threat to his life should have been, but apparently was not, shaken by an incident which occurred in the summer of 1786. In that year Ramadan, the great Islamic Fast of thirty days from moon to moon, ended on August 29th. The Fast, always a trying period for the health and tempers of Moslems, is most severe in its effect when it occurs in the height of summer. The hours of daylight are much longer, since the Fast lasts from sunrise to sunset, and the great heat makes the need for water almost insatiable, and the short periods of darkness, during which the sufferer stuffs himself with rich foods and sweetmeats, lead to alimentary and digestive troubles, so that the body becomes bilious and gives off an offensive odour. This acute condition leads to an irritation of temper, outbursts of violence and fanaticism, familiar to anyone who has lived among practising Moslems.

The feast of Bairam which follows the end of Ramadan is always made the occasion of a ceremonious exchange of formal visits between Moslems. Consuls, officers of state, religious dignitaries make and receive a round of official calls, playing Box and Cox between their various establishments.

The first call was on the head of State, and the Karamanli Bashaws always made this into a reception held with great pomp. Here, in the large audience chamber in the Castle, with its carved and coloured marbles, its Chinese tiles and fretted stucco, the Bashaw on the first day of Bairam sat in state to receive his visitors.

The rules of etiquette obliged the Bashaw to hold a full audience, in which his ministers, the foreign consuls, the tribal chiefs, the representatives of the religious minorities, and the leading merchants paid their respects, while he received them surrounded by the Princes, his sons, and the Grand and Little Kehya.

At this ceremony, both etiquette and security required that all visitors except the consuls should appear before the Bashaw without weapons. As a further precaution, two of the Bashaw's *hampas* stood at the elbow of each visitor, as he approached to kiss the Bashaw's hand, ready to seize him by the arms should he make any move beyond the simple courtesy etiquette demanded. To the surprise of the visitors, the Bashaw's three sons were not, as usual, standing behind their father when the audience opened.

Tully, as his precedence allowed, was probably closest to the Bashaw, and it was from his lips that Miss Tully, with her indefatigable pen, no doubt gives this account 'when suddenly, the entrance doors were flung open:

The drawing room, in honour of the day, was extremely crowded; when all the courtiers were, in a moment, struck with a sight that seemed to congeal their blood; they appeared to expect nothing less than the slaughter of their sovereign at the foot of his throne, and themselves to be sacrificed to the vengeance of his enemies. The three princes entered, with their chief officers, guards, and blacks, armed in an extraordinary manner, and with their sabres drawn. Each of the sons, surrounded by his own officers and guards, went separately up to kiss the Bashaw's hand. He received them with trembling, and his extreme surprise and agitation were visible to every eye. The princes formed three divisions, keeping distinctly apart; they conversed with the consuls and different people of the court as freely as usual, but did not suffer a glance to escape to each other. They stayed but a short time in the drawing-room, each party retiring in the same order they had entered; and it became apparent that their rage was levelled against each other, and not against their father, though the Bashaw seemed only to recover breath on their departure.

Féraud states that shortly after this alarming incident, the Bashaw in a private audience asked the advice of the French consul, Vallière. Vallière found the weak old man almost in tears, and replied bluntly to his request for advice as to what he should do:

Of your three children, the most dangerous is Yusef. His pride and ambition have no limits: he is ferocious and bloody, and he uses the fondness you have for him to make a ground against his brothers. He is also a favourite with 'Queen Esther', who detests Prince Hassan and Prince Ahmed, since they despise her. If you want peace between your children, send them away from the intrigues of the Court.

It was sound advice and was partly followed. The Bashaw's weak predilection for his youngest son, the hatred Yusef had for the Bey, and the utter weakness, incapacity and easily wakened fears of the middle brother Ahmed, together with the apparent indifference of the Bey to the growing danger which surrounded him, continued to supply fertile ground for the intrigues of their adherents and the casual women of the Castle, those 'common instruments of mischief' as Miss Tully calls them. Cut off from the outer world, separated one from the other by locked doors, closely guarded by eunuchs and blacks, the *harims* of the Bashaw and those of his three sons, each inspired by differing hopes, ambitions and fears, continued as hotbeds of rumour, gossip and malicious intrigue, easily exploited by those Castle women—the Jewesses and others, who had easy access to all of them and who, for money or malice, would tell any tale, repeat any calumny, and give vent unchecked, to their own fears, ambitions and lusts. Indeed, to Lilla Halluma, the Bashaw's lonely wife, to Lilla Ayesha, the Bey's wife, and to the separated *harims* of the

Princes Ahmed and Yusef, where the painted, bejewelled women, in their stiff silks and brocades, sat out the long days and nights in isolated splendour, the appearance of these freely-moving Jewesses, whose creed and sex released them from the Islamic restrictions controlling Moslem women, were often the only means of communication with each other and with the world outside.

No one was more aware of their value than Prince Yusef, who flattered and paid these creatures, using them to stir up dissension and fear where he thought it most appropriate to his plans. Miss Tully reports a Castle rumour that this clever and fearless man, facing almost certain death by discovery, moved among the *harims* himself, disguised as a woman.

The constant rumours of Castle plots, the Bashaw's growing dislike and fear of the Bey, carefully fostered by the other two sons, and the continual reports of the Bashaw's ill-health, with all the alarming possibilities of bloodshed which his death would provoke, filled the city of Tripoli, during the latter part of 1786, with a ceaseless sense of dread and alarm. According to Miss Tully:

So many plots are laid by each contending party that no chief officer can consider himself safe, nor can be assured that he is not the one singled out for destruction. If the Bashaw sends unexpectedly for any one of them to the castle, the consternation of his family is beyond description. They take leave of him as if for the last time, and his family tremble with despair till he returns. These fears are rendered natural and unavoidable by the secret and sudden manner in which deaths happen to victims at the castle, who at various times have been massacred there without a possibility of avoiding their fate.

Such a state of affairs could not continue indefinitely. A pointed insult was offered to the Bey when, in the autumn, he was setting out in state to collect the annual taxes. This occasion was always made an affair of great ceremony with a large crowd of ministers and leading townspeople assembled to see him off. Some of the ladies of the consular corps watched the scene, as did Miss Tully, from a vantage point on the Castle wall.

Neither of his brothers or their adherents appeared. In fact, they were nearby disporting themselves on the sands. This, according to court etiquette, was an example of disrespect verging on insolence. 'This want of attention was so striking,' wrote Miss Tully, 'that the Bey's people murmured much at this disrespect shewn him by the princes; but the Bey, with his usual policy of forbearance, did not appear to notice it. Many of the Bey's friends tremble at his safety.'

It is possible that what seems an almost wilful disregard by the Bey of the behaviour of his brothers, was in fact the result of a positive decision in his own mind to rid himself of them the moment his ailing father died. This would account for his seeming indifference to their threats and plots which must have reached his ears. If so, then Sidi Yusef's fears of being murdered on his father's death were not entirely without reason and it makes more explicable, if no less reprehensible, the way he now acted.

During the early part of 1790 both Ahmed and Yusef were absent in their governorates where the Bashaw, acting on the French consul's advice, had sent them. It seems, however, that Yusef was growing increasingly uneasy at the Bashaw's state of health, and from the fear of what might happen were his father suddenly to die, or decide to abdicate in favour of his eldest son.

It was now that he carried out a plot he must have long considered, and he instructed his slaves in its accomplishment. On July 20th he returned suddenly and unexpectedly to the Castle. Ahmed was still absent at Zanzur, and only the Bashaw and the Bey were in residence. Entering the gateway without any sign of disturbance and with only a few slaves, he passed through the *saquiffa*, where sat as usual the Grand Kehya, a venerable old servant of many years, and made his way swiftly through the many dark passages and open courts to his mother's apartments.

Leaving his slaves at the door, he entered unarmed, saluted his mother and sat down. He told Lilla Halluma that he had come to ask her to intercede because he wished to make his peace with the Bey. He hoped she would send a message to the Bey saying that Yusef was awaiting him unarmed, and that he was prepared to swear an oath of reconciliation in front of their mother. Lilla Halluma, who had for so many years feared the passions and intrigues of her youngest son, was overjoyed by the suggestion, and agreed that in front of her they should join their hands in reconciliation.

A messenger was sent to the Bey, whose first inclination was to go armed with pistols and sword. But his wife, Lilla Ayesha, who was with him at the time he received the message, begged him to observe the strict rules of the *harim* and leave his weapons behind. Nothing, she said, could threaten him from a *shaqiq*, a blood brother, in the *harim* of their mother.

This was a belief to which any strict Moslem would subscribe. The Bey hesitated, then took off his arms; but as he was leaving the *harim*, Lilla Ayesha, moved by some premonition of danger, suddenly threw herself at his feet and begged him to take his sabre. Armed therefore with this, he went unaccompanied to his mother's apartments.

Lilla Halluma, according to tradition, greeted him with joy but begged him to lay aside his sabre, as she knew his brother had no arms with him. The Bey allowed her to take it from him and lay it on the window-sill, and followed her to a sofa where, sitting between the brothers, she took both her sons' hands in hers and spoke in happy phrases of their unity at last. The Bey then turned to his brother and told him that he bore no animosity at all towards him and that, being himself now without a son, since his two only sons had died in the plague, he regarded both Ahmed and Yusef as his sons and heirs. To please his mother, however, he would go through the ceremony of an oath.

Yusef expressed himself as pleased with this and suggested they should both swear on the *Qur'an* an end to enmity. The Bey assented. Yusef rose quickly to his feet and called loudly for a *Qur'an*.

This was a signal to his slaves. With his back to the Bey and his mother, he now received from the waiting slaves, not a *Qur'an*, but a brace of pistols. He turned and immediately fired at the Bey who was still seated at his mother's side.

Lilla Halluma, who had risen quickly on seeing the pistols, put out a hand to stop Yusef, and had it mangled by a shot which struck the Bey in the side. He staggered to his feet, reached for his sabre, and made a cut at his brother who then fired the second pistol into the Bey's body, killing him instantly. As he fell, he turned his eyes to his mother, who with horror thought she saw in them an accusation of treachery. She threw herself on the body of the Bey, screaming as she did so, and Lilla Ayesha, who had waited outside, tearing herself from her women, entered and threw herself likewise on the bleeding body of her husband. But both were now torn aside by five of Yusef's slaves, who rushed in on his command to kill, and hacked the Bey's body with their knives.

Led by Yusef, covered with his brother's blood, the whole party fled from the apartments. In the entrance *saquiffa*, the Grand Kehya, alarmed, rose to stop them, or perhaps to remonstrate, but Yusef sprang on him and stabbed him to the heart, while the slaves dragged his body out into the street. The party now mounted their horses which had been kept in readiness, and—a fearful sight since they were all covered in blood—fled from the city to the *menshia*.

A dragoman from the British consulate saw the fleeing party as they dashed out of the town gates, and came to the consulate with the news. During the rest of the day, while news of the Bey's death began to circulate in the city, Miss Tully, watching no doubt from the consulate rooftop, noted the ensuing disturbance:

The people began to arm and assemble in the streets in numbers: the Arabs and Gibeleens [i.e. Beduin and Berbers], with their long guns and knives, and the Moors, with their pistols and sabres, making a most terrific appearance, each dreading to meet an enemy in his neighbour. . . . The general alarm in town, made it necessary to shut the consulary houses. Ours had been shut but a few minutes when two of the late Bey's officers hurried in despair to the door, and intreated to be let in, as they expected to be massacred every moment by those attached to Sidi Useph, for being favourites of their late master.

Downstairs in the consulate, Tully was writing a more sober appreciation that might well be the epitaph of the Bey:

> This morning, Sidi Yusef, the Bashaw's third and youngest son murdered his eldest brother, Hassan Bey, in the apartment of their common mother. The affability and good qualities of the deceased, make his death an irreparable loss to the natives, as well as to the Christians, who reside here. Sidi Hamet, the second and now eldest son of the Bashaw, who was out of the way at the time, is expected this afternoon. The predilection the Bashaw has for his brother, whose ferocity is detested by the people and several other circumstances, render it highly probable that more bloody scenes will take place incessantly.

The behaviour of the Bashaw on receiving the news was so extraordinary, that it must be inferred that either he was out of his mind with fear, or worse, had prior knowledge of the plot against his eldest son. While Sidi Ahmed came post haste to the Castle with his followers, the Bashaw sent a messenger to Yusef, asking him to return, sending his own rosary in token of his safe conduct.

This order was of course ignored. Instead Yusef, who had now occupied the Bashaw's palace in the *menshia*, held a celebration with his followers which could be heard in the city. 'The sounds of music, firing, and women hired to sing and dance, were louder than at a feast or a wedding.' Yusef also sent a message to the wife of the murdered Grand Kehya Mustafa, whose country house adjoined that of the Bashaw and whose women were preparing to go through the ceremonial wailing for the old man's death, that if he heard any sound of the funeral dirge he would have her strangled.

It being midsummer, the funeral of Hassan Bey could not be delayed and he was buried almost immediately. A long cortege of mourners followed his body to the Karamanli mosque, and minute guns were fired from the ships in the harbour, while the consulates flew their flags at half-mast.

The only contribution of Sidi Ahmed to these events was, on arrival, to swoon for several hours in his *harim*.

Yusef's adherents now began to come in from all sides, and the

Bashaw put out an order that the former adherents of Prince Hassan, who were now in fear of their lives, were not to be molested. But no move was made against Yusef, and when in fact, surrounded by several hundred of his supporters, he did eventually present himself at the Castle, it was noted that the Bashaw instructed Ahmed to go and welcome him in the *saquiffa*, an honour usually only given to visiting royalty. A further sign of the Bashaw's fear of, or favour for, his youngest son, was that when the period of mourning for the late Bey was over, and Sidi Ahmed applied to be made Bey in his place, the Bashaw instructed him to get Yusef's consent to the appointment.

This was obtained, and in a grand ceremony the two brothers went to the Karamanli mosque, where, in the Beduin fashion, they swore blood oaths to be faithful to each other. As Miss Tully rather quaintly reports it, 'they approached together the altar of Mahomet, and after swearing by the Koran each to hold the other's life sacred, they wounded themselves with their knives, and, mixing their blood in a vessel, shocking to relate, they both sipped it'.

Following this ceremony, Yusef retired to his governorate at Zavia, in spite of continued requests from the Bashaw that he should return and take up residence in the Castle. For a time, however, it seemed as if relations between himself, his father and his brother, might become less acute. He probably kept out of sight, not only from fear of some murderous *coup* against him from the former partisans of his murdered brother whom he had not been able to destroy, but also to collect support for his future plans.

It was not until the summer of 1791, a year after the murder of the Bey, that news began to come to Tripoli of armed men collecting round Yusef in Zavia. A week later he was in the *menshia* surrounded by his followers, and from here he sent a message to the new Bey inviting him to come and visit him. The Bey, rightly fearing treachery, refused to do so even though his father urged his compliance. Armed men now began to stream in to the *menshia* from all sides. Yusef's adherents included most of the *Kuloghlis* in the *menshia*, including the Mahmid tribe, the Sheikh of Gharian with a large number of Berber tribesmen, and Beduins from the tribes with whom Yusef had spent much of his absence from Tripoli.

On the other hand, adherents of the Bashaw and the Bey flocked into the city; these included tribesmen from the Nouail tribe near the Tunisian frontier, and a large contingent from Misurata. The streets of Tripoli were now filled with savage looking tribesmen, to the alarm of the Christian houses, whose fears of being pillaged by these fanatics were not probably all imaginary.

In a despatch dated August 9th 1792 Tully outlined the situation and made the point that the occupation of the *menshia* was probably the key factor in the impending struggle. The Karamanli Bashaws, he pointed out, have always depended in the final resort, on the people of the *menshia*. 'So long as these last stand by the capital (and there was hardly any instance of their doing otherwise), it need not be apprehensive of any successful attacks by land.' But he goes on also to show how Yusef, with his usual cunning, was utilising the divisions in the *menshia* itself: 'Profiting by local discontent at one of the mukhtars or governors in the *menshia*, Yusef rallied to him the opposition; others flocked to join them, and by June the city was apprised of the defection of the whole *menshia* to Yusef, by a stream of refugees flowing from thence into the city. The Bashaw hastily recruited the assistance of several thousand tribesmen, 'so that in the article of cavalry His Excellency is considerably superior to the enemy', but it was difficult, 'without field artillery, and with a force chiefly composed of horses, to dislodge a much superior number of desperate men, entrenched in a compact body of gardens, mostly fenced and walled in and with buildings of one kind or another which give them advantage over an enemy that must attack them unsheltered'.

On June 22nd Yusef made an attack on the city but was driven back by inaccurate but sufficient cannon fire, directed by an elderly Russian. The cannon had no trunnions, and most of the shots, observed by Miss Tully from her rooftop, 'fell into the sea on his left, instead of the *pianura* exactly before him'. The consular houses were now in great fear of what would happen to them if Yusef's hordes broke into the town. From their rooftops, the consuls could watch the whole progress of the fighting, the daily engagements between galloping Bedouins, yelling *Kuloghli* horsemen, small phalanxes of heavily armed *janissary* soldiers, single combats, ambuscades among the palm trees, decapitations, throat cutting, all interspersed with the boom of cannon and the constant screams of women.

The scene in the British consulate was now reminiscent of the days, eighty years earlier, of the *janissary* revolts. Since the large building, originally constructed to house the Bey and some of his troops, was solid and roomy, and protected on three sides by walled buildings, it became a centre of refuge, not only for members of the other less well protected consulates, but for other refugees. The kind Tully opened his doors to all he could. His sister wrote:

> The Greeks, Maltese, Moors and Jews brought all their property to the English house. The French and Venetian consuls also brought their families; every room was filled with beds, and the galleries were used for dining rooms. The lower part of the building contained the Jewesses and the Moorish women, with all their jewels and treasures. There was likewise a great quantity of jewels belonging to the Bashaw which were in the possession of some of the consuls to be returned at a future time. For a while, the Venetian consul brought some Slavonian sailors, from a Venetian ship, with small cannon to protect the consulate, joined by other European sailors from any ships in the harbour. A determined attempt by the Europeans to help the Bashaw was made in a visit the Venetian consul made to the Castle, in which he offered to put ashore a large body of Slavonian sailors, from some Slavonian galleots refitting in the harbour, but this the Bashaw refused, probably because they were Christians, who could not be used by a Moslem to shed the blood of other Moslems.

In spite of the turmoil in the British consular house, the alarms and excursions in the streets outside, and the constant firing of matchlocks and the crash of cannon, Miss Tully covered her unhurried pages with her careful observations. One can picture her writing by a candle in a more secluded room, noting every move from the Castle and the *menshia* and every rumour brought to her brother from outside, and joining him and the other menfolk from time to time on the roof, then returning to her table to record such a picture as the following:

We remained till near daybreak, this morning on our terrace, observing the efforts made on both sides to maintain their ground. . . . While we remained on the terrace we had a most perfect view of all that was passing in the Pianura. It was one of those clear, still nights only known in the Mediterranean: the bright beams of the moon from a brilliant sky discovered to us the greatest part of the Messeah with every object in it distinctly. The silence in the town was striking. The greatest part of the inhabitants were without the ramparts, guarding the town, and the rest of the Moors, instead of being seen sitting on their terraces, were, by their fears and the Bashaw's orders, retired within their houses. In the streets, no objects were visible but the town guard, with their pack of hungry dogs, prowling about in vain, for some strolling victim to repay them for their vigilance. Near us, not a sound broke upon the ear, but that of the slow swelling wave that washed the walls of the town; while at a great distance on a calm sea, the white sails of the passing vessels, were distinctly visible by the clearness of the night. Opposed to this calm were the confused screams and the incessant firing in the Pianura, accompanied by the loud song of war and the continual beating of the tambura or drum to call Moors and Arabs to arms. Frequent parties of Moorish horsemen and foot soldiers we distinctly saw by the light of the moon passing with incredible swiftness over the sand in pursuit of the Arabs. The death song breaking from different parts of the country, often announced to us, the loss of some distinguished person on either side, who at that moment was numbered with the slain.

Retiring at intervals from the *menshia* into the Gharian mountains, allowing it to be reoccupied by the Bashaw's forces, then swooping down again to attack, Yusef kept the town for some months in constant alarm never knowing where or when he would strike next. At each appearance of Yusef's hordes of

Beduins beneath the walls, there was a rush of frightened people to the consulate. Yusef had now obtained a number of cannon, which he approached to the town walls and began firing. To the city, under constant threat of invasion, blockaded by land, and half-starved because of intermittent supplies from the *menshia*, this new menace of cannon fire brought the inhabitants near to panic.

Yusef even fired some cannon balls at the Castle, which at last induced the terrified Bashaw to have an offer circulated through the city, that he would pay 2000 sequins to anyone who would bring in Yusef's head.

It was too late. Suddenly on July 19th all firing stopped, and consternation struck both the Libyans on the city ramparts and castle, and those in the *menshia*.

A small fleet of ships, crammed with troops and flying the Ottoman flag, had appeared in the harbour.

Before following this new episode in the history of Tripoli, it is necessary to go back to the affairs of Richard Tully and the British consulate. Miss Tully, whose busy pen usually covered all aspects of life in Tripoli, makes no mention in her published letters of the arrival in Tripoli in October of an Englishman, Simon Lucas, who had come to attempt a journey to the Fezzan on behalf of the newly formed African Association in London.

Lucas had had an unusual career. As a boy, he had been sent to learn the wine trade in Spain, but *en route* to Cadiz, his ship had been captured by a Moroccan corsair, and Lucas had been sold as a slave to the Moroccan court. He had passed three years in slavery before redemption, during which time he had acquired a wide knowledge both of the Arabic language and of the customs of the North African arabs. He had, as have so many since, been attracted by the Moslem way of life, and on return to Gibraltar after slavery, had gladly accepted an offer to return to the Moroccan court as British vice-consul. After sixteen years in Morocco, he had returned to England to take an appointment as Oriental Interpreter at St. James, Here, the newly formed

African Association, established in June 1788 for 'Promoting the discovery of the interior parts of Africa', had found him, and sent him to Tripoli with instructions to cross 'the Desert of Sahara, from Tripoli to Fezzan'.

Tully naturally invited Lucas to take up his residence at the consulate, and what he saw there so shocked him, that he was constrained to add a few sentences to a report he sent to London, on his travel prospects:

> Consul Tully has been so obliging as to offer me an apartment in his house, which, indeed, I accepted rather with reluctance, for the misery of his wretched situation as a British consul in this country beggars all description; when you consider a man with a large family merely dependant on a set of sordid creditors in Europe who receive his salary and scarce allow him out of it sufficient to support nature in a place where I can assure you living is as dear as in England; and under the circumstances still obliged to keep up the false appearance of rank, you will not be surprised how it is possible he could have held out so long. If he has any enemies, they are only among his creditors.

By 1788, destitute of any personal income, of any possible trading profits or shipping dues because of the political and economic chaos in the country, and reliant only upon what his European creditors allowed him, Tully's state was indeed desperate. He could only support life by sinking deeper into debt with the local traders, the Jewish money-lenders, and with the Bashaw and the Bey. It is a tribute to the charm of his personality that so much forbearance was shown to him. When in November 1788 he made one more despairing attempt to enlist financial help from London, the old Bashaw Ali himself wrote a letter in his favour to King George III:

> Consul Tully has resided near twenty years in this our country in your service, during which time he has not only given us any displeasure, nor occasioned to us any disgust, but has even increased the harmony between our two Courts, on which account we love him very much.

The eulogy fell on deaf ears, for by now the Home Department had had enough of Tully and his debts, and perhaps their main problem had been to find a successor. In July 1790, in a letter which was not to reach him for several months, the blow fell. 'I have the King's command to acquaint you,' wrote the Secretary of State, 'that His Majesty has judged it necessary for his service that you should be removed from the office of his Consul General in Tripoli.' It was probably expected by Tully, and it was still three years before he could be replaced, but it was a sad end to a long record of devoted service.[1]

It seems likely that Simon Lucas, whose attempted journey to the Fezzan foundered at Misurata owing to the unsettled state of the caravan routes, and who had returned to London in 1789, had given, perhaps not without some expectations for himself, a report to the Secretary of State on Tully's wretched finances and general condition of life. He himself was offered the post of Consul-General in Tripoli, and gave up that of Oriental Interpreter to accept it, while Tully, on return to England was offered the post of Oriental Interpreter and *faute de mieux*, accepted it; and with it he disappears, certainly unaware that the busy hours his sister had spent with her candle and quill pen in the long, hot nights in the consulate, were to give future historians the only first-hand glimpse of life in the Barbary Regencies in the 18th century.

The usurper

Simon Lucas, newly designated British Consul General, arrived off Tripoli on July 24th 1793 in some style. He had chartered his own ship, the packet boat *Hampden*, and was accompanied by a large household, which included a secretary Mr. Langford, a surgeon Mr. McDonough, a butler Mr. Trent, and several house servants. He had been delayed at Gibraltar through the new outbreak of war between Britain and France,

[1] *The Gentleman's Magazine* of February 1794 contains a report of an approval by the House of Lords for the payment of Mr. Tully's debts of £2111. 1. 0.

and because of this was escorted into Tripoli by two British frigates, *Iris* and *Tisiphone*.

The party and their escorts swung into Tripoli harbour at the height of the struggle between Ali Bashaw in the city and Yusef in the *menshia*, and must have watched with amazement the violent engagements between the city walls and the palm groves beyond. It was immediately decided that Lucas and his family should remain aboard *Hampden* until the situation cleared up. Meanwhile some officers from the frigates went ashore to inform the Tullys of their arrival. It was while arrangements for the Tullys' departure from the consulate were being put in hand that the harbour was suddenly invaded by the fleet of Turkish ships.

The events of the next few days were covered by Lucas's first despatch from Tripoli dated August 22nd 1793, addressed to the Secretary of State:

I have the honour to acquaint you with my arrival here in the *Hampden* packet, under convoy of H.M. ships *Iris* and *Tisiphone* the 24th July. I am sorry to say that, contrary to my expectations, I found this poor devoted country in the utmost distress and misery, the old Bashaw shut up in his citadel, the gates of his city shut, and closely beseiged by his second son, Sidi Joseph, who, about three years since, murdered his eldest brother, and fled to the interior parts, where, being well received by several of the Arabs, he collected an army of two or three thousand men with whom he marched down in order to dethrone his father, and must have miserably succeeded, as all manner of supplies were so effectually cut off and provisions and stores of every kind so scarce, that the city and garrison could not have held out fifteen days longer.

But, unfortunately for both parties, a Turkish fleet consisting of two xebecs of 12 guns, a Venetian polacca and a Spanish brig with about three hundred and eighty Turkish troops and ammunition on board arrived here July 29th, coming from Constantinople with a Turkish Bashaw named Ali Bashaw invested with full powers from the Grand Signior to take command of this government in his name. The next morning he landed without the least opposition and took possession of the Castle and City, the Old man having made a precipitate retreat with his youngest son [*sic*], his brother and Prime Minister, attended by a very few of his Friends and domesticks. . . . All the neighbouring Arabs and the Tripolines who live in the gardens have declared against the usurper, as they still call him, and prevent all supplies coming into the Town. The gates are shut and all communication by land cut off. . . .

Miss Tully who in the midst of all these excitements had, about five o'clock in the afternoon, taken a walk on the terrace of the consulate, saw the fleet arrive:

We were taking our usual afternoon walk upon the terrace when we perceived a fleet of Turkish vessels anchor in the harbour. We were immediately informed that a Turk, named Ali ben Zool was on board with a firman from the Grand Signior to depose our Bashaw, and mount the throne himself. . . . As hazardous as we considered our situation a few hours since, it is now infinitely more so, and increasing in danger from one moment to another. The Commodore with whom we are to return to Europe, with that delicacy of feeling and attention and from which he has never in the least deviated, sent to us, the moment the arrival of the Turks was known, the most pressing messages by his officers to come on board his ship. They informed us that the frigate's boats would lay in waiting for us at the Marine, as late as possible; and that afterwards they would be kept in readiness during the night, when, on any signal being made from our terrace, they would be at the wall again before we could get there ourselves.

Though immediate advantage of this offer could not be taken, the arrival of the Turks was soon to show itself as a nightmare period for the city of Tripoli.

Ali Effendi el Jezairli, or Ali Burghol, as he was popularly known from his propensity to feed the men under his command with 'burghol', or parched corn, was one of those Mediterranean semi-official pirates who hung around the Ottoman court, extracting permission to rob the remote Turkish principalities under the guise of controlling them.[1]

He was a renegade Georgian, who had recently been expelled

[1] Of such, no doubt, were the 16th-century corsairs Sinan and Dragut, who seized Tripoli for the Ottoman Sultan.

rom Algiers by the Dey, for his behaviour while holding office as Rais of the Marine. To be expelled by an Algerian Dey for cruelty and rapacity puts Ali Burghol very high on the list of bad rascals. He was to maintain his reputation during the short period he ruled Tripoli. On his expulsion from Algiers, he had returned to Constantinople, where his brother was acting as vice-admiral of the Turkish fleet, and where, aided by his brother, he was searching for a new lucrative field of endeavour.

While he was there a deputation of Tripoli merchants, despairing of the fratricidal warfare between the Karamanli family and the consequent anarchy in the country, arrived to beg the Sultan to bring the Regency back under direct Ottoman rule. The Sultan, with his treasury and his armed forces impoverished by the long war with Russia, was in no state to assist them directly. He was therefore agreeable to a suggestion from Ali Burghol that he should be appointed Bashaw of Tripoli, under *firman*, in return for which he would equip and pay for a force of his own, and duly render to the Sultan the annual dues of the Regency.

A weak Sultan in a moment of indecision, agreed and a *firman* was issued to Ali Burghol, who hired a few vessels and embarked with what proved to be a mere horde of corsairs—Greeks from Zante and the Morea, Turks, and Arnauts.

The first action of Ali Burghol's troops on arrival in Tripoli harbour was to seize one of the outlying forts and turn its cannon on the city. But the sight of the Ottoman flag flying from the ships' masts had paralysed the city, so that a *capiji bashi*, or official messenger, and about four hundred men were ferried ashore without difficulty, where they seized control of the Marine gate, from which the *capiji bashi* proceeded to read aloud the Sultan's *firman* deposing Ali Karamanli and appointing Ali Burghol in his place.

The consular corps, equally bewildered by the sight of the Ottoman flag, hastily sent their dragomen to the Marine gate to find out what was happening. The dragomen returned in despair. Miss Tully wrote:

They declared that the Turks were not from Constantinople, but that they were a banditti, and only came to sack the place; that the Marine gates were strongly guarded by the Turkish soldiers, and not a Moor was to be seen near the spot. It was with great difficulty they themselves escaped being detained by them, as the Turks would not let them go till they were convinced they were a guard belonging to a consular house, but no person was suffered to go in or out of the gates; the Turks stood with their sabres drawn. They had nearly killed a Jew, who was under the French protection, for endeavouring to pass the gate in his way to the Marine. He lay on the ground almost lifeless.

Before dawn the next day, July 30th, she took up her pen again, and a vivid picture of her final days in the consulate begins:

Worn out with anxiety and fears, the greater number of the ladies of the party are retired to rest for a few hours. The consuls have determined to keep watch themselves through the night, relieving each other every two hours. Not a servant in the house, whether Christian, Moor or Black, but is completely loaded with knives, guns and pistols, and little else is heard at this moment but the din of arms. The dead silence of the night at intervals is surprising, while so much was going forward. Nothing is seen or heard in the town, except from time to time a sudden burst of noise, from the clinking of arms of large parties of Turks, who parade the streets.

Without information, without communication, with fears in their hearts, the consular corps, armed at all points, waited for dawn huddled in the British consulate and the only sign of succour for them was the two British frigates lying silently at anchor in the outer harbour.

Ali Burghol, having by now complete power, was beginning to run true to form. His soldiers in Tripoli went through the Castle seizing all those remaining of Ali Bashaw's officials. Ferried out quickly to the flag ship where Ali Burghol still remained, they were one by one, strangled to the firing of a gun. Only when the last of them was despatched did Ali Burghol come ashore in great state. As he landed at the Marine, all the consular and official houses flying the Karamanli flag changed their colours for the Ottoman flag. The Bashaw's orchestra, or *nubar*, awaited him and played as he proceeded through the city. As Ali Burghol and his Turks advanced, the watchers from the rooftops saw the flying black-clothed figures of a horde of terrified Jews driven with violence down the streets, while 'all the Turkish vessels saluted him, and the batteries from the Marine fired, till he reached the castle'.

The Castle had been evacuated only hours before by Ali Bashaw. Half-paralysed from a stroke brought on by all the recent events, and accompanied by the Bey and about two hundred of his retainers, Ali Bashaw had fled, not towards the *menshia*, eastwards of the city, but westwards on the road to the Tunisian frontier. From the *menshia* itself, where Yusef's adherents watched the movements of the fleet, all was quiet. Prince Yusef was for the moment nonplussed.

From the harbour, the British frigates watched the situation with some dismay. The Sultan of Turkey's official *firman* had to be regarded as valid, and the change of government legitimate, but it was soon clear that the invaders were little more than a horde of pirates, and a careful watch was kept on the safety of the inmates of the British consulate. However, diplomatic courtesies had to be observed, and when Ali Burghol was installed in the Castle, it was necessary for the consular corps to call on him and pay their respects. Lucas the new consul, Tully, and some officers from the frigates made arrangements for a ceremonial visit, but were checked by an order from the new Bashaw which insisted that Christians visiting him must as in Algiers, leave their swords behind, remove their shoes and kiss his hand.

This the consuls and naval officers refused to do, and there was an awkward pause of several hours. Maybe some movements from the two frigates whose gunports faced the castle, persuaded Ali Burghol to change his mind. An apology was sent to the consulate, and Lucas, Tully and Commodore Lumsden of *Tisiphone* proceeded in state to the Castle, where they were received, according to Lucas, by the new Bashaw, 'in a becoming style with all his guards drawn up under arms, and without any other ceremony than a shake of the hand and the usual compliments; we sat on chairs in his presence and were served with coffee'.

The last few days of Miss Tully's stay in the city was a long tale of scenes, 'too shocking to relate', as Ali Burghol's troops seized and tortured the Jewish merchants to extract their money, chained Ali Bashaw's 'Queen' Esther in a dungeon in the Castle until her family paid 100,000 pataques (£5000) for her, and strangled any citizens suspected of favouring the Karamanlis. But before she and the consul and his family left safely on *Tisiphone* she could write prophetically, 'The reign of this tyrant is not imagined to be long, he is making the best of his time in plundering the wretched inhabitants, forcing them by every method to declare their property, which he immediately seizes.'

Miss Tully—if that was her real name—now vanishes from the scene, but before she embarked at the Marine, she bravely made her way through the turbulent city to the house to which Lilla Halluma, the Bashaw's wife, had fled from the Castle. She had come to take her leave. Lilla Halluma, sad and ill, and alone except for her slaves, greeted her affectionately. Her last words as the English ladies took their leave were:, 'The Consul's sun and the Bashaw's sun have set together; their day closes, and their night begins at the same time: but may the Prophet yet wake them to a brighter *adan*, which I am hardly likely to behold again.'

It was Miss Tully's last adieu from Tripoli after ten years' residence.

From the comparative safety of the *menshia*, Sidi Yusef must have watched the change of fortunes with dismay. The flight of his father and brother towards Tunis, the appearance of the Ottoman flag on the Castle walls, and the news of the turmoil in the city left him with little alternative but to continue the blockade of foodstuffs from the *menshia*. It could now indeed be increased in effectiveness, because Arabs from the Gharian area and from the tribes of the *Sahel*, were flocking to his standard to repel the *mughteseb*, the Usurper as Ali Burghol was styled.

By the end of August, the city was more closely invested than before and the plight of its inhabitants became more desperate. There was practically no food to be found, and the consular corps, pooling their resources, were obliged to charter a small sailing vessel to go to Malta and bring back some basic foodstuffs for their families. Even this relief did not last long, and Lucas in desperation wrote to London asking if he and his family might be removed to safety in a British warship, since, after striking their flags both the Dutch and Venetian consuls had departed: 'I cannot sufficiently describe to you the wretchedness of our residence in this place, hemmed in for these six months between four walls, closely besieged by the Bashaws two sons at the head of 8 or 900 wild Arabs'. No reply came from London, and somehow the Lucas household held out through the hot summer months.

In September with that melodramatic suddenness of affairs in Tripoli, the situation in the *menshia* changed. The Beduins who had flocked into the oasis to help Sidi Yusef in his attack on Tripoli, had already begun characteristically to melt away to their autumn harvests in their *diras*. Agents of Ali Burghol had insinuated themselves with bribes into the *menshia*, and succeeded in turning some of the sheikhs against Sidi Yusef. Warned in time, he fled suddenly by night with his adherents and took the road to Tunis, where he joined his father and elder brother—united once more against a common enemy. In one day the *menshia* surrendered, the gates of the city were opened, and the needed supplies of food began to come in.

Lucas's domestic problems were for the time solved, but he began now to have other problems with the new Bashaw. The first of these was the consulate cook, who was suddenly seized by Ali Burghol's men, accused of treachery, and in spite of vehement protests from Lucas, publicly hanged. This alarming circumstance had scarcely taken place when news was brought to Lucas that an English sailor had escaped ashore from the *Hampden*, and had apostasised and turned Moslem. Lucas called on the Grand Kehya and had the story confirmed. The Scottish mate of the *Hampden*, a man called Peter Lyle, accused of theft aboard ship had fled ashore, approached the Turks at the castle gate, and asked to join them. He had already gone through the act of conversion, had been circumcised, and was dressed as a *janissary* before information reached the British consulate.

Lucas demanded an audience with the Bashaw, and protested against this behaviour in direct contravention of Article 19 of the Treaty of Peace and Commerce, which explicitly stated: 'No subject of the King of Great Britain shall be permitted to turn Turk or Moor, in the city and kingdom of Tripoli unless he voluntarily appear before the Dey or Governor, with the English consul's dragoman, three times in three days, and each day declare his resolution to turn Turk or Moor.'

The Bashaw's reply was curt, and regrettably, true. He had so far signed no Treaty of Peace and Commerce with Great Britain. Peter Lyle remained with Ali Burghol and was later to return and become a famous name in the Regency under his Moslem title of Murad Rais.

There were further exacerbations of relations between the British consulate and the Castle. In October, two British frigates called again in Tripoli on what was now a routine visit. Ali Burghol refused to give them the requisite courtesy gun salutes unless he was paid for the gunpowder expended. And he insisted that in their ceremonial call ashore, the officers should follow the example of the recently arrived Spanish consul, and remove sword and shoes and kiss the Bashaw's hand. Lucas refused this humiliating request, and a ceremonial call was not made ashore. This behaviour by the Bashaw induced Lucas, with the approval of London, to refuse to give Ali Burghol the usual presents brought from England on the appointment of a new consul. His retention of these gifts of money and weapons put him in some danger from Ali Burghol's troops, but Lucas, as were the rest of the consular corps, was sure that such a regime could not long survive.

Reports coming to the consular corps from Tunis supported this view. Ali Karamanli, now united with his sons against the common danger, was active in trying to get the Bey of Tunis to raise troops to regain his throne. The Karamanlis had established themselves on the island of Jerba in southern Tunisia, and their agents were busy recruiting men from Tripolitania to join them. In an attempt to forestall them before it was too late, Ali Burghol embarked troops and sailed to Jerba, and, while the Karamanlis fled in time, sacked the island with much slaughter, assisted by 2000 Beduins of the treacherous Nouail tribe. He sent back to Tripoli five ship-loads of plunder, remaining himself in possession of Jerba.

This foolish act, more than any of the manœuvres of the Karamanlis, at length aroused the Bey of Tunis to action. On November 2nd while the Tunisian fleet moved to blockade Jerba, a force of 20,000 men, with Ahmed and Yusef at their head, and six siege guns, ten field pieces and three mortars, under the general command of a Tunisian General marched down the Tunisian coast, retook Jerba, rapidly advanced across the Tripolitan frontier taking a salutary revenge on the Nouail tribe as they passed through its *dira* and marched towards Tripoli. At the same time, a party of Tripoli and Tunisian merchants sailed for Constantinople, where they reported to the Grand Vizier the situation which had arisen through Ali Burghol's depredations, and succeeded without much difficulty, in getting the Sultan to rescind the *firman* which had created Ali Burghol's appointment, and replace it with a new *firman* reappointing Ali Bashaw to the throne. Armed with this they sped back to Tripoli.

By January 16th 1795 the Tunisian army, now swollen to nearly 30,000 men, arrived at the *menshia* and set up camp in it and across the *sahel*. Here they started to loot the area and were only with difficulty controlled by their General. By the 18th the blockade of the city was once more complete and the Tunisian gunners were advancing their siege guns to bombard the Castle. Ali Burghol, who never seemed to lack for courage, made a desperate sally at nightfall to seize the guns but after a fierce struggle was driven back with heavy losses. He must have realised that the odds against him were now too great, and summoning his leading captains to the Castle, he gave the orders to evacuate after pillaging the city.

While two ships in the harbour were loaded with Ali Burghol's plunder, including the most valuable of the Christian slaves, a scene of appalling slaughter and destruction took place in the recesses of the Castle. A squad of executioners moved among the Moorish, Jewish and Arab prisoners in the dungeons, killing everyone. The Castle was completely gutted. What could not be taken away was destroyed, and the seaward guns on the ramparts were spiked. In the city the murder gangs roamed about, looting and killing, purposively destroying any remaining members of the senior Tripoli families. On the night of January 18th Ali Burghol, who had determined to turn corsair once more, sailed with his men and his plunder to Egypt—then as now—the refuge for every disaffected Levantine. With him sailed the Scots mate Peter Lyle.

These last hours of the Turk's frightful rule were a time of great anxiety to the shut consulates. Lucas had been warned that he was marked for murder by the revengeful troops, and wisely took his precautions: 'I not only armed my own household, but privately engaged eight or ten of my own neighbours well armed, and before ten o'clock at night: I could muster about twenty muskets, ten pair of pistols . . . and sat up all night determined to sell our lives at a dear rate.'

Several of the other consular houses put themselves in the same defensive posture, and it was probably this prudence that saved them from the attack by Ali Burghol's hordes of pirates.

The news of the tyrant's departure reached the Tunisian camp on the morning of the 19th, and the Tunisian troops, avid for plunder, began to flock to the city gate still firmly shut, while the Tripolines once again manned the ramparts. Failing in their attempts to enter by the main gate, the Tunisians had brought up a gun to blow it down. But one of their generals threw himself across the muzzle of the gun as it was about to fire. There followed a quick conference between Sidi Yusef and the Tunisian Commander-in-Chief and the latter was induced to withdraw his troops with a present of 100,000 mahbubs, (about £15,000) paid on the spot, and immediately distributed it among his men. The Tunisians withdrew, and that evening the Karamanli family once more entered their capital.

In the weary British consulate, Lucas could now sit down and write another despatch:

> I am happy to acquaint you, we are not only freed from the despotism of an arbitrary Tyrant, but once more restored to the peaceful enjoyment of our former rights and privileges by the restoration of the lawful Princes of the Caramanli family to the throne of their ancestors. . . .

A month later, on February 24th, the old Bashaw, Ali, returned. from Tunis in a British frigate with his family, to join his sons.

But they returned to a Castle gutted and full of rubbish and the rotting bodies of Ali Burghol's victims. When it was at length cleared it was found that nothing usable was left, and Ali Bashaw was forced to borrow furniture and silver from the consuls. It was with pleasure that the old man received the presents of firearms, watches and English cloth, which Lucas had prudently retained for him.

But, if peace was once more established in the Castle, it was only short lived. As if all the adversities of the past year were forgotten, the father and two sons were soon at odds again. Lucas found the old Bashaw, crippled with age and paralysed from a stroke, unable to do more than stammer a few words. In the Spring of 1795 he abdicated, appointing his elder son Ahmed in his place. Sidi Yusef accepted the appointment, assisted in the coronation celebrations, and bided his time.

On June 11th 1795 while the new Bashaw was absent in the *menshia* with some of his followers, Sidi Yusef struck. He ordered the gates of the city to be shut, and publicly proclaimed himself as Bashaw. At the same time an order was sent to Sidi Ahmed to leave at once for Derna, or face the consequences. Helpless, the town gates shut against him, and the *menshia* gladly proclaiming for Yusef, he fled to Gharian, but here also the Berber sheikhs declared against him. The long years that Yusef had spent assiduously cultivating the friendship of the tribes now began to bear fruit. Ahmed's followers melted from his side, and, virtually alone, he fled as instructed to Derna, and from there, fearing for his life, to Tunis.

Lucas, in a despatch of June 30th 1795, reporting the event, did not regret the change:

> Sidi Ahmed having at best but a very weak understanding, gave himself entirely up to his pleasures, was almost in a constant state of inebriation and consequently neglected his government. Sidi Yusef, who is quite the opposite character of his brother's neither drinks nor smokes, and, having studied for some years in the school of adversity, acquired a thorough knowledge of the constitution of the government and disposition of his subjects, who love him, almost to adoration.

4

YUSEF KARAMANLI

1795–1835

Yusef succeeds to the Throne

The 'love and adoration', enthusiastically described by Consul Lucas, in the first flush of relief at this sudden change in affairs, might perhaps more realistically be described as 'admiration and fear'. For the Karamanli who had at last ascended the throne of Tripoli by virtue of the murder of one brother and the forced exile of another, was a strange mixture of qualities.

Strong and resourceful, ambitious, callous and calculating, he could yet be swayed easily by momentary emotion. In this, he resembled more than any other Karamanli the character of the founder of the dynasty, his great-grandfather Ahmed Karamanli. This was to show most in his dispensation of justice. The recalcitrant Arab or Moor dragged before him in the audience chamber might find a hand extended in genial forgiveness, or raised for the sword of the executioner to fall. The rage and violence that were never far from the surface, might be suddenly turned aside by a quirk of circumstances—a right gesture or an appealing word. This very unpredictability of their ruler was something that his subjects understood and admired; his very human wrath might be turned, and every sinner must take his chance of it. To the oriental mind, this was understandable, human and fair.

His seizure of the throne and control of affairs, in a turbulent Regency still divided by civil war, weakened by lawlessness, and almost destitute from economic stagnation, soon manifested itself.

At his first full Divan he announced the death penalty for even the smallest offence, and this was sternly imposed both in the city and the *menshia*. Thieves were hanged by busy squads of Jews or strangled by the *hampas* immediately on conviction, raiding tribesmen instantly beheaded, the adulteress tied in a sack and thrown into the sea; even pederasty, a common failing among the Turks, was severely punished.

The results were immediate. Banditry, robbery, and tribal

raiding ceased; violence against the person disappeared. In the city and the villages of the *menshia*, Arab, Moor, Christian and Jew[1] could pursue their vocations undisturbed. Trade began to revive, markets reopened; numbers of Jews—who provided the economic life-blood of the Regency—returned from Italy, where they had fled from Ali Burghol's extortioners, and took up their trading ventures again. Shipping appeared in Tripoli port, and, as Yusef's *Kuloghli* troops began to make their force felt among the tribes of the interior, peace descended on the central African trade routes. The caravans from Bornu, from Ghadames and from Chad began once again to cross the Sahara, with their long lines of black slaves, their camel-loads of gold-dust and ivory, while the Tripoli merchants started to form their own caravans to carry cloth, beads, gun-flints and gunpowder to the far south. The Fezzan oases came back to life, and the market places of Mourzouk, of Socne, of Ghadames and Hon became the scenes of violent activity.

Since the Castle was gutted[2] and his treasury empty, Yusef raised money by summoning the consular corps—with the exception of Britain and France—demanding advance payments on their annual subsidies. From eight countries he received a total of 320,000 piastres, and it was with this that he was able to pay his troops and despatch them on their pacification of the country. He may well, in his audience with the assembled consuls, have drawn their attention to the work going on below the castle walls at the Marine, where Spanish shipwrights from Cartagena were busy building new, fast corsair vessels for future raiding. For this, the future looked bright, for the outbreak of war between Britain and France would leave the smaller nations of the Mediterranean at the mercy once again of the Barbary corsairs.

It was now that Peter Lyle, the Scots mate who had turned

[1] The Bashaw, realising the economic importance of a thriving Jewish community, relaxed many of the impositions on them. An example of this is that they were no longer obliged to wear black clothes. They could dress as Moslems, with only caps and slippers remaining black.

[2] The Castle was practically refurnished by France and Britain.

Moslem and joined Ali Burghol, returned to Tripoli, where the Bashaw, a good judge of men, appointed him Rais of the Marine. Lyle was to turn the Tripoline navy, small as it was, into an efficient and lucrative source of income for the Regency.

Those foreign visitors calling on the new Bashaw of Tripoli at this time, found an energetic looking young man of about thirty, of short stature and with the fair complexion of his Georgian mother. '*Di bella Prezensa,*' noted an Italian traveller,[1] who also remarked that the Bashaw spoke excellent Italian.

He received his visitors in the newly furnished audience chamber of the Castle, where the gilded furniture, the carpets, mirrors and clocks, gifts from England and France, were set out in surroundings of some taste and luxury. He was already embarked on rebuilding the Karamanli quarters in the Castle, and improving those of himself and his *harim*, and nothing was spared to give an impressive effect. '*Amante del fasto, si circondo di una corte veramente principesca, spiegando grande magnificenza. . . .*'

One of Yusef Bashaw's chief qualities was the air he gave to visitors of a winning, humorous and relaxed charm—the Karamanli *bashasha.* Few of those who did not know his history, could believe that this short, almost jolly, Arab Prince was capable of a cold, ambitious and callous cruelty that had murdered a blood brother at the actual feet of their mother. Here in audience, surrounded by his Divan and *taiffa*, a circle mostly of newly appointed European renegades or Arab officials who had spent some time at the courts of Europe, headed by a Greek Grand Kehya, and a Scottish Rais of Marine, he would speak to his visitor with a lively and penetrating intelligence of the events in Europe which were at that time pressing ever closer to his small Principality.

Yet, amid these scenes of luxury and expense, his personal life remained essentially simple. Unlike his predecessors, he drank little and did not abandon himself to the willing women of the Castle. He had only two wives—one white the other black—by both of whom he had children, for whom he showed an equal

[1] Della Cella, P. *Viaggio da Tripoli di Barbaria alla frontiere dell' Egitto.*

fondness. It seemed as if this simplicity of personal life, which of course did not last, was the result of his long years among the Beduin tribes of his allies, and the Berbers of Gharian.

In August 1795 the last of his dynastic worries seemed to be removed. Ali Bashaw, sick and half paralysed after his stroke, his constitution weakened by drink, died in seclusion in Tripoli, resigning an unhappy life as the French biographer neatly puts it, '*sous les poids des années et des chagrins*'. With his death, and with the weak Ahmed exiled in Tunis, it seemed as if Yusef's lifelong ambition to be unfettered ruler of Tripoli was at last realised. Now, with a country pacified and economically improving daily, with resources flowing in from subsidies and from the raids of his corsair fleet, he could turn his full attention to the problems facing the Regency from the turbulent world of Europe.

The year 1799 ushered in far-reaching developments in the Mediterranean which were to have a gradual effect on all the Barbary Regencies. The upheaval of the French Revolution had so far left the North African Regencies untouched but, politically, the declaration of war between Britain and France, and the subsequent virtual withdrawal of the British from the Mediterranean area, must naturally have led Yusef Bashaw to listen more readily to French wishes and pretensions. In this policy he must have had the compliance of his immediate advisers, for both the Divan, from the despatches reaching them from their representatives in Paris, and the *taiffa*, from the reports of their vessels observing the movements of French shipping on the sea routes, must have realised that a new force was making itself felt in Europe and was reaching out its tentacles into the Mediterranean seas.

Perhaps the first immediate warning of these changes was the arrival in Tripoli in 1798 of an emissary from Napoleon called Naudé, who opened secret discussions with the Bashaw, not only about a renewal of the Peace Treaty, but also about the possible use of Tripoli as a channel for the despatch of French troops, supplies and information between Paris and Cairo. The Bashaw agreed to all these proposals, and the reason for them became clear in June of 1799, when news arrived that Napoleon, with a stratagem worthy of any oriental despot, had seized Malta and driven out the hereditary rulers, the Knights. He had released 600 Turkish and 1400 Moorish slaves from the Maltese *bagnios*, perhaps in the hope that this would mollify the Sultan of Turkey over the projected conquest of Egypt, and he had simultaneously sent a stiff Note to the Barbary rulers, ordering them to release all their Maltese slaves, containing these instructions: 'Let the Bashaw see that the power, which, in three or four days has taken Malta, will be in a state to punish him if he lapses for a moment from the respect which he owes the Republic.' This was language which Yusef understood.

But as the year progressed, Yusef's problems increased. For one thing, Britain in the form of admiral Nelson and a fleet of battleships was suddenly back in the Mediterranean and Lucas, the British consul, alarmed at the French manœuvres, had been in touch with him about the situation in Tripoli. At the same time, a *capiji bashi*, or official messenger, had arrived with instructions from the Sultan that made alarming reading. Turkey also was at war with France. The navies of the Barbary Regencies must combine to blockade Toulon and Malta, and they should also assemble their forces of *janissaries* to advance eastwards to Egypt and attack the French. All French subjects in their dominions should be at once imprisoned.

The Bashaw did nothing about the first two of these instructions, although, while the *capiji bashi* remained at Tripoli, he made a token arrest of all the French nationals, merely putting them into a hostel, from which they were immediately released when the *capiji bashi* had left the harbour.

Lucas, meanwhile, after a series of angry exchanges with the Bashaw, had struck his flag saying that he could no longer remain as consul in a Regency which had defied the orders of the Sultan, and he had sailed for Leghorn from whence he sent letters of complaint to Nelson now at Naples.

Nelson had already realised the importance of the Barbary ports as harbours and channels for supplies for his fleet, which was virtually cut off from any other Mediterranean sources. He sent *Vanguard* under Captain Hardy to extract from the Bashaw a retraction of the treaty entered into with the French and a request that all French nationals should be arrested and expelled. He was afraid of Tripoli falling into French hands.

Hardy seemed to be successful. He left with a letter to Nelson from the Bashaw agreeing to all the requests. But the moment *Vanguard* was out of sight the promises were repudiated. The thought of the French frigates at Malta, only two days away from his weak batteries, kept the Bashaw to his pro-French policy. He hoped that procrastination would extricate him from his difficulty.

If so, he did not know Nelson. On receipt of a letter from Lucas giving news of the state of affairs in Tripoli, Nelson detached a warship, *Alfonso*, seconded from the Portuguese fleet and commanded by Commodore Campbell, and despatched it to Tripoli with a stern letter addressed to the Bashaw:

When I received your Highness's letter by Captain Hardy of the *Vanguard*, I was rejoiced to find that you had renounced the treaty you had imprudently entered into with some emissaries of General Bonaparte, that Man of Blood, that Despoiler of the Weak, that enemy of all good Mussulmen, for, like Satan, he only flatters that he may the more easily destroy. . . . I had sent your letter to the King, my Master. I had done the same to the Grand Signior, for I never believed that your Highness would say a word that was not most strictly true, a lie is impossible for a true Mussulman to tell, at least I had always believed so. What then must have been my astonishment to have heard from His Brittanic Majesty's consul, Mr. Lucas, that the moment the Vanguard sailed, the French consul and all the French were liberated, and French vessels in port allowed fit for sea.

Why will your Highness be thus led astray by evil Counsellors who can have no other object in view than your ruin?

Your Highness knows that although a powerful squadron of Portuguese ships has been since last August under my command, that, by every means in my Power, they have been prevented from cruising against the ships of your Highness, or from approaching your Coast. It is now my duty to speak out and not to be misunderstood. That a

Nelson who has hitherto kept your Powerful Enemies from destroying you can and will let them loose upon you unless, in two hours, the following terms are compiled with:

Viz. That the French consul at Tripoli, and every Frenchman are delivered on board Her Most Faithful Majesty's ship, *Alfonso* to Commodore Campbell, in two hours of Mr. Lucas setting his foot on shore. . . . There shall be no reservation or trick about the French consul at Tripoli. He shall be on board, in Two Hours from the demand being made. . . .

If these proper terms are not complied with, I can no longer prevent the ships of Her Most Faithful Majesty from acting with vigour against Your Highness. . . .

Nelson's instructions to Campbell were explicit. He was to see that the terms in the letter were complied with, or to act vigorously against the Bashaw's shipping. He was also to oblige the Bashaw to accept a treaty of peace with Portugal. Campbell, however, sailed without consul Lucas.

On May 8th 1799, *Alfonso* appeared off Tripoli roads and Bryan McDonough, who was acting for Lucas as chargé d'affaires, went out to call on Campbell. No gun salutes were fired from the shore, where there was some consternation as the great 74 gun warship was slowly warped into the bay. McDonough returned and went into audience with the Bashaw, carrying Nelson's letter which he left for the Bashaw's consideration.

There was, no doubt, an immediate conference with Beaussier, the French consul, who, aided by the Rais of the Marine who had recently, on French advice replaced Peter Lyle, and who was actively pro-French, urged the Bashaw to refuse the request for their expulsion.

For some reason, *Alfonso* instead of staying in port, now left and sailed for Tunis. With the immediate threat of her guns removed, the Bashaw, hoping again to play for time, sat down and wrote an evasive reply to Nelson, which he sent off by a Danish frigate then in port. It was a hopeless gesture. Two days later, *Alfonso* reappeared, and seeing no salutes fired or flag of truce flying from the Castle, immediately went into action. With one broadside she crippled a corsair vessel of 18 guns which ran ashore in heavy surf. Campbell sent in his boats to burn her, while with grape-shot and canister he swept the beaches.

At this juncture, either attracted by the sound of gunfire, or by pure chance, three ships appeared in the harbour. These were the *Betsy*, an American capture from Boston, now converted by Peter Lyle into his flagship, and two Swedish prizes he was bringing into port. Peter Lyle, better than most, knew the conclusive arguments of a broadside of 74 guns, and he immediately struck his colours. His ship was boarded and he was made a prisoner of his fellow countrymen.

The whole of these manœuvres had been observed by the Bashaw, who, fearing to lose his best captain and his best ship, capitulated, summoned Bryan McDonough and sent him at once aboard *Alfonso* with a flag of truce. A white flag appeared on the Castle battlements, and the Castle guns fired a salute to which *Alfonso* immediately replied.

Capitulation was now complete, and by 4.30 the same afternoon a procession of some forty Frenchmen, headed by Consul Beaussier, were assembled on the Marine. From here, as Beaussier reported to Talleyrand, '*dans le plus absolu negligé, avec les seuls vêtements que nous avions sur le corps, abandonnant tous les meubles et effets à la discretion des Maures,*' the French party was ferried aboard *Alfonso*.

Peter Lyle, who, with his Scots accent, Tripoline oaths and fearsome pirate accoutrements, must have astounded the English officers, was allowed ashore on parole; and a Portuguese Captain called on the Bashaw and drew up and signed with him a peace treaty between Tripoli and Portugal, which, among its terms, included the payment by the Bashaw of a sum of 12,000 piastres for damage done to Portuguese shipping.

Peter Lyle was now released, the *Betsy* and the two Swedish ships were handed back to him, and after an exchange of 21 gun salutes, *Alfonso* carrying the entire French population of Tripoli, set sail for Palermo, whence the French were sent on to Genoa for release.

Lucas returned to Tripoli a few weeks later, and flew his flag again. Amicable relations of a sort between himself and the Bashaw were resumed, and the Bashaw had little difficulty in hiding from Lucas the fact that the French agent Naudé, had secretly returned to Tripoli and was acting as a channel for communications between Napoleon's forces in Egypt and the Directory in Paris. In fact, this secret was so well kept that Lucas was easily constrained by the Bashaw to send a letter to the Sultan, confirming the Bashaw's statements that he was now a declared enemy of France and had carried out the Sultan's instructions.

Lucas was failing. Although, with his large English domestic staff and rich appurtenances—he had lent the Bashaw large quantities of table-silver when the latter took over the gutted castle in 1795—he must have had considerable private means, the climate, the hardships and political vicissitudes of life in Tripoli, the usual delays in receiving his emoluments from London, had all combined to shake his judgments and weaken his concentration. He had once been a slave in Algiers, and when in 1799 his English wife died, perhaps some memory of the gentleness, the devotion and the sense of comfort which Arab women can provide, inspired the old man to marry a local Moslem woman—'A dame of easy virtue in Barbary'—as one of his contemporaries described it. He had no children, and for lack of any family successor to whom to leave his property, he adopted his surgeon Bryan McDonough as his son. In 1800, he received instructions to make an agreement with the Bashaw for the despatch of regular supplies of food to H.M. ships and garrisons in the Mediterranean, and this he did. It was almost his last act.

He died on May 4th 1801, leaving the consulate in the hands of his adopted son Bryan McDonough.

The Bashaw though obliged to cede to British and Turkish *force majeure*, continued to maintain in secret his pro-French policy. He ordered his corsairs not to attack any French merchant shipping but, with his habitual cunning, he seized the opportunity of the Sultan's declaration of war against France to break some of the peace treaties with the minor maritime powers by allowing his navy to attack and capture any vessels of these countries which were carrying supplies for France. Danish, Swedish and Genoese shipping in particular began to arrive in Tripoli harbour, and gangs of slaves were once more driven ashore to fill the castle *bagnios*, recently emptied of the Maltese slaves.

The Danish consul in particular vainly invoked the peace treaties and solicited practical help from the Porte in preventing further seizures. When he handed the Bashaw a *firman* from Constantinople ordering the latter to hand over the captured Danish shipping, and release the crews from slavery, the Bashaw, in a brief and brusque audience, told him contemptuously 'You think a *firman* is something big. I can tell you that in Constantinople, you can obtain one for 40 Levantine piastres. It is nothing but a piece of paper!'

There were those in the Divan who opposed his policy towards France, either from their natural pro-Turkish feelings or fear of British reaction, and could not understand the reason for it. Only a very few of his closest counsellors knew that in his recent peace treaty arranged by Naudé, he had extracted a protocol agreeing that France, in the event of her eventual victory over Turkey, should in any treaty of capitulation by the Sultan oblige Constantinople to give complete independence to the Barbary Regencies, thus removing for ever the fear that another Ali Burghol might be sent to wrest control from the Karamanlis. In the Bashaw's eyes, Napoleon's victories in Egypt made French victory over Turkey an almost certain probability. Not yet could he know of the full impact of Nelson's Battle of the Nile.

It was for this reason also that he allowed the secret return of the French emissary, Naudé, who managed to sustain the system of communications between the French forces in Egypt and the Directory. When Naudé asked for facilities for the French to land troops and supplies at the ports of Derna and Benghazi, the Bashaw sent orders to the Governors of these towns to allow free passage of these munitions of war, destined for Cairo.

But here the Bashaw received a rebuff. In June 1801, a French squadron under Admiral Ganteaume, convoying transports with 4000 troops and supplies to be landed at Derna and taken to Cairo, slipped out of Toulon and avoided Nelson's blockade. But as the boats landing troops approached the shore, the population of Derna rushed down to the beach and opened fire on them, driving them back. The landing had to be called off for, clearly, Yusef's instructions to the Bey were not being carried out. The French squadron was obliged to return to Toulon.

The Treaty of Amiens in March 1802, put an end to these intrigues. Peace between Britain and France, the two major powers in the Mediterranean, and the defence their navies could once more offer to the minor powers, cut down the field of venture for the Barbary corsairs. Yusef was now obliged to look elsewhere for the replenishment of his treasury and his *bagnios*. There remained only one maritime nation whose unprotected shipping lay at the mercy of the corsairs. This was the newly independent Republic of America.

War with America

As early as the mid-eighteenth century, small, sturdy and competently handled merchant ships had been creeping into the Mediterranean from the American continent. They brought dried codfish from the Newfoundland fishing grounds, grain, marine stores and even rum.[1] As they increased in numbers, they began to enter the competition for the carrying trade between the Mediterranean ports, and the reports from both British and French consuls in the area warned of the dangers of their competition. For this reason when the Americans, who possessed no navy until Congress authorised one in 1794, approached first France and then Britain to ask for protection against the corsairs, they were refused. Once again, both Powers saw in the Barbary

[1] They had also secured a virtual, though discreet, monopoly of the opium trade from Smyrna, adulterating and exporting the drug to China.

States a useful check on maritime competition. 'The Americans', asserted Lord Sheffield in a debate in the House of Commons in 1783, 'cannot pretend a navy, and therefore the great nations should suffer the Barbary pirates as a check on the activities of the smaller Italian states and America.'

Refused protection for their shipping, the Americans tried the traditional method of subsidy to the Barbary powers, but it was not until 1797 that they appointed three resident consuls in North Africa.

To Algiers, they sent a former ship's captain, named O'Brien, who had spent ten years in the city as a semi-slave of the Dey: to Tunis, William Eaton, a New England soldier, and to Tripoli, a man called Cathcart who had once been a foremast hand.

If British consuls in the past had shown a curious measure of antipathy one to the other, the American consuls were to prove worse. Cathcart, regarded by both Eaton and O'Brien as a man 'of repulsive habits', and—a curious analogy from them—the 'servile manners of a slave', lived in a state of perpetual feud with O'Brien. There may have been a conflict of business interests here, for O'Brien had many businesses in Algiers, and Cathcart when a slave had owned seven taverns there. In any case Eaton, placed geographically between them, had to suffer as a channel for their constant mutual reproaches and suspicions.

Cathcart arrived in Tripoli in April 1799. Lucas was then absent, and in any case would not have helped him, and he could get no help from the French consul, Beaussier. Until he could have an audience with the Bashaw and present his letters of credence from Washington, he had no status, and the Bashaw, who had no wish for a peace treaty with America, showed no interest in seeing him. Eventually, he struck on the idea of giving an expensive bribe to Bryan McDonough whose medical skill had given him an easy *entrée* to the Divan, and McDonough arranged for an audience with the Bashaw.

The result of this seemed at first very satisfactory, and a treaty was signed between Tripoli and America, comprising an annual payment of 18,000 dollars to the Bashaw, plus an immediate consular present of 4000 dollars. Cathcart must have caught the Bashaw in a very good mood, for these payments were much below those paid in Tunis and Algiers, and it was not long before Yusef found this out. His attitude to Cathcart began immediately to change. 'There is no stability in our tyrant,' Cathcart resentfully informed Eaton with foreboding, in August. 'He frequently issues orders in the morning and countermands them in the evening. . . . There is no confidence to be placed in him; he would sacrifice his mother if she interfered with his interest.'

Cathcart must have had an unhappy stay in Tripoli. The only maritime power with any influence on the Bashaw was Britain, since the French consul had now been expelled. But McDonough, having had his bribe, did nothing further for Cathcart. Indeed, he had now become a bosom companion of Peter Lyle the renegade Scot, who had a hatred of all Americans, and now once again was in command of the Marine. Cathcart referred to him as 'that Satanic Scot'.

Cathcart continued to run his consulate as best he could in these circumstances; but the Bashaw's attitude was rapidly hardening, and lack of sufficient money from the Americans, and the booty he was losing by allowing their shipping freedom, were constantly in his mind.

The first ominous signs appeared early in 1800. A Tripolitan cruiser brought in an American brig under the pretence that its passports were not in order. After earnest representations by Cathcart, and the payment of a bribe to the *taiffa*, the ship was released, but Yusef was clearly looking for an excuse to break the treaty. He had been needlessly annoyed in December 1799, when Cathcart, unlike Eaton and O'Brien who had kept the news secret, publicly announced the death of George Washington by flying his flag at half-mast, and was then unable to pay the consular present to the Bashaw, to which he was liable under the peace treaty on a change of regime.

During March and April of 1801, Yusef made increasingly insistent hints to Cathcart that he was receiving much less money than the rulers in Tunis and Algiers, and that the old treaty must be accordingly revised. Any new treaty, he informed the American consul, must include a yearly subsidy of 250,000 dollars, and an immediate present of 25,000 dollars. To all these representations Cathcart could make no acceptable reply, cut off as he was, by months of sailing time from home, and the slow deliberations of a parsimonious Congress.

The Bashaw waited tactically until the opening of the Spring cruising season for his corsairs. Then on May 11th 1801, without any further diplomatic niceties, he sent a file of *janissaries* round to the American consulate, who forced a way into the building and cut down the American flag, refusing a final attempt at bribery by Cathcart from the few dollars he had left in the consular safe. Tripoli had declared war on America.

Thirteen days later, Cathcart and his family sailed for Leghorn, and the old sailor must have watched with foreboding, as his ship cleared Tripoli harbour, the swift corsair vessels slipping out one by one across the skyline to lie in wait for the stream of unprotected American merchant ships now beating their way eastwards from the New World.

In Washington, spurred on by the ominous reports of its three Barbary consuls, the American administration had not been entirely idle. One month after Cathcart's expulsion from Tripoli and the Bashaw's declaration of war on America, a squadron of three frigates, under the command of Commodore Richard Dale, sailed for the Mediterranean. It included *President*, under the command of Captain James Barron, *Philadelphia* under Captain Samuel Barron, and *Essex* under Captain William Bainbridge. With them, was the schooner, *Enterprise*, under Lieutenant Andrew Sterrett.

Congress had not yet met to declare war on Tripoli, so Dale's instructions were to take his squadron to Gibraltar for supplies, and then pay official calls on the three Barbary Regencies, to present letters to the consuls, call on the Rulers, and generally show the flag. If, on arrival in the Mediterranean, Dale found that the Barbary States, or any one of them, had declared war on

America, he was 'to chastise their insolence by sinking, burning or destroying their ships and vessels wherever you shall find them'.

By this time, Dale must have had news of the declaration of war by the Bashaw of Tripoli, for on arrival at Gibraltar, the Americans found two Tripolitan cruisers, which had come to water there, held in quarantine, with their commander Peter Lyle. Dale immediately took action. He ordered the frigate *Philadelphia* to remain in the Straits, blockading the Tripolitan ships, while *President* and *Enterprise* sailed for Tunis and Tripoli.

Off Tripoli, Dale remained for two inconclusive weeks, while he tried to enter into negotiations with the Bashaw through the agency of the Danish consul, M. Nissen. The Bashaw played skilfully his usual delaying tactics until Dale ran out of provisions, and had to make for Malta, thus lifting the blockade.

En route for Malta, the schooner *Enterprise* of 12 guns and 94 men fell in with a Tripolitan cruiser of 14 guns and 80 men. A fierce battle ensued, in which American seamanship and gunnery soon showed their superiority. After hand-to-hand fighting, the cruiser was boarded by the U.S. sailors; all her guns and gear, with the exception of an old spar and enough sail to give her seaway were thrown overboard, and the cruiser, with a total of 20 dead and 30 wounded, the latter including her *rais*, Mohammed Sous, was allowed to limp back to Tripoli. Here, the Bashaw, enraged at the poor showing of his corsairs in equal fight, ordered Mohammed Sous to be paraded through the city mounted on a jackass with a sheep's entrails hung round his neck.

This success of *Enterprise* was however the only action by the American squadron that season. With the autumnal storms coming on, *Enterprise* returned to the U.S., *Philadelphia* went into winter quarters at Syracuse, and *Essex* was left blockading the Tripolitan corsair outside Gibraltar. Peter Lyle, however, leaving a small maintenance crew aboard the cruiser, took the rest of his crew aboard a British ship, sailed for Malta, now in British hands, and from thence to Tripoli.

The Philadelphia *captured*

The following Spring of 1802 found another American squadron in the Mediterranean, this time with stronger powers. An Act passed by Congress in February gave control of the U.S. navy into the hands of the President, and thus enabled him to give instructions to the squadron, not only to burn or destroy any enemy shipping, but also to take prizes.

The new squadron, under Commodore Richard Morris, consisted of six vessels, led by the 36 gun frigate *Chesapeake*. Its orders were to maintain a strict blockade of Tripoli. Morris, whom U.S. naval historians have dismissed as 'a more incompetent officer could hardly be found', began a half-hearted blockade of Tripoli on May 20th. This blockade was so ineffective that three corsairs had slipped out of harbour, and one had even returned with a captured American prize, which it had brought safely in through the blockading ships.

Morris' squadron, though badly commanded, had some resourceful young officers, and several gallant attempts were made by a Lieutenant Porter, who had already won fame in the capture of the Tripolitan cruiser in hand-to-hand fighting, to enter Tripoli harbour and burn some of the Tripolitan gunboats moored there. But his efforts were nullified by the failure of Morris to take risks. Some damage to Tripoli's shipping was done, and Porter was wounded, but the Americans were obliged to withdraw before any decisive destruction could be achieved.

On May 29th, some tentative moves were made by Morris to discuss peace terms through the Danish consul Nissen. Morris at length went ashore for an interview with the Bashaw's new Grand Kehya, Mohammed d'Ghies. Morris could only offer the derisory sum of 500 dollars as a consular present, and a promise of a further 10,000 dollars to be paid at the end of five years. The Bashaw's demands were for an immediate payment of 200,000 dollars, and a reimbursement for his losses from American attacks on his shipping. There was nothing for Morris to do but return to his flagship and continue his half-hearted blockade.

There was no further incident until Morris sailed for Malta on June 10th, leaving the squadron behind. His departure was followed by the only American success of the season. A Tripolitan gunboat was attacked, driven ashore and partly burned. On June 26th Morris ordered the blockade to be lifted, and all the ships were withdrawn to Malta. The blockade was not resumed that year.

Morris' poor performance, which led to a court martial and his dismissal from the Service, had other lessons which the American naval Captains now appreciated. Their frigates were not sufficiently heavily armed—they carried no bombards—to attack effectively the shore defences, and with no gunboats smaller than a schooner, they could not run sufficiently close inshore to follow the shallow draught of the speedy Tripolitan cruisers.

The following year, 1803, a third American squadron under Commodore Preble in the frigate *Constitution* reached the Mediterranean in August, somewhat late in the sailing season for those waters. Preble's orders were virtually the same as those given to Morris, but he was instructed to base himself on Malta for supplies, and to attempt to hire, either from the British or the Neapolitans, the small gunboats necessary for inshore attacks against Tripolitan shipping.

At Gibraltar, the frigate *Philadelphia*, now under the command of Captain William Bainbridge, was ordered to take up the blockade of Tripoli again, accompanied for inshore action, by the 12 gun schooner, *Vixen*. *Philadelphia* reached Malta on October 5th, and two days later took up her station off Tripoli.

It was a reflection of American naval ignorance of conditions in Mediterranean waters, that a decision was made to blockade the North African coast so late in the year. The autumnal gales which, blowing strongly from the north, put sailing vessels on a potentially dangerous lee shore, were just beginning, and most shipping was making for its winter anchorages. The schooner *Vixen* found it so difficult to keep station off Tripoli bay with its line of treacherous reefs, that Bainbridge ordered the schooner to leave him, and take up a patrolling position off the coast of Cap Bon, westwards of Tripoli, where there was a report of enemy cruisers still at large. *Philadelphia* was therefore left to continue the blockade alone.

The winds were now growing severe. Towards the end of October, a violent west wind had blown the frigate far eastwards of her station, and she was speeding back, when she sighted a Tripolitan cruiser running for shelter closer inshore. The date was October 31st. The Tripolitan cruiser hoisted the Tripoli flag, perhaps to lure the frigate nearer inshore, and firing between the ships began.

About eleven o'clock in the morning, *Philadelphia* was approaching the Kaliusa reef, which curves across the bay of Tripoli. The enemy vessel was now drawing away, and Bainbridge seeing that the range was increasing, and he was now in only seven fathoms of water, gave up the pursuit and was bearing off the land still running before the wind, when *Philadelphia* with an appalling crash, ran on an uncharted reef in a depth of only four fathoms. She struck hard under the following wind, and remained immovable.

Bainbridge immediately ordered a boat to be lowered, and finding that soundings gave a greater depth of water astern, laid back his sails and tried to sail the frigate off, without success. Another attempt to get out an anchor and wear the ship off the reef also failed, as the small boats could not carry the heavy anchor. The frigate lay fast, tilted on the reef so that her guns could not be brought to bear.

Her predicament was soon seen by the Castle lookouts, messages were sent to the Marine, and Tripolitan gunboats began to approach the frigate, under their lateen sails. Peter Lyle, knowing the state of the tide, and seeing a chance to capture the vessel, had given the gunboats instructions to fire only at the masts and rigging, and for four hours at a safe distance, they pounded her with their guns.

Unable to reply effectively and firmly fixed on the reef, the frigate was soon lying in a tangled mass of masts and rigging. Bainbridge called a council of officers and about 5 p.m. they came to the sorry conclusion that they would have to strike their flag and surrender. The few guns on the frigate that would fire fell silent, and the American flag was lowered, while the officers and crew watched fearfully the advancing gunboats.[1]

Their worst fears were to be realised. As the gunboats swung alongside the vessel, their crews with terrifying yells scrambled aboard and hurled themselves on the helpless Americans, stripping both officers and men of their clothes, while others went below to loot the cabins and storerooms. The ship's crew, clad only in their undergarments, were ordered into the boats and forced to row themselves and the officers ashore, while the corsairs took possession of the ship.

They landed about ten o'clock at night, and after being paraded through the city between lines of armed men who helped only very ineffectively in keeping the mob from abusing them, they were taken to the Castle, and herded through its long winding passages to the audience chamber, where the Bashaw, sitting on his throne and surrounded by his Grand Kehya, ministers, officers and guards, awaited them.

It was found, on making a count, that the officers and crew totalled 308 men. The Bashaw was polite and friendly to the officers and even discussed with Bainbridge some details of the engagement. The officers were then sent into an adjoining room where supper was served to them, following which they were led through the town to the house formerly occupied by the expelled American consul, Cathcart, where they were to be housed. Here

[1] Some of the frigate's crew wanted not to surrender, but to wait for the tide and a shift of wind to bring the frigate off the reef. The ease with which the Tripolitan sailors, the following day, succeeded in doing this, made Bainbridge's action seem all the more precipitate, especially as the frigate was not in any danger of boarding. The Bashaw certainly regarded Bainbridge as a coward, and Peter Lyle, on his orders, interrogated both officers and men of the frigate as to their opinion of his behaviour in striking his flag so easily on a 44 gun ship.

awaiting them was the Danish consul M. Nissen, who was to act for them during their imprisonment.

A different treatment awaited the American sailors, who to the Tripolitan mentality, were only a sort of slave. They were taken to a large room where some rags were given them to cover their nakedness, and they were forced to pass their first night without food at all. The following day they were lodged in an old storehouse, where there was barely room to lie down, and their first meal, after forty-eight hours, was the daily ration of a slave—a small loaf of bread apiece.

Bainbridge deeply felt the humiliation and disgrace of his surrender, which was indeed accentuated when the following day he learned that his attempt to scuttle the *Philadelphia* had failed. The Tripolitan sailors had plugged the holes made by the ship's carpenters in her bottom, and waiting for high tide, had sailed her off the reef and made a prize of her.

Bainbridge had been given a room to himself, and it was here, in the depths of depression, that a letter dated Nov. 1st., written by his officers, reached him. It did much to relieve his feelings:

> We, the late officers of the United States frigate, *Philadelphia*, under your command, wishing to express our full approbation of your conduct concerning the unfortunate event of yesterday, do conceive that the charts and soundings justified as near an approach to the shore as we made, and that after the ship struck every exertion was made and every expedient tried to get her off and to defend her, which either courage or abilities could have dictated....

He was further comforted when a few weeks later a letter from Preble[1] reached him, dated December 19th 1803, in which his commander wrote, 'I have not the slightest doubt but that you all have done everything which you conceived could be done.'

No one better than Bainbridge realised what a loss to the already stretched and unsupported American navy, the capture

[1] Preble had by then recovered from the anger with which he had received the news of the surrender, and which caused him to write to his Secretary of State 'Would to God... the crew... had one and all determined to prefer death to slavery.'

of the *Philadelphia* entailed. This powerful and well-appointed frigate was not only lost, but could now become a very potent threat to American merchant shipping. In the hands of corsairs as skilful as Peter Lyle, she might well upset the balance of American naval power in the Mediterranean. Bainbridge conceived his first task therefore to prepare plans either for the frigate's enlargement by American forces, or her destruction. He called a conference of his officers, and it was decided that the difficulties of cutting the frigate out and steering her under fire through the tortuous channels of the harbour in which she lay, were too great for success, and that she must be destroyed. His officers were instructed therefore to collect as much information as they could of the size and disposition of the sea batteries, the system of harbour guardships, the winds and tides in the harbour, and the general disposition of the Tripolitan navy, so that a plan of attack could be drawn up for the destruction of the frigate by Preble's squadron.

Permission had been given by the Bashaw for the American officers to open up a correspondence, though under Castle censorship, and when a plan for the destruction of the *Philadelphia* had been discussed, Bainbridge, using the old stratagem of lemon juice to send invisible writing, incorporated these plans in between the lines of a letter couched in general terms, which he sent via the Castle censor to Preble. The letter reached Preble at a time when he was discussing a similar plan with his own officers, and Bainbridge's information on tides, currents, harbour defences and guardships proved invaluable to Preble in preparing his daring plan. Preble had recently captured a Tripolitan ketch, the *Mastico*. Her crew had been made prisoners and the ketch, renamed *Intrepid*, was attached to Preble's squadron as a gunboat. It was now proposed that she should be carefully re-rigged to present again the appearance of a Tripolitan ship, and should be sent in to the harbour, accompanied by the brig *Siren*, under cover of darkness, and attempt to reach the frigate. After loading the frigate with explosives, and firing a train, the crew were expected to escape out of the harbour in *Siren*. It was a bold scheme, and as hazardous as any planned by any naval commander in the history of any nation. Its essentials were disguise and surprise, and the first had to be effective in order to obtain the second.

Having drawn up this plan in all its details, it remained to find an officer prepared to lead the expedition. This presented no difficulty. A young lieutenant, Stephen Decatur, in command of *Enterprise*, had volunteered while the plan was still under discussion. Decatur was one of those courageous, almost reckless, officers whose careers end either abruptly in sudden death, or in fame.[1]

His offer was accepted, and, during January 1805, he and his scratch crews went through a period of rigorous training, the most important part of which was the practice of carrying combustibles at speed, in silence and darkness, aboard a frigate and placing them in the vital parts of the ship's carcase. Eighty men had been selected for this task.

By the end of January training was finished. *Intrepid* and *Siren* were loaded, and with Decatur and his special crew in the former, the two ships set sail for Tripoli, which was sighted on February 7th. But now, one of the sudden gales which sweep this coast caught the two vessels and drove them eastwards. While *Siren* managed without difficulty to ride out the gale, *Intrepid*, the open-decked, lateen rigged, shallow draught corsair boat, gave Decatur and his crew a terrible experience of discomfort and danger. In this small ship, five American officers, six midshipmen, eight marines and fifty sailors struggled to keep going for several days. One of the accompanying midshipmen named Morris was later to write:

> The commander, three lieutenants, and the surgeon, occupied the very small cabin. Six midshipmen and the pilot had a platform laid on the water casks whose surface they covered when they lay down, and at so small a distance below the deck that their heads would reach it when seated on the platform. The marines had corresponding accom-

[1] His exploit at Tripoli was to be followed by a brilliant naval career, broken, characteristically in 1820, when he was killed in a duel with a brother officer.

modation on the opposite side, and the sailors had only the surface of the casks in the hold. To these inconveniences were added the want of room on the deck for exercise, and the attacks of innumerable vermin which our predecessors, the slaves, had left behind. . . .

By the 16th of the month, the storm had abated and they were back off Tripoli in a fairly calm sea. They were, of course, sighted by the Tripoli look-outs but, as they had expected, were taken for local coasting vessels and were unmolested as they beat slowly into the bay. Here *Siren* anchored, and *Intrepid*, waiting for dusk to fall, began to creep in through the channel between the reefs towards the outer harbour. Everybody remained below except a Maltese pilot, brought specially with them, and a few of the officers dressed in Maltese costume.

By the time they were through the channel, night had fallen and a moon gave a half-light to the scene before them. A guard-boat slid up to them in the darkness and hailed them, and the Maltese pilot replied that they had come from Malta to collect a cargo of bullocks. The guard-boat, unsuspicious, let them pass, and with every outward appearance of acting casually, they crept nearer to the place where *Philadelphia* could be seen lying at anchor in the inner harbour. She was crippled, but was seen to be both manned and gunned.

These were critical moments, as the slow-moving vessel crept towards the towering frigate. Any alarm would have meant the end. *Intrepid* had only an armament of four small guns while around her the frigate and harbour armaments amounted to nearly 100 heavy cannon.

Another guard-boat approached *Intrepid*, and called on her to sheer away from the frigate. The Maltese pilot prompted by Decatur, replied that they had lost their anchor during the night, and he requested permission to tie up to the hull of the frigate. After some parley, permission to do this was given, and the guard-boat began to turn away. But just as *Intrepid* drew alongside the frigate, the wind changed, and blew her back. 'It left us', wrote Lieutenant Morris, 'at rest abeam and about twenty yards from her. This was a moment of great anxiety. We were directly under her guns motionless and powerless, except by exertions which might betray our character.'

At this moment, *Siren*'s longboat, which was in tow to the ketch, drew alongside with a leisurely movement, took a rope from *Intrepid* and rowed towards *Philadelphia*. At the same moment, some of the guards on the frigate dropped into a boat, and brought out another rope to help the ketch. The two crews met in the darkness, the ropes were joined, and *Intrepid* hauled herself alongside the frigate.

Just as the two vessels bumped, one of the frigate's guards saw something suspicious, and raised the alarm, and across the harbour rang out the cry 'Americanos.' Decatur immediately gave the order to board, and the U.S. sailors and marines swarmed aboard the frigate. The crew of the frigate, huddled in the stern, were taken completely by surprise. No firearms were used, and in virtual silence about twenty of them were killed by cutlass and dirk before the rest fled into their boat.

By the dim light of the moon, the combustibles and explosives, already disposed in the ketch, were quickly hauled aboard the frigate, while each sailor ran to a prearranged place in the ship's hull to put his burden. So efficiently was this carried out, that it took only a few minutes to plant the explosives. The train was then lit and, under a welter of flame and smoke the Americans leaped back into the longboat, Decatur being the last to leave. Then, under sweeps, they pulled rapidly back to the ketch just as a violent cannonade of the harbour's powerful guns broke out over the bay.

At the entrance to the harbour, which they reached unscathed in the turmoil and confusion, midshipman Morris looked back at the blazing frigate:

> The flames in the interior illuminated her ports and, ascending her rigging and masts, formed columns of fire which, meeting the tops, were reflected into beautiful capitals; while the occasional discharge of her guns gave an idea of some directing spirit within her. The walls of the city and its batteries, and the masts and rigging of cruisers at anchor, brilliantly illuminated and animated by the discharge of artillery,

formed worthy adjuncts and an appropriate background to the picture. . . .

By the time the boat had reached *Siren*, it could be seen by the bright glow in the harbour that *Philadelphia*'s cables had burned off and she had drifted ashore, where, shortly afterwards she blew up. *Intrepid* and *Siren*, with no losses at all except one slightly wounded man, ran for Syracuse with a favourable wind.

The success of this exploit, which, rightly holds a high place in American naval annals, helped considerably to strengthen the morale of the small American squadron, and news of it soon circulated round the Mediterranean. It reached Nelson, in his ship on blockade off Toulon, and he gave it the accolade of 'the most bold and daring act of the age'.[1]

To Bainbridge also, watching it perhaps from the rooftop of the American consulate, it must have brought relief. No longer was the ship within view, a reproach to himself and his nation.

Although the loss of *Philadelphia* was a blow to his prestige, the Bashaw knew that it had not altered his bargaining position. He had 308 American captives to be ransomed, and he now raised his price for peace talks to half a million dollars. It was this sum that he demanded in March when *Constitution* appeared off Tripoli to discuss ransom and peace. During this visit, the self appointed mediator between the Bashaw and Preble was the French consul, Beaussier. Beaussier when he boarded *Constitution* with the Bashaw's terms, added privately that he thought the Bashaw would accept 200,000 dollars. But even this suggestion was far above what the American commander was authorised to discuss. *Constitution* sailed away, only to return in June with further proposals.

On June 13th, the former American consul-general in Algiers, O'Brien, who had been relieved of that post by Tobias Lear, and

[1] Twenty years later, when Decatur, now a Captain, visited Tripoli, an American writer reported: 'the old Pasha received in the most friendly manner the commander of the squadron, who, when a young man, had destroyed his frigate, and bearded him under his very batteries. . . .'

had been taken aboard the flagship, was sent ashore by Preble with a renewed offer. This time the offer was to ransom the captives and not discuss peace terms, for fear of inflated reports of the Bashaw's price affecting the other Barbary rulers. O'Brien was authorised to offer a ransom of 200 dollars for each American prisoner, a total of about 62,000 dollars for the crew of *Philadelphia*. The Bashaw refused the offer with scorn. Bainbridge, who was deeply suspicious of Beaussier, believed that the Frenchman had an interest in keeping the price high. 'The consuls', he added gloomily, in a letter to Tobias Lear, 'are all intriguing for themselves and against us and do not wish us to have peace with Tripoli, as they are certain that such an event will be the Signal for War with some of them', and he concludes ominously, 'The Bashaw is daily gaining in strength—he has now 14 gunboats—and a gang of carpenters from Spain are building him several more.'

Meanwhile Commodore Preble was in a serious predicament. Although the danger to American commerce had been partially removed by the destruction of the *Philadelphia*, over 300 Americans were still captive in the Bashaw's hands, and the terms he was demanding for their release was far above anything Preble was authorised to consider. Normally, there would be one effective answer, and that was a bombardment of Tripoli, to force the Bashaw to come to terms. But would this not risk the lives of the American captives on whom reprisals might be taken?

It was probably the advice of some of the experienced American consuls which decided Preble to press forward with an attack, persuaded by the argument that the Bashaw would not willingly remove the American captives while they were so useful a bargaining counter while alive. Their possible deaths must be accepted as a risk.

Once this decision was taken, preparations for the bombardment were pressed ahead at Syracuse where the fleet was based. *Constitution* was now re-armed with 30 long 24 pounder guns to attack the shore batteries, and six 26 pounders. Six brigs and schooners were to be attached to the squadron for blockade purposes, and the King of the Two Sicilies had leased six flat-bottomed gunboats, with their Neapolitan crews, for close inshore work. Two of the latter were bomb vessels. With this miscellaneous squadron, Preble appeared off Tripoli on July 24th. But for over a week action had to be suspended while the mixed squadron fought out one of the now familiar gales.

By August 3rd this had subsided and the squadron, approaching as near the dangerous reefs as was safe, opened fire on the Castle. While the long guns played on the Castle batteries, the shallow draught gunboats crept close inshore to loose their fire and their hissing bombs on the shore batteries. The results of the first attack were indecisive. The Tripoli defences, prudently rebuilt and reinforced by the Bashaw, were now very strong. Several new forts in the bay, including one which the American captives had built, had been equipped with guns and brought to bear on the American squadron. The full weight of 115 Tripoli guns could now be turned on the squadron tacking slowly across the bay.

After some hours, Preble drew off, to reappear four days later, and renew the contest. This time, by pressing hard his attacks inshore, he sank a few boats in Tripoli harbour (where they were soon re-floated); but he was forced to draw off again when a red-hot shot, fired from one of the Tripoli batteries hit one of the gunboats which immediately blew up, killing two officers and eight men.

Between these attacks the Bashaw, unlike his forebears, had refused to leave the city for the *menshia*, and had remained in the Castle, in a bomb proof shelter. After the first attack he had brought the American captive officers from the comparative freedom of their house in the American consulate into the Castle, where they were kept closely imprisoned. Only the American surgeon Jonathan Cowdery, was allowed a certain freedom, and he saw the Bashaw emerging from his shelter when the American gunboat blew up in the harbour, wearing 'a small piece of paper on the top of his head with a Turkish or Mahometan scrawl with assurances that it would entirely secure him from all danger'.

On August 9th, the squadron reappeared off the City and again opened fire. Some 48 bomb shells and 500 twenty-four pound shot were hurled at the batteries and the town. A mosque was hit, and several shells were seen to fall on the house of the Danish consul, Nissen, who ironically had been so kind to the American captives.[1]

This bombardment had some effect, for the next day, a signal was observed flying from the French consul's house, and O'Brien, under a flag of truce, went ashore. O'Brien now carried a new offer though this was based on ransom only and not on peace terms. He offered 80,000 dollars ransom, plus 10,000 dollars as a consular present. The Bashaw countered this with a demand of 150,000 dollars to include peace terms, and an agreement for annual tribute. Preble countered by a final offer of 100,000 dollars, plus the same consular present, but refused to discuss tribute or peace terms. This the Bashaw, with signs that he already regretted having been so lenient, rejected and O'Brien withdrew.

Preble resumed the offensive with three more attacks, all equally inconclusive, and he began to think of a final withdrawal as he was running short of ammunition. With memories of Decatur's great exploit, a final attempt was made to damage the harbour and shipping by sending in a fireship. Once more the now famous *Intrepid* was used. Filled with combustibles and explosives it was planned to send her into the harbour, where her crew of volunteers—two American officers and six sailors—were to lay her alongside the harbour shipping, fire her, and then be rescued by two of the fastest of the squadron's longboats, who were to follow close behind her.

On the night of September 4th, this fireship with its crew of desperate men, glided out from the squadron towards the harbour, and on to the inner harbour. But this time the Tripolitan

[1] Nissen had been advised by Bainbridge to leave his consulate and go with the other consuls to the safety of the *menshia*. He had remained behind, although nearly killed by a round shot from *Constitution*, in order to see that the American captives, left without food during the bombardment, should receive something to keep them alive.

gunners were not to be caught napping. Fire was quickly opened on the brig, and it was apparently suddenly hit by a hot shot, for it exploded with dreadful force, hurling the mutilated bodies of its crew high into the air. The bodies of several of these sailors were seen by Bainbridge and Cowdery a few days later on the shore considerably mangled by dogs. The Bashaw refused to allow them to be buried, as they were a considerable help to Tripolitan morale. They were eventually buried south of the town.

The American squadron had scarcely recovered from this blow when an American frigate appeared from Gibraltar, bringing orders for Preble's recall. Leaving his frigate and the two ships *Argus* and *Vixen* to continue the blockade, Preble boarded the frigate and sailed for Gibraltar, carrying with him a casualty list of thirty killed and twenty-four wounded. It was a sad end to another inconclusive attempt to bring pressure on the Bashaw of Tripoli by sea. 'I must candidly tell you', wrote Nissen to the American chargé d'affaires in Tunis in a letter of September 30th 1804, 'that all the attacks of the squadron, except that of the 3rd August have had very little effect, and the damage done of absolutely no consequence'.

Nothing remained for the Americans but to continue the blockade with their meagre forces, and await some new plan to unseat the Bashaw, whose success in resisting them might well lead to awkward repercussions among the rulers of the other Barbary states.

Before considering what this new American plan was to be, it must be seen what the results of the recent bombardment were on the American captives in Tripoli.

The American bombardments naturally affected the life of the 308 American captives. The Bashaw, partly, it is fair to say, for fear of public reprisals, had moved the officers from the relatively comfortable quarters in the former American consulate to cramped quarters in the Castle, where, they alleged, they were even worse housed than the men. Here, with some few exceptions they were closely confined for six months. Bainbridge and

Cowdery the ship's surgeon, who as a doctor became of great use to the Bashaw, were given separate rooms. Though Bainbridge was not allowed out of his, Cowdery was given comparative freedom to wander over the Castle and tend the Bashaw's family, the American sailors and the Bashaw's Neapolitan and negro slaves, who, with some few Swedish slaves, made up the working population of the Bashaw's *bagnios*.

Down in their cell in the castle basement, the American officers had passed the difficult and dangerous days while the castle batteries thundered near their heads and the shells and shot of the American squadron crashed into the masonry about them. In the engagement of August 24th, one 36 lb. ball burst through the wall of Bainbridge's room where he was sleeping, missed him by inches and covered him with nearly a cartload of masonry and rubble, from which he had to be virtually dug out.

Surgeon Cowdery kept a brief journal of his experiences, and since he had access to the battlements, could watch the engagements between his own squadron at sea and the shore batteries. He thus had an interesting view of how the Turks and *Kuloghlis* fought. On the alarm gun being fired, they all went to their stations and then, in serried ranks by their guns, went through their prayers 'kneeling and kissing the ground several times with their faces towards the east, all with as much regularity as the exercise in a well disciplined army'. As the firing started, they ran to their guns, many of which were being served with powder and ball by the unfortunate American sailors, while from the tops of the battlements and high places on the city walls. the *marabouts* in their strange costumes, exhorted the soldiers to fight, at the same time shouting snatches from the *Qur'an*, and curses and spells at the American ships, whom they strove by magic to draw on to the rocks, as they believed they had drawn the *Philadelphia*.

During all this the Bashaw sat in a bomb-proof room emerging from time to time to watch the contest, with a holy paper, with 'a Turkish or Mahometan scrawl', as Cowdery noted, still sealed to his head by a *marabout* to protect him from danger. He remained quite calm during the bombardment, sitting sometimes joking with Cowdery, to whom he had taken a liking, about his value as a slave:

He said he would not take 20,000 dollars for me; to which I replied I might then expect to remain in slavery for life; he patted me on the shoulder and said I must then content myself to stay with him.

Cowdery also saw another side to the Bashaw, which perhaps explained his hold over his troops:

Many Turks were killed and wounded, and several men much burnt by the explosion of their own powder . . . The Bashaw has all of his wounded brought to an apartment in the Castle, where he visits them, and makes them a present of ten dollars each. He then orders his surgeons and mamelukes to dress their wounds, and he often assists with his own hands.

Cowdery was astonished to see how the Arab treatment of the wounds with honey seemed to lead to quick recovery.[1]

This curious mixture of courage and generosity, cruelty and indifference in the Bashaw was reflected in the treatment of the American officers and sailors. Until the bombardments began, the officers had been allowed considerable freedom, making excursions with a small guard into the *menshia* where they visited at some houses, including that of the Bashaw's eldest son, the Bey. Cowdery was surprised at the courtesy of their reception which showed 'as much respect as could be expected or desired from a foe who held us prisoners of war'. Indeed one evening a dance was held at the Bashaw's own garden, where Turks, Arabs, Berbers and American officers gave the guests examples of their different modes of dancing to the amusement of the Bashaw and the Bey.

Very different was the treatment of the sailors captured in *Philadelphia*. These poor men were treated as the commonest white slaves, and put to hard labour like their thousands of Christian fellow sufferers in the terrible *bagnois* of Algiers, of Tunis and Tripoli. They were allowed no communication with

[1] The traditions of the Prophet state that the three cures for ills, are 'honey, cupping and branding'.

their officers, but occasionally smuggled letters to them. Cowdery saw them several times in the streets of Tripoli, worn, emaciated, heavily chained and dragging great loads of stone for the repair of the fortifications. They were given a bare ration of two small loaves of bread and a little oil each day, and were constantly beaten and flogged by their brutal overseers, though in these respects it is only fair to repeat that their condition was no worse than the Christian and Moslem galley slaves at Marseilles, Toulon or Venice. Five of them died during the captivity, and six became renegades. One of the latter, Herkimer, known to the Tripolines as 'Hamet American' was able by intercession with the Bashaw to get his comrades' lot ameliorated; another, West, a carpenter, became a useful builder of gunboats for the Bashaw, and a third, a bad character called Wilson, who made life difficult for the prisoners by carrying tales of projected plots of escape to the Bashaw, was employed to teach the Turks 'how to throw bombs, hot shot and hand-grenades'.

Of the officers, Bainbridge as the commander, suffered most. As late as December 1804, although he had carefully reported to his government, and sent a number of very useful letters of information both naval and political written in secret ink over his normal correspondence to Tobias Lear, the U.S. consul in Algiers, he could write to the latter, that he had received 'not one word from Government since my unfortunate captivity'. Through the helpful and completely honest Danish consul Nissen he had been able to alleviate the lot of his officers and crew in the matter of clothing and a little money, but he felt bitterly the fact that he was kept completely incommunicado from the Bashaw and from the other consuls. He fell ill from a fever which attacked the officers in the autumn months, and Langford, the newly arrived British consul, interceded with the Bashaw for him to come and reside under supervision in Langford's house—a request that was refused since the Bashaw believed that the harsher the treatment of this senior officer, the more disposed the U.S. government would be to pay a ransom for him. 'It requires', wrote Bainbridge in another letter to Lear from his prison, 'more than the fortitude of man to bear my daily reflections: Injurious reports, loss of services to my Country, wife and child in America, are painful subjects in contemplation in a close prison in Tripoli.'

Nevertheless, distressed and sick, he continued to send out a stream of sensible advice to the U.S. government. The theme of these letters was that the Bashaw was a strong, proud man and in complete control of his people. He must be treated with the respect due to an independent ruler in any negotiations for a treaty and for ransom of the prisoners, and it was therefore useless to try to use the intercession of the Grand Signior, the Bey of Tunis, or even Napoleon—all ideas mooted by Washington—to bring pressure on him. Further, any attempt to unseat him through assistance to his brother, was doomed to disaster. This was advice that might have saved the U.S. government considerable expense, if taken, but would not have led to the undertaking of one of the most courageous and daring enterprises in American history.

William Eaton's march

As early as 1802, William Eaton, while American consul in Tunis, had been considering a plan, first put forward by his colleague, Cathcart, for using Yusef Karamanli's elder brother, Ahmed (called by the Americans Hamet), as a means to unseat the Bashaw of Tripoli. There was some legal basis for the idea. Ahmed, second son of the old Bashaw, was senior to Yusef, and had indeed been appointed to succeed his father, when Yusef drove him out. From Tripoli, Ahmed had fled to Tunis, under the protection of the Bey, and it was here that Eaton had met him and seen in him the possibility of bringing about Yusef's downfall.

Eaton was an interesting character. He had been in turn professional soldier, school teacher and clerk. As a Captain in the army, he had served in the Indian wars in Ohio and Georgia. He was then, for reasons which seem difficult to elucidate, appointed a Consul in Tunis. In character he was courageous, direct, and extremely practical. But he had a rather devious financial history, and was inclined to ignore authority and follow his own schemes. In personal relationship also, he had not the character for dealing with orientals, and after only a few years at Tunis was expelled by the Bey and returned to the United States. Before he left Tunis, however, he had broached the idea of returning Ahmed to the throne of Tripoli with that Prince, and had secured his agreement. The reason for Eaton's expulsion seems to have been partly this intrigue with Ahmed,[1] for at the same time as Eaton's expulsion took place, the Bey withdrew his protection from Ahmed, who then fled to Malta.

Back in Washington, Eaton, vigorous, plain-spoken and persuasive put his plan to a government still recovering from the news of the loss of the *Philadelphia*, the capture of a large number of American sailors, and the defiance by the Bashaw of the repeated attacks of a strong naval squadron. At this distance from North Africa it seemed to ignorant congressmen to be a clever *coup de main*. The plan was simple. It was to take Ahmed, with sufficient adherents and a strong contingent of American forces, to Derna by sea, from where they would march overland for the capture of Tripoli.

Eaton had set out the details of this plan in convincing terms. Its advantages were, he wrote:

> (I) By investing Tripoli in the rear, through the co-operation of Hamet Pasha, we cut off the enemy's retreat from the country, and effectually prevent him receiving supplies from any quarter whatever,
>
> (II) The dread of our retaliation when thus invested will deter the enemy from treating our captives with cruelty,
>
> (III) The experiment will cost very little, even if it fails of success; nor shall we lose any ground by the failure. The success of the measure will save both life and cash.

The logistics of this hazardous enterprise, which depended on accurate information which Eaton either did not possess, or

[1] It was typical of him that in order to finance Ahmed for his assistance in the plan, Eaton had borrowed money from the Bey's own commercial agent.

ignored, appealed to the authorities in Washington, none of whom asked what seems to have been a question of vital importance. This was, what would be the attitude of the population of Tripoli to the arrival of Ahmed as their ruler? Instead they accepted the plan in its entirety, authorised Eaton to carry it out, provided him with money and arms, and instructed him to join Commodore Barron, who had now succeeded Preble as Commander of the American Mediterranean squadron. He was thus commissioned with the curious title of Agent of the American Navy. Under this title, and with Barron as his chief, Eaton sailed for the Mediterranean in December 1803.

The optimism of the authorities in Washington was not echoed by those American naval officers nearer the scene of action. They saw fatal flaws in Eaton's plan, and their misgivings were echoed both by Tobias Lear in Algiers and Bainbridge in Tripoli, both of whom had received secret information about it.

Lear wrote urgently to Washington:

> I presume the co-operation of the Brother of the Bashaw of Tripoli will not be attempted. . . . Indeed, I should place more confidence in the continuation of peace with the present Bashaw, if he is well beaten into it, than I should have with the other . . .

Bainbridge, who during his captivity had learned a great deal about Yusef's character, wrote with equal urgency:

> I sincerely hope that such an Impolic [*sic*] and extraordinary measure has not intruded itself on the wisdom of our Government. . . . Whoever has advised such a measure must be entirely ignorant of the power of the present ruler and the disposition of his Subjects, who always detest the miserable exile. . . . It is not a natural supposition that he should have any friends in this Regency that they will abandon (the Bashaw) the moment they find (Ahmed) is joined with Christians against Mussulmen. . . .

And Commodore Barron also warned that Yusef was a person 'of pertinacity of character not unmixed with bravery and other qualities belonging to the Soldier. . . .' Barron dutifully prepared to help Eaton, but his misgivings were voiced in another despatch in which he feared that Eaton's character might make him take, 'a wider scope in his Engagements to the exiled Prince than is compatible with the ideas and intentions of Government or with the authority vested in me as relates to the subject of co-operation. . . .'

All these warnings and sound advice were unheeded by Eaton. He thought the attitude of Barron and his officers as symptomatic of the American navy, for whom he had some contempt which he did not hesitate to express. He thought Bainbridge as little less than a coward for striking his flag, and the present U.S. squadron in the Mediterranean as wavering and without purpose. 'The government', he had written earlier about the U.S. navy, 'may as well send out a Quaker meeting to float about this sea. . . .'

It was not an attitude to make for harmony in what was to be a combined operation against Tripoli.

Ahmed Karamanli meanwhile had remained in Malta only a short while. Yusef was shrewd enough to recognise his potentialities as a rival when settled so close to the frontiers of Tripoli. He sent him a series of peaceful messages, inviting him to return and take up the traditional post of a junior in the Karamanli family—the governorship of Derna, in Cyrenaica. Ahmed eventually accepted this, but his stay in Derna was short. News came to him, probably founded on fact, that his brother intended to murder him. He did not wait; but fled to Egypt, where he had joined with one of the Mameluke Beys who were then at war with the Turkish forces of the Grand Signior.

Eaton, who had hoped to find Ahmed still in Malta, had therefore to make a change of plan. The original scheme had been that Ahmed would have been shipped from Malta to Derna, with his adherents and some American forces; and these had been Commodore Barron's instructions. Barron would now have been glad to leave Ahmed Karamanli somewhere in Egypt, and drop the plan altogether. But Eaton proved both stubborn and persuasive. After some demur a new plan was agreed. It was arranged that Eaton should travel to Alexandria in the American brig *Argus*, and would make an attempt from there to get into touch with Ahmed. To assist him in his enquiries in Egypt, the Americans approached Sir Alexander Ball, the British Governor of Malta, who supplied letters of introduction to the British resident in Cairo, Major Misset, and to the pro-consul in Alexandria, Mr. Briggs.

Armed with these documents, some money and a small number of assistants, Eaton sailed from Malta on November 4th 1804 in the *Argus*, whose captain, Isaac Hull, carried written orders to proceed to Alexandria and convoy some American vessels back to Malta, but whose oral, and secret, orders were to assist Eaton in every way to carry out his plan.

Alexandria was reached, without incident, on November 27th, and Eaton went ashore to find further difficulties awaiting him. The British pro-consul agreed to furnish him with money and such assistance as he could, but he warned him that Egypt, still suffering from the chaos following Napoleon's defeat by the British, and the evacuation of the country by both armies, was still completely disrupted by the fighting which was going on between the Mameluke leaders and the Turkish troops. Cairo was in a state of virtual civil war, and Major Misset, the British resident, had been obliged to move his consulate to Rosetta. The main action between the Mameluke *janissaries* and the Turkish troops was going on south of Cairo, and among the former somewhere was Ahmed Karamanli.

Eaton was undeterred. He sat down and wrote two letters addressed to Ahmed, giving them to two separate messengers. In these he begged the Prince to give him a rendezvous where the plans for his return as Bashaw of Tripoli could be discussed. He then prepared to leave for Rosetta.

It was Ramadan, the month of the Moslem fast, and not the best for Christians to travel. Eaton, however, obtained a small boat and laboriously made his way, with his few companions, towards Rosetta. He had begun a diary, which is almost our only source for the near epic story which follows; and at Aboukir, where they camped for the night, Eaton wandered among the wreckage and French skeletons still littering the shore from the great battle of six years earlier. 'Ghastly monuments', Eaton mused, 'of the Savage influence of avarice and ambition on the human mind.'

At Rosetta, he received a warm welcome from Major Misset, an old soldier himself, and a promise of any assistance possible. Although Sir Alexander Ball's letter to the Resident referred to Eaton's visit in only general terms as 'to transact affairs of a temporary nature for his Government', Eaton was so impressed with Misset's welcome that he decided to take him into his confidence about the real nature of his visit.

It was a gesture that was appreciated; and Misset promised all assistance. Eaton was not ungrateful. 'The attention of Major Misset,' he wrote in a despatch to the Secretary of the Navy, 'though it cannot exceed my gratitude, far exceeds any means I have of expressing it. Finding him a frank, open-hearted generous soldier, I unreservedly unveiled to him the object of my voyage. He took every step which the nature of his situation would justify, to facilitate that object.'

Misset, in fact, not only helped Eaton to charter boats to continue his journey to Cairo, but lent him his own private secretary, a Captain Vincent, to accompany him and see that he was lodged in the English House in the city.

On December 4th 1804 two boats left Rosetta, flying respectively the British and American flags. Eaton made a note in his diary of the composition of his small force.

Our strength consisted of Lieutenant O'Bannon, of the Marine Corps, Midshipman Mann and Danielson, Mr Farquhar (an Englishman from Malta). Selim, a *janissary*, Ali, a dragonmen with six servants; all well armed. Captain Vincent and Doctor Mendrici in another Boat, mounting two swivels, besides muskets pistols and sabres, and about an equal number of people; Precautions necessary to resist the predatory attacks of the wild Arabs, who infest the river banks and during this general suspense of justice, prey upon the defenceless....

It was well that the party was large and well armed. Not only were parties of Mamelukes sweeping the area, but the tribes were in revolt, and parties of Turkish troops containing the dreaded Albanian levies, and the even more savage Kurds, were quartering the countryside, their violence falling more hardly on the helpless villagers than on the enemy.

By December 7th, however, Eaton's party had reached Boulak without incident. A messenger had been sent on by Vincent, and horses were awaiting them; and mounting they entered the city of Cairo, 'followed by a vast concourse of people of all ages and sexes, whom curiosity or want had collected about us; but at that distance peculiar to people of the East towards strangers of distinction.'

The Viceroy[1] had been apprised of their arrival, and his interpreter was awaiting them at the English House to call them to attend an audience on the following day.

Eaton, the simple New Englander, found the audience with the Viceroy, impressive. 'The court which attended the Viceroy surpassed in magnificence everything I have ever seen of the kind.'

At length, after the usual courtesies, Eaton, speaking in French, which was translated into Turkish for the Viceroy, enlarged on the reason for his visit; the bad relations between America and Tripoli, the deplorable state of Tripoli under its present ruler, and the necessity for his replacement by the legal heir to the throne, Ahmed Pasha.

'Varying a little the subject,' reported Eaton, 'I touched upon the affinity of principle between the Islam and American religion. ... He listened with attention and evident gratification.'

The visit was successful. The Viceroy was no doubt glad on any account to get rid of Ahmed Karamanli. Messengers were sent out, and Ahmed was found with the troops of the Mameluke

[1] In the anarchy then prevailing in Egypt, it is difficult to know who Eaton means by the Viceroy. Presumably it is Ahmed Pasha Khorshid, who was overthrown by Mehemet Ali a few months later.

chief, Elfi, in the village of Miniet, in upper Egypt. The Viceroy, under Eaton's persuasion, sent him an amnesty and a safe conduct through the Turkish forces, and only mildly reproached him for taking part with the Mamelukes.

While these necessary documents were going to Ahmed, and the Prince was preparing to leave with his supporters for the rendezvous with Eaton, Eaton himself remained in Cairo to recruit men for the small detachment of troops he needed for the hazardous journey ahead.

Cairo was full of a strange medley of races and professions, the remnants of the Napoleonic, the Turkish and the Mameluke troops, who had passed through. Eaton recruited a German engineer, 'late a Colonel in the Tyrol battalions', and with him a deserter from Napoleon's army, a Frenchman, turned Moslem, called Selim Comb; he collected Greek gunners, and an Italian A.D.C. Perhaps it was the last who took him to the only relaxation recorded in his brief diary, a Cairo entertainment. 'Dancing women', wrote Eaton severely, 'Haggard prostitutes, disgustful, obscene monsters who exhibit savage nature in gestures of studied and practised depravity.'

In the midst of these activities, a reply from Ahmed Karamanli arrived. It contained what must have been an unwelcome surprise. After giving a rendezvous for their meeting, Ahmed announced that he did not approve of the American plan that he and his adherents should be transported to Derna by sea. He would make his way there overland.

Provided his confidence in himself was justified, and he would be welcomed on his arrival at Derna, Ahmed's plan was not without some common sense. The more adherents and followers he picked up on the way, the stronger the force which would present itself at Derna. But the plan presented Eaton with a dilemma. As a practical soldier he knew that it was one thing to embark a party of Arab troops on a warship for a short sea journey to a destination where they could disembark, fresh for action and under a protective naval screen; it was another to take them overland across some five hundred miles of desert country exposed to all the hazards of travel, of supply difficulties, of illness and possible exhaustion; and deliver them at their goal to face what might prove a determined enemy.

Nevertheless, there is no record in Eaton's diary of any hesitation on his part in undertaking this much more difficult task. It is possible that since he had no maps of the area, he relied on the protestations of Arabs who had made the journey, that the way was easy, water was available en route, and the tribes were friendly. At all events, without demur, he returned to Rosetta where he arrived on January 14th to inform the captain of *Argus*, and prepare plans for the journey.

He had already replied to Ahmed's message, agreeing to make the journey to Derna overland, and suggesting they now rendezvous at Rosetta. But after several days waiting for a reply, he pushed on to Alexandria, where a letter eventually reached him from Ahmed changing the rendezvous again to the banks of Lake Fayoum.

In the unsettled state of the countryside, this was a difficult place to reach, but Eaton started off at once, taking with him two ship's officers, Lieutenants Blake and Mann, and a detachment of twenty-three Marines. They had hardly covered seventy miles of the difficult journey before they were surrounded by Turkish troops and made prisoners by the Governor of the province. Eaton now learned that he had been arrested at the instigation of the French consul in Alexandria, who had informed the Turks that the Americans were in reality British spies.[1]

Here they languished, under guard for a few days, until Eaton by blandishments and a small bribe of money to a Sheikh of the Wuld Ali tribe, in whose *dira* they had been arrested, sent a message to Ahmed telling him of their predicament. After what seemed endless delays and procrastinations, mainly caused by Ahmed's incapability to help the Americans under duress, the Governor was induced to let them go; and they returned to Alexandria again on February 16th.

[1] It seems likely that the French, anxious to keep on good terms with Yusef Karamanli, arranged for this embarrassment.

Here they found more difficulties. The machinations of Drovetti, the French consul, had persuaded the Governor of the City and the Admiral of the Port to refuse entry to Ahmed Karamanli. In these circumstances, Eaton and his whole party moved round to the west of the city, and set up camp; and from here, in a letter home, Eaton announced his historic decision: 'We shall therefore take up our line of march through the Desert of Lybia towards Derna next Wednesday.'

The last few days in Alexandria were spent recruiting men to provide an escort for him to Derna; through Selim Comb, the French gunner, and Litzendorf, the Austrian, he managed to find sufficient men to have 38 Greek and 25 other Christian mercenaries, mostly gunners. As Ahmed Karamanli's men came in, followed by some Beduins recruited on the way, Eaton guessed his total force to be about 400 men. For this number, rations were organised, camels and camel drivers hired, and a store of weapons and ammunition served out from *Argus*. In a final discussion with Captain Isaac Hull of *Argus*, it was arranged that while Eaton's party made their way overland, *Argus*, and some reinforcements from Barron's squadron, should follow by sea, meeting them off Derna. Here, further supplies would be landed, and the whole expedition, with the ships following closely off shore, should advance across the country to Tripoli, picking up adherents on the way to swell the army.

Before finally setting out, Eaton sat down and drew up a written Convention, which he induced Ahmed Karamanli, to sign. In this, the Prince agreed, on taking over the throne, to reimburse the American government for the expenditure it had undertaken for him; these payments to be guaranteed from the Swedish, Danish and Dutch annual subsidies. In a secret Article, attached to the Convention, and not forwarded to Washington, Karamanli also promised to deliver up to the Americans as prisoners both Yusef Karamanli and the Scotsman, Peter Lyle.[1]

[1] Lyle the renegade Scotsman had become Commander-in-chief of the Bashaw's pirate fleet.

This Convention, excluding the Secret Article, was forwarded to the U.S. Secretary of State on February 23rd. Attached to it was a brief note which merely stated: 'The camp moves tomorrow for Derna.'

On March 5th 1805 those sections of the great Wuld Ali beduin tribe, whose *dira* lay westwards of Alexandria, and who were now pasturing their flocks in the spring herbage along the foothills overlooking the sea, must have watched, with some wonder, a strange cavalcade winding slowly along the rough camel track between Burg el Arab and el Omeiyid.[1]

In the van rode an American general officer, in full regimentals and cocked hat. Behind, in order, came a Marine subaltern, two naval midshipmen, a warrant officer and a file of six uniformed U.S. Marines, the latter marching in careful step, with their muskets at the slope. Behind these came a less disciplined company of twenty-five artillery men, clothed in a variety of uniforms, and dragging an equally varied collection of weapons, including a field gun. Behind these again came a strangely dressed party of thirty-eight Greek mercenaries. Around this little party, as it moved slowly but inexorably westwards, cavorted a party of about ninety Arab horsemen, led by a Prince of Barbary, dressed in all the *Kuloghli* finery of coloured silks, gold embroidery, silvered saddles, and profusion of guns, pistols and daggers. Behind toiled a long line of camel-men, camp followers, servants, and a string of 109 camels carrying supplies.

From Eaton's journal, we have a rough list of the principal participants in this epic march to Derna. Besides himself, there was Lieutenant O'Bannon of the Marines, Mr. Peck and Mr. Mann, midshipmen from *Argus*, and a warrant officer. The commissariat was in charge of Mr. Farquhar, an 'Englishman from Malta'; and a Dr. Mendrici, formerly from Tunis, had come as surgeon. The French deserter, Selim Comb, commanded the gunners, assisted

[1] Twenty years after Eaton's adventure, J. R. Pacho, the French traveller, passed along most of Eaton's route. His map, the first of this area, helps roughly to estimate where Eaton's army camped.

by Lieutenants Conant and Rocco, and the thirty-eight Greek mercenaries were in the charge of Captain Luco Ulovix and a Lieutenant Constantine. Close behind Eaton rode his Italian A.D.C., Davico. Ahmed Karamanli's escort was commanded by his Selectedar, or sword bearer; and the vital office of control of the camels and camel-men was in the hands of two Beduin sheikhs, el Tayyib and Mohamed.

Slowly, this ill-assorted caravan of conflicting hopes and ambitions moved across the foothills of the coastal plain, while the watching Beduin herdsmen and their women working in the scattered barley patches must have gathered together in fear and wonder. These were not Mameluke troops riding on foray, nor Turkish *janissaries*, nor the *ghazzu* of a Beduin tribe sweeping down for their animals. In fact, though they could not know it, the watchers were looking at history being made. The first land force of the new world of America was marching on African soil towards a planned invasion.

Eaton's route, except for divergences imposed by the search for water, was virtually that so well known to thousands of British soldiers in the second world war. It lay along the coastal track which, since antiquity, has followed the 500 miles that separate Alexandria from Derna. In 1805, it was still what it had been for centuries, a mere camel track threading its way from well to well by the shortest route, worn by the feet of countless pilgrims to Mecca, by couriers from the Maghreb, and by the few merchants who dared the risks of the road to carry their merchandise. Across gravel desert steppe; sandy *wadis* filled with rocks and oleanders; salt marshes, treacherous underfoot, called *sebkhas*, and covered with a rank alkali herbage, which even camels refuse; sometimes within sight of the sea and the white beaches of the coast, but more often presenting to the traveller no view but a low horizon of yellow desert covered with tufts of the plant *shih*, a horizon broken only occasionally by the foothills of the coastal ranges with their steep dry watercourses. In March, this desert, after the winter rains, would be covered here and there with a fine delicate mist of green, as a thousand tiny plants sprang up, a brief spell of colour quickly killed by the advancing summer sun. But this green was no evidence of water, which was scarce and usually confined to wells often far apart and sometimes soon dried out, and to the few waterholes, known only and jealously preserved by the Beduin shepherds.

This was a route where climate, lack of food and water, and marauders were all a danger to travellers. In March, the equinoctial gales would have begun, bringing either dark clouds of stinging dust from the Sahara to envelop the caravan, or sudden floods of rain from the west, which in the space of minutes would turn the dry watercourses in the foothills into raging torrents, or pools of mud; the dust storms, sudden and blinding, can cause the track to be lost by carelessness and a watering place missed, while the parching air rapidly brings on a raging thirst in men and animals. Of food, there is scarcely any, except occasional purchases of milk or *leben* from the Beduin, or barley bread and a few dates at the rare caravan stops near any cultivation. Water is even scarcer and therefore dependence on the occasional wells is vital for life. Last of all were the marauders on this well travelled route, bands of robbers made up of disaffected soldiers, rapacious tribesmen, political and criminal refugees from Egypt or Cyrenaica, who hung about on the horizon of caravans ready to swoop down and attack any unprotected travellers. Between Sollum and the border of Cyrenaica there was a sort of independent tract of country entirely controlled by these refugees from both Egypt and Cyrenaica, who wielded a sort of rule, and waged a levy on all travellers from whom they could get it. Beyond the touch of the authorities of either country they had a stranglehold on the route between the two.

All these hazards faced Eaton with his small section of six disciplined Marines, his yet untried troops of mixed Christian nationalities, and his almost uncontrollable Arab auxiliaries. Yet not a qualm appears in his brief journal; not even the very great difficulty of no common language among most of his supporters seems to have worried him. He knew some French, a little Italian, and a few words of Arabic; it is not known if any of the Christians knew any language with which to communicate with the wilder members of his army.

Indeed, perhaps Eaton's saving grace was his ignorance. With a map of the route and more knowledge of its hazards, he might have drawn back, or waited for a better occasion. With any sort of knowledge of Beduin temperament, he might have questioned the easily given promises and agreements of the sheikhs in control of the camels carrying his supplies. And surely, if he had known Ahmed Karamanli better, this Prince whose whole career had exhibited nothing but cowardice, weakness and indecision, he might have paused for thought. It was well perhaps that the words of Pacho, the French traveller who crossed this route only a few years after Eaton, could not be known to him.

Dès que les Arabes sont entres dans les solitudes du désert, alors se trouvant dans leur domaine, ils parlent en maîtres. En vain le voyageur rappelle les accords faits et les ordres reçus, les accords deviennent illusoires, et les ordres sont aisément eludés.

The first few days' march of Eaton's small army passed without incident; and it was not until they reached the area of Dresieh on March 10th that Eaton had his first taste of what was to become a familiar scene:

The camel drivers, and footmen who followed the horses, revolted and made a stand. The Chiek el Taiib[1] had insinuated a suspicion among them that if they performed their services before being paid, the Christians would be apt to defraud them. The Bashaw seemed irresolute and despondent. Money—more money was the only stimulous which could give motion to the camp. The forenoon was consumed, and no appearances of a disposition to proceed ahead. I ordered the Christians under arms, and feinted a countermarch, threatening to abandon the expedition and their Bashaw, unless the march in advance proceeded immediately. This project took effect; the mutiny was suppressed; and we marched twelve miles.

The next incident occurred three days later. On March 13th a man on horseback was discerned approaching the party from the

[1] Eaton's own spelling is followed throughout.

west. He dashed up to Ahmed Karamanli's horsemen, who were ahead of the column, with the news (afterwards proved false) that the population of Derna were in revolt against the Governor, and had imprisoned him. This news was greeted with great excitement by Karamanli's men, who without waiting to inform the rest of the column, began celebrating in their accustomed way, by firing their guns in the air. This noise of firing reaching the rear of the column was heard by the footmen accompanying the camels. Believing that this was an attack on the Christians, they themselves turned on some of the Christians in the rear and attacked them, hoping to disarm and kill them. Order was hastily restored by some of Karamanli's horsemen, but the augury was a disturbing one to the Christian commander.

Eaton, worried by the state of his rations, was for pressing on as fast as possible, and he soon found that he had grossly miscalculated the speed at which the column could move, its progress constantly being impeded by trouble with the camel drivers. By March 16th they had reached Bir Gerawiya, a few miles east of Mersa Matruh, where heavy rain flooding their camp again delayed them. Two days later, at a small caravan halt called Massouah, more trouble broke out.

Eaton, to his exasperation, now learned for the first time that Ahmed Karamanli, who had been charged with the recruiting of the Sheikhs, and the camel-men, had only paid them as far as Massouah. They refused to go further without more money. Eaton faced this problem as philosophically as he could. After emptying his own money chest and borrowing from the Christian officers and men, he gave Karamanli the sum of 673 dollars, which, with further sums collected by the Prince from his own adherents, was handed over to the two sheikhs. During the night, however, all the camels, except forty, now disappeared, having turned back for Egypt. The sixty remaining beasts were also prevented from moving forward by their drivers.

Fearing treachery, in which Karamanli himself might be involved, Eaton now threatened to occupy the small fort which protected the wells and hold it until help came to him by sea. This threat had its effect, and after some hours of waiting, fifty of the lost camels returned, and on March 21st the journey was resumed.

The next day, the little army debouched on to a wide plain stretching down to the sea, which Eaton learned was called '*Oak kerar ke barre*'.[1] Here they found the whole area covered with the tents of a section of the Wuld Ali tribe, with a large number of horses, camels and cattle. They were friendly, and ready to barter, but Eaton's funds were now reduced to only a few sequins. He managed, however, to exchange some rice for some excellent dates and some barley for the horses; and while they rested here, Eaton wrote some despatches, which he sent by courier to Bomba to await the arrival of *Argus*.

They moved on again the next day, and some eighty warriors of the Wuld Ali decided to throw in their lot with Karamanli, and joined his party. Eaton felt them to be merely an added burden. He had no money and, as he wrote in his diary, 'cash, we find, is the only deity of Arabs . . .' It was also necessary to draw up new contracts with the two sheikhs, to freight the camels on another stage to Bomba. Perhaps the presence of the Wuld Ali induced the two camel dealers to accept the promise of payment ahead. The party now moved off, and Eaton found that it was followed by forty-seven tents of the Wuld Ali, with about 150 more warriors, their wives and children.

On March 26th more trouble arose. A courier riding in again from the west reported another rumour. This was that the Bashaw of Tripoli had sent a large force of troops to oppose Ahmed, and that they would arrive at Derna before him.

> The alarm excited by this information arrested our motions, [wrote Eaton]. The Bashaw seemed to hesitate whether to proceed further. The camel drivers fled with their caravan, and there seemed to be combination among the Bashaw's people and the Arabs of Behara to return to Fayoum.

Eaton checked this by immediately cutting off their rations.

[1] I take this to be 'aqra kebir' which can mean in Arabic 'dry, sandy slopes'. It is not to be found on Pacho's map.

There ensued a rowdy council of war. Sheikh Tayyib swore he would return home, and after quarrelling with Eaton, who had refused a request by Karamanli that he should beg Tayyib to stay, the latter left with some of the camel-men.

Eaton did not hesitate.

I ordered a march. We got under way at 7.30. At 10, a messenger came from the Sheikh to assure us that he had taken up his march for Behara. . . . Continued the march. At 12 o'clock another messenger. 'The Sheikh el Tayib will join if we camp seasonably.'

The party then halted, and Eaton, sitting in his tent, received Sheikh Tayyib, 'who presented himself . . . with visible chagrin on his countenance.'

There was some further trouble with Karamanli on March 28th, and Eaton, perhaps rightly, surmised that the news of his brother's troop movements had brought out all his old cowardice and fears. Undeterred, Eaton pressed on, and, somewhere east of Sidi Barrani, feeling himself well on the way to his objective, sat down in his tent and wrote out a proclamation to the people of Tripoli.

Headed: 'Desert of Libya', and addressed to: 'The inhabitants of the kingdom of Tripoli', it was a curious mixture of admonitions, threats, biblical exhortations and promises. Yusef Bashaw was 'a bloodthirsty scoundrel', who, 'led by Jews and others', was encouraged 'to commit outrages against foreign nations'. It was, the document announced, the 'just retribution of the Lord' that had brought war and famine on the people of Tripoli for supporting Yusef. 'Woe', it went on, 'to all those who would strive to prevent the punishment which God has meted out to him. Be assured that the God of the Americans and of the Mahometans is the same. Be loyal to the Grand Signior. Be loyal to the rightful prince, Hamet Bashaw of Tripoli. . . .'

By what means, and through whom, this extraordinary document was to reach the almost completely illiterate population of Tripoli, the Eaton papers do not disclose. It must have been sent off in English, for there is no evidence that any of Eaton's companions could speak, let alone write, intelligible Arabic. It was, in fact, probably read by no one, and only remains to make the historian muse on the vast gulf which stretched between this brave New England soldier's beliefs, and the reality surrounding him.

On March 30th the march was about to be resumed when a dispute broke out between the Arabs themselves. Eaton left them, and pushed on with his Christians, but was, at length, obliged to retrace his steps a few miles, as, without guides, he had missed the wells. The next day, the sheikhs, Tayyib and Mohamed, in another squabble, took their camels back several miles, and had to be pursued by the Karamanli horsemen and brought back. There was another exhausting reconciliation in Eaton's tent.

'I exhorted them . . . to union and perseverance, to which they gave pledges of faith and honor—and orders were accordingly given to resume the line of march, at reveille beating tomorrow.'

On April 5th the army—if it could be so called—now swollen, with its Beduin followers and their families, to about 700 persons, arrived at the bay of Sollum, and saw, looming above them to the west, the steep cliffs of the escarpment, leading through the pass of Halfaya to the Jebel Akhdar foothills beyond. They were now very short of water, and the horses in particular were suffering. By April 7th they had completed the weary toil up the steep road of the pass, and pressed along the top of the escarpment for about eighteen miles, where they camped, with excellent fodder for the animals, but again no water.

The next day, however, they reached some wells, and were able to water their exhausted animals.[1] The Arabs naturally wanted to rest here, but Eaton, who was rapidly running short of both time and rations, was determined to press on.

While the animals were watering, he went ahead to reconnoitre the route. It was an unwise move, as, on his return, he found that Karamanli, against his orders, had pitched camp, and was determined to take a day's rest.

Eaton protested vigorously. He had only six days' rations of rice left, and no other food of any sort. He returned to his Christian

[1] From Pacho's map I take these wells to be Biar Zemleh.

contingent, who began to make preparations to move. Meanwhile, anger and frustration began to show among the Arab followers.

'The day passed confusedly among them' wrote Eaton, who was not unduly surprised when once more they turned back for home.

At 3 p.m., the Bashaw, compelled by his Arab host, struck his tent, ordered his baggage packed, mounted and took up a march for Fayoum. I waited without emotion the result of this movement. Discovering however, an intention in the Arabs to seize our provisions, I beat to arms. My Christians formed a line in front of the Magazine tent. Each party held an opposite position, the space of an hour.

Faced by the small but menacing line of Marines and Christian gunners, Karamanli wavered, then temporised, called his horsemen to order, and, dismounting, pitched his tent.

It was a sensible attempt at reconciliation. But then, Eaton did something that, in the circumstances, was extremely foolish.

Supposing the tumult tranquillised, I ordered the troops to pass to manual exercise, according to our daily practice. In an instant, the Arabs took alarm, remounted, and exclaimed, 'The Christians are preparing to fire on us!' The Bashaw mounted and put himself at their head, apparently impressed with the same apprehension. A body of about two hundred advanced in full charge upon our people, who stood their ground motionless.

Behind Eaton's clumsy prose style, the picture leaps to the eye; the galloping Arab horsemen; the small file of American Marines, with firelocks at the ready—as steady as any square of British infantry—the line of Christian gunners, with here and there a wavering as a man left the ranks and fled. As usual, the very steadiness of the troops had its effect on the advancing throng.

The enemy withdrew at a small distance, singled out the officers, and with deliberate aim, cried—*fire!* Some of the Bashaw's officers exclaimed: 'For God's sake do not fire! The Christians are our friends.' Mr. O'Bannon, Mr. Peck, and young Farquhar stood firmly by me. Selim Agha, Captain of Canoneers, his lieutenants and the two Greek officers remained stedfast at their posts. The others were agitated, and in fact abandoned us.

It was touch and go. Eaton, a veteran of the Indian wars, and who never lacked for courage, now stepped forward from the ranks and addressed the Bashaw, who was in a state of great, excitement.

At once, a column of muskets were aimed at my breast. The Bashaw was distracted. A universal clamor drowned my voice. I waved my hand as a signal for attention. At this critical moment, some of the Bashaw's officers and sundry Arab chiefs rode between us with drawn sabres and repelled the mutineers. I reproached the Bashaw for his rashness or rather weakness. His Casnadar[1] asked him if he was in his senses. The Bashaw struck him with his naked sabre. The fracas had nearly resumed its rage, when I took the Bashaw by the arm; led him from the crowd and asked him if he knew his own interests and his friends.

Once again this weak man wavered, and his anger and perhaps shame at his behaviour diminished.

He called me his friend and protector, said he was too soon heated, and followed me to my tent, giving orders at the same time to his Arabs to disperse. After a moment's breath, he said, if I would give orders to issue rice, it would quiet everything. This I would do on no other condition than his promise to march tomorrow morning at reveille beating. He promised and provisions were issued.

With comparative tranquillity once more restored, Eaton sat down in his tent to transcribe the events of the last hour in his diary. It was the first time his small force of Christians had been in imminent danger of attack, and he could assess their value as troops in the arduous days ahead. He was generous in his report: 'The firm and decided conduct of Mr. O'Bannon, as on all other occasions, did much to deter the violence of the savages, as well as support our own dignity of character. After the affair was over,

[1] The Bashaw's Khasnadar, the Treasurer, and senior official of his suite.

the Bashaw embraced him with an enthusiasm of respect, called him *the Brave American.*'

Mr. Farquhar, too, the Englishman, came in for praise: 'Mr Farquhar conducted with manly firmness. One of the Arabs, during the agitation, snapped a pistol at his breast. Happily, it missed fire.'

But, of his own A.D.C., and his doctor, he had little praise: 'The Chevalier Davico, my Aide de Camp, acted a part which I would rather attribute to an amiable disposition than to weakness of nerve. My Doctor behaved like a coward, and a base one.'

Then, perhaps, laying down his pen for a moment to listen to the sounds of the camp outside—the voices of his Marines around their camp fire, the shouting, and the snarling of weary camels from the Arab camp fires in the distance; beyond it all, the surrounding silence of the desert, through which he had yet many days to lead this strange host of followers, short of food and water, and not even sure of the route. 'We find', wrote this indomitable man, 'it is impossible to inspire these wild bigots with confidence in us. . . . We have a difficult undertaking.'

Karamanli kept his word to Eaton, and the next morning the long straggling column moved forward again, covering about eleven miles, before it reached a water cistern, at which, in spite of the bodies of two men lying in it, the party were glad to water.

From here, the march continued with increasing slowness, dragging itself across a landscape of low hills, broken with *wadis* giving distant views of the sea. By April 10th, they were down to half rations of rice and water, and all eyes were straining forward for a sight of the courier from Bomba.

At 3 o'clock that afternoon the caravan halted while a council was held. No news had come, and once again the half-hearted Semites were talking of turning back. Once again, Eaton had to harangue the ring of sullen faces and try to whip some further resolution into them. Just as it seemed as if he was about to fail, the courier they had sent ahead some days earlier was sighted hurrying back. He brought news that American vessels had been sighted off both Bomba and Derna. 'In an instant, the face of everything changed from pensive gloom to inthusiastic gladness. Nothing more was heard of mutiny. The Arabs resumed confidence, and the Bashaw promised to force the residue of our march to Bomba. . . .'

Acutely short of food, Eaton's army could only make small daily marches. Eaton found that his starving Marines were cutting the buttons off their uniforms and selling them to the Beduin women in exchange for a few dates. The next three days were a long tale of growing hunger. A camel was killed and eaten, and some of the Arabs were subsisting on roots. Eaton and his men were driven to eat fennel and sorrel plants.

On the afternnon of April 15th, the tired, hungry little army, struggling slowly across the now almost endless ravines of the coastal cliffs, reached a small inlet of the sea. One of the Arabs who pretended to be a guide told Eaton that this was Bomba, and he wearily climbed down the slopes to the beach and turned his glass on to the horizon. To his dismay, he saw nothing in sight. There was not a sail to be seen, nor did the beach show any signs that anyone had landed there. 'Not a foot-trace of a human being, nor a drop of water,' he noted gloomily in his diary, supposing that the ships had sailed in, and lain off-shore, whence, seeing no one, they had sailed away.

As was to be expected, the easy suspicions of the Arabs were once again aroused. 'They abused us as impostors and infidels, and said that we had drawn them into that situation with treacherous views.'

He tried to calm them, advising that the best thing to do, in fact, the only thing, was to push on to Derna. It was probably hunger and thirst which prevented them from being more violent, and they retired to their own camp, resolved to leave him the next morning.

Night, Eaton recorded, fell on a scene of disorder. For safety, Eaton took his Christian party up a steep cliff, where they made camp, lighting large fires, which they kept burning all night.

The following morning, Eaton emerged from his tent to find the Arabs packing up to depart and take their several ways. He called his officers to discuss what to do.

It was at this moment that the Bashaw's khasnadar, an intelligent man, clambered to the top of the steep cliffs to have a last look at the horizon. Suddenly, the parties below saw him waving frantically, and heard him crying, 'A sail, a sail!' The eyes of all were strained out to sea, and slowly a vessel came into sight.

As it drew inshore, Eaton, with relief, recognised it as the brig *Argus*, which had seen the signal fires. 'Language', wrote Eaton, 'is too poor to paint the joy and exaltation which this messenger of life excited in every breast.'

From signals from the *Argus*, it was discovered that their Arab guide had misled them, and that Bomba, in fact, still lay to the west, around an intervening headland. But there was little difficulty now in getting the whole camp to up-sticks and move; and later in the same day, they reached the small beach of Bomba, where *Argus* could come inshore and unload the much needed supplies. Two days later, the American sloop, *Hornet*, arrived, with more provisions, arms and money, and, for three further days, supplies were ferried ashore for Eaton's army, whilst preparations were put in hand for the final march on Derna.

On April 23rd the motley army resumed its historic march towards Derna. The landscape had now dramatically changed, and the concourse of men and animals moved across the cultivated uplands of Jebel Akhdar, which bordered the steep cliffs dropping down to a blue sea below. Here the camp followers of the army found the small farms and houses on the road irresistible objects for loot; but Ahmed Karamanli, who perhaps felt he was now coming into his own, sent a warning to the tribes that looters would have their right hands severed, if caught.

They camped that night at the edge of a steep ravine near the cape of *Ras et Tin*; and next day, a distance of fifteen miles was covered through the lovely fertile landscape of waving corn of the region known as Barce. As they camped that night, even the severely practical Eaton was obliged to remark on the beauty of their surroundings, so different from the desert they had left behind them.

But as hourly the prospect awaiting them at Derna approached, Karamanli's indecision and timidity grew. Derna was now only about five hours march away, and, already couriers were coming out, with increasing news of the Governor of Derna's knowledge of their approach and preparations for resistance. More ominous, they carried reports that Yusef Karamanli's troops from Tripoli were only a short distance away, and might reach Derna before them. There was as yet no sign of any of the population appearing to welcome their 'rightful Prince'.

That night, Eaton broke in on the councils of Karamanli and his supporters, and spoke to them urgently, trying to encourage a little stability of purpose in them. But he had at length to retire to his tent and report gloomily in his diary: 'The night passed in consultations among them, at which I was not admitted.'

The next morning, the inevitable happened. 'The Arabs mutinized.' Sheikhs Tayyib and Mohamed began leading their beasts back down the track to Egypt, and the Beduin contingent refused to strike their tents. Eaton again harangued them. 'After much persuasion, some reproach, and a promise of two thousand dollars to be shared among the chiefs,' they were prevailed on to advance. Slowly they straggled along the last ravines and headlands separating them from the steep declivity leading to Derna, passing through the ancient Greek city ruins of Cyrene, until they looked down at the scene far below: the white buildings, the green verdure of fig and palm, the curving bay of rocks enclosing a small, secure harbour—the dazzling blend of white, and green, and blue—the town of Derna.

Here, above Derna, the little army camped, to await the arrival of the partisans of Ahmed Karamanli. When, eventually, in small groups, they arrived, they were few in number, and the information they brought was not reassuring. They estimated that though about two-thirds of the population of Derna might be favourable to Ahmed Karamanli, both the Governor of the town and at least one-third of the most influential of the population remained loyal to Yusef Karamanli; and these had swiftly reacted to the news of Eaton's approach.

The Governor, with about 800 troops, had occupied all the fortifications and seized all the arms in the town, and had dug his troops well in to hold the town until the arrival of Yusef Karamanli's troops, now reported to be only a few miles away. More disturbing still, a heavy gale which had blown up had clearly blown the American ships off course. There was no sign of them on the horizon.

Eaton and his officers reconnoitred the towns's defences, and then called a council of war. The defences, according to Eaton:

consisted of a water-battery of eight 9 pounder guns. Towards the north east, some temporary breastworks and walls of old buildings; towards the south-east, and along the front of the bay, a department of the city of about one-third of the whole number of inhabitants, who were in the interest of Joseph Bashaw, had provided their terraces and walls of their houses with loopholes.

In addition, the Governor had a 10-inch howitzer mounted on the roof of his palace. He was, in fact in possession of all the gun batteries and the city's breastworks. 'We shall find it difficult to dislodge him,' wrote Eaton in his diary. But the rules of 18th-century warfare still obtained. Eaton sat down and wrote to the Governor:

April 26 1805. Environs of Derna.
Sir, I want no territory. With me is advancing the legitimate Sovereign of your country. Give us a passage through your city, and for the supplies of which we have need, you shall have fair compensation.... If you are a man of liberal mind, you will not balance on the propositions I offer. Hamet Bashaw pledges himself to me that you shall be established in your government. I shall see you tomorrow in a way of your choice. Eaton.

This was despatched by a courier into the town. A reply came almost by return. The Governor was not, alas, a man of liberal mind. He merely wrote: 'My head, or yours. Mustafa.'

While these messages were being exchanged, Eaton's men had climbed to the top of the cliffs overlooking the bay and lit smoke signals. By two o'clock, to everyone's relief, the brig, *Nautilus* was sighted, and four hours later Eaton was shaking the hands of Captain Dent, her commander. Eaton told Dent that if the other ships appeared in time he intended to attack the town the following day. Dent agreed to this plan, and immediately began disembarking from *Nautilus* supplies of shot and powder.

By dawn the following morning both *Argus* and *Hornet* had appeared, and, as soon as they were at anchor, Eaton called a meeting of the Captains to discuss immediate plans for action. He stressed to the sailors that Yusef Bashaw's troops were only a few hours away, and it was necessary that the town should be in Ahmed Karamanli's hands before their appearance.

A joint attack on the town from sea and land was necessary, and plans for this were put in hand immediately. *Argus* first landed two field guns, which Eaton had requested; she then drew off into the bay of Derna, and took up a position whence her 24-pounder guns could be brought to bear on the fortified buildings round the fort called Bu Mansour. Meanwhile, *Nautilus* and *Hornet* drew close inshore, to a point where they could sweep the Governor's batteries on the Matariz promontory.

At 12 a.m. *Argus*'s 24-pounders opened fire on the 8 gun site of the Governor's water battery, and, after an hour of heavy pounding by the superior American guns, the water battery was silenced and the gunners were seen to evacuate it and take refuge in the town and surrounding gardens. At the same time the brigs *Nautilus* and *Hornet* poured a galling fire of ball and grape shot at the parties of Derna troops skirmishing for the protection of the town wall and buildings.

On land, the fighting during that day between Eaton's mixed and widely scattered troops, and the loyal defenders of Derna, was confused, spasmodic, and vigorous. It was an affair of whirling mêlées of horsemen; of Beduins snapping off their matchlocks from behind palm trees; of disciplined Marines loading and firing with the precision of trained troops. It was, indeed, the steadiness of the Christian elements of Eaton's army coupled with the fire of the naval vessels that kept the Governor's forces from making any serious headway in a situation where they had many advantages.

Eaton, as a precaution against the sudden appearance of the troops from Tripoli, who were now supposedly close at hand, sent Ahmed Karamanli and his mounted troops to a position to the south-west of the town. Here they were split, and while one half took up a position covering the entrance to the foothills, the other was sent to take up a line from whence they could make a flank attack.

Simultaneously with this move, Eaton detached Lieutenant O'Bannon, with his detachment of six Marines, the Christian gunners and thirty-six Greek mercenaries together with some Arab irregulars, to make a new attack on the town walls from the south east.

This attack was held up by a hot fire directed from the loop-holed houses along the walls, and the attackers were forced to take cover. Here, the defenders poured such a sustained fire at them that the mercenaries and the Arab irregulars began to show signs of confusion. At this moment, Eaton, with a small reserve of troops that he had kept in hand, arrived and took command.

The fire of the enemy's Musketry became too warm and continually augmenting. Our troops were thrown into confusion and, undisciplined as they were, it was impossible to reduce them to order. I perceived a charge—our *dernier* and only resort. We rushed forward against a host of Savages, more than ten to our one. They fled from their Coverts, irregularly, firing in retreat from every palm tree and partition wall in their way. At this moment I received a Ball through my left wrist, which deprived me of the use of the hand, and of course of my Rifle. Mr. O'Bannon, accompanied by Mr. Mann of Annapolis, urged forward with his Marines, Greeks, and such of the cannoniers as were not necessary to the management of the field piece, passed through a shower of Musketry from the Walls of houses, took possession of the Battery, planted the American flag upon its ramparts, and turned its guns upon the Enemy, who, being now driven from their Out Post fired only from their houses, from which they were soon dislodged by the whole fire of the Vessels . . . a little after 4 o'clock, we had complete possession of the Town.

This report, written hastily that evening, while his troops laboured to repair the town walls to repel the attack of Yusef Karamanli's troops due to arrive at any hour, counted up his casualties. One of his gallant and precious Marines was killed, and two were wounded; the rest of the wounded came to eleven persons, including himself. There must have been other deaths, but, since he only gave a count of Christians, they were ignored.

He found time to praise the courage of Lieutenant O'Bannon, Mr. Mann, and that shadowy figure, 'the young Englishman, Mr. Farquhar'. Of the Greek mercenaries he wrote, 'they well supported their ancient character'. Nor did he fail to praise the dispositions of the naval forces, who could not have managed their fire, 'with more skill and advantage . . .'

It was now urgently necessary to put the town in a proper posture of defence, the more so as the first troops of Yusef Karamanli's army were expected at any moment. While Eaton rapidly placed his guns at strategic points covering the entrance to the town, he made persistent attempts to arrest the Governor, Mustafa, who had prudently taken refuge in the *harim* of the household of Sheikh of Misurata, from whence he was enabled to send messages and signals to the advancing troops from Tripoli.

The sanctuary laws of the Moslem *harim* were such that neither Ahmed Karamanli, nor any of the Arab troops under him, would obey Eaton's request that the Governor should be removed by force. Karamanli's reply to Eaton's request that he should demand the hand-over of the Governor was, reported Eaton, that, 'should he suffer himself to transgress that sacred principle, the vengeance of God and the odium of all mankind would justly fix on him and his posterity'.

By May 8th, the army from Tripoli, advancing by a circuitous route, had established themselves on that site, overlooking the town, that Eaton's own forces had held before their attack. The Governor's continued presence in the town, protected by Moslem law, now became a real security problem. The fickle townspeople, who had accepted the arrival of Ahmed Karamanli as a *fait accompli*, now began to fear that, if they assisted Eaton's forces, they would be massacred by the new invaders. The removal of the Governor was now very urgent, since he could easily become the centre of fresh resistance.

Eaton realised the danger, and, ignoring Karamanli's requests that he would leave the Governor alone, assembled about fifty of his Christian mercenaries and marched them, with fixed bayonets into a Quarter nearest the Sheikh's *harim* in an attempt at intimidation. The townspeople immediately began to assemble to resist any attempt by the Christians to penetrate the *harim.*

Once again, Karamanli urgently beseeched Eaton not to act too precipitately, and doubtless his experienced Christian officers urged the danger of such a move. Eaton thereupon marched the armed men back again.

But the move, though dangerous, succeeded in its purpose. The Governor, feeling his position was unsafe, decided to leave. During the same night, aided by the Sheikh of Misurata, and with a party of fifteen of his adherents, he stole out of the town and escaped to the Tripoli lines. Eaton was astonished to find that this discharge of a sacred trust by the Sheikh of Misurata, by no means impeded him from fighting against the Governor the following day and publicly asserting his loyalty to Ahmed Karamanli.

That night, the watch-fires of the Tripoli troops could be seen closely investing the routes into the town; and at dawn the next day, May 13th, they attacked, their primary objective being, probably on the advice of the Governor, the capture of Ahmed Karamanli who was commanding his troops from the Castle.

At first they met with success. Their advancing horsemen broke through a detachment of Karamanli's cavalry screen covering the road, and, in spite of fire from the American ships, advanced rapidly into the courtyard of the Castle. Just as it seemed as if the attacking horsemen would overwhelm the Castle's inner defences, the guns from the ships found the range and round shot began to fall among them. At the same time, Eaton's artillery piece opened fire from close by, killing several of them. They recoiled and were finally driven off by a charge of Karamanli's reformed cavalry. The effect of this set-back on the Tripoli troops soon began to show itself, as a trickle of deserters to Ahmed Karamanli began to come in.

There was stalemate for some days. Then, on May 29th, a detachment of some sixty Tripoli *janissaries*, led by an officer, made a sudden raid upon some of Karamanli's adherents camped on the hillside behind the town. This was warfare more to their stomachs than attacking fortified positions.

Capturing some livestock, they were hurrying back to their lines when they were overtaken by a detachment of Karamanli's cavalry; several of them were killed and the livestock was recovered.

This skirmish had been seen by Eaton. Quickly assembling his American officers and Marines and accompanied by Mr. Farquhar and about twenty-five of his Greek mercenaries he led them across the ravine and rapidly up the heights where they could cut off the returning *janissaries*.

Another brisk skirmish ensued, which ended in a bayonet charge from the Americans, which killed the *janissary* officer and several of his men, while two others were made prisoner.

The reaction to this further defeat in open warfare led to more defections from the Tripoli troops, who, on arrival in Eaton's camp, complained that the Americans had fought unfairly by attacking them with the bayonet before they had time to reload—contrary to their principles of warfare. There were further desertions to Ahmed Karamanli and the townspeople of Derna took further heart.

But, in spite of these successes, Eaton was aware that his problems were increasing. He now knew the exact value of his Arab allies, and the worth of the support given so reluctantly to Ahmed Karamanli by the people of Derna. His dream of a nation rising to support the legitimate heir to the throne of Tripoli had vanished. There were now only the realities of the situation for him to face.

These were grim enough. Without the assistance of the off-shore ships, in guns and supplies, the situation was hopeless. On that unpredictable coast, a sudden violent storm might drive the ships out to sea, and without their support he doubted if his few Christians could long hold out against a concerted attack from the Tripoli troops, aided by treachery in the town.

While in a state of some indecision as to his next move, he received a letter from Commodore Barron, his commanding officer, which contained some news and a distinct order which must be obeyed.

It was from Malta, and dated May 19th. In it, Barron told Eaton that direct negotiations had been re-opened between America and Yusef Bashaw for the conclusion of a peace treaty and the release of the American prisoners. Further direct assistance to Ahmed Karamanli was therefore unnecessary. Some specious reasoning was added to this information. America, by bringing Ahmed Karamanli to Derna, had now 'fulfilled every pledge' to him. If he could not now carry out the conquest of Tripoli by himself, aided by discreet naval support from the sea, 'he must be held as unworthy of further Support'.

In brief, Ahmed Karamanli whose conquest of Derna had been used as a lever to extract better peace terms from Yusef Bashaw, must now be deserted, and left, with his troops, to their own devices. In earnest of this, the supply ships shuttling between Syracuse and Derna had been instructed to bring no more rations for the Arab troops, but only sufficient for the Christians, who would now be evacuated by sea.

Eaton was bitter about the negotiations which had gone on while he was struggling to bring the 'legitimate heir' across the deserts to Derna; and he protested vigorously about the cutting down of the rations to his army. Was it fair, he complained, to distribute rations on the basis of religion, or to supply one part of any army and not the other?

But his protests were in vain, and, while he awaited the expected orders for the evacuation, his thoughts were mutinous at what he called the treachery of the American government.

Orders to prepare for evacuation were received on June 11th; and on this same day, the commander of the Tripoli forces, aware that through desertion and failure his strength was failing and that he must take Derna immediately or leave the territory, launched a final desperate attack. Already, the treasurer of the Tripoli troops had deserted to Egypt with the soldiers' pay, and the commander himself had no other alternative than to flee should this final attack fail. To return to Tripoli would be death.

In this final attack, the Tripoli *janissaries* approached the town by means of a narrow ravine, which sheltered them from the gunfire of the ships. Here they drove in Karamanli's screen of horsemen, and rapidly approached the town walls, where they were halted by heavy fire. For four hours the engagement, an affair of charge and counter-charge, punctuated by shots from the guns of *Argus*, continued. But the attacking troops could not keep up their impetus; and they were forced to retreat. It was their last attack, and now they began to melt away, fleeing both east and west into the hinterland.

It was ironic that, at this moment of final victory, Eaton had to set in hand the evacuation of his Christians aboard the frigate *Constellation*, which had arrived off Derna just as the firing died down.

The Captain of the *Constellation* now came ashore with the news both of the signature of the peace treaty between Tripoli and America and of the evacuation. Fortunately the treaty contained conventions, one of which guaranteed that Yusef Bashaw would release the family of Ahmed, now prisoners in Tripoli, and allow them to join him; and another which guaranteed a pardon to all those who had taken up arms against him. Eaton must have doubted if the second guarantee would have much value.

Eaton had now, in great secrecy, to inform Karamanli of the facts and persuade him to accept evacuation for himself, and the desertion of his own followers.

Ahmed Karamanli received the news with great dignity. Perhaps, weak and undecided in character as he was, he had, for some time, secretly hoped for such an outcome to the adventure.

He agreed that for his own safety he must leave the kingdom, but he warned Eaton that the utmost secrecy must be kept, or his adherents would certainly turn on them and prevent their departure.

Eaton carried out the evacuation with great skill. He instructed his Christians to carry out all their normal duties and even go through the preparations to repel another attack from the enemy.

I accordingly sent ammunition and extra rations to be distributed among our moorish and arab troops, and despatched spies to ascertain the enemy's position. With the same apparent view, I inspected the garrison; ordered them to be divested of all heavy baggage, and to be held at their posts ready to advance at the word. At eight in the evening I placed patroles of marines to stop intercourse between our post and the town . . .

The ruse was successful. While the marines stood at their posts in full view of the town, the *Constellation*'s boats came ashore and silently embarked the Christian gunners and the rest of the Christian party. With them safely aboard:

I sent a message to the Bashaw requesting an interview. Understanding the purport of this message, he immediately repaired to the fort with his retinue; dismounted, and embarked in the boats. The marines followed with the American officers. When all were securely off, I stepped into a small boat which I had retained for the purpose; and had just time to save my distance, when the shore, our camp, and the battery, were crowded with the distracted soldiery and populace.

It was a harrowing scene—the air filled with shrieks, execrations and shots, while voices calling imploringly on Karamanli and Eaton could be heard slowly fading into the distance. The last sight of Karamanli's adherents was of a mass of men carrying off the tents and horses left behind and pillaging the baggage before they fled into the night.

As *Constellation*, with her Arab prince and his mamelukes, her mixed group of Greek, French and English mercenaries, her little group of heroic American marines, drew away from the fast fading shore, Eaton, down in his cabin, drew out his diary.

'In a few minutes, more,' [this indomitable soldier wrote] 'we shall loose sight of this devoted city, which had experienced as strange a reverse in so short a time as ever was recorded in the disasters of war; thrown from proud success into an abyss of hopeless wretchedness. Six hours ago, the enemy were seeking safety from them by flight—this moment we drop them from ours into the hands of this enemy for no other crime, but too much confidence in us. . . .'

It was at once a condemnation, and an epitaph.

The rest of the tale of Ahmed Karamanli is soon told. He was taken by the Americans to Syracuse, where he lived in some penury on an allowance from the U.S. government. In 1807, Yusef Bashaw released his wife and family to join the exile. In 1809, he was once more appointed Bey of Derna but two years later, again in danger of his life, fled to Egypt, where, in 1811, he died.

Feeble, vacillating, cowardly, Ahmed Karamanli has only one claim on history. He inspired a feat of American arms which became a legend in a young, fast growing nation.

Peace with America

From Tripoli, the progress of Eaton's army had been followed with an anxiety which the Bashaw strove to conceal. He had no faith in his elder brother's capacity to force the issue and replace him on the throne, but equally he had no faith in his own followers, whose fatal predilection for collapsing into anarchy he well knew.

Meanwhile he was taking counter-measures. By March he had collected sufficient troops to send against Derna, and Jonathan Cowdery saw them assembled at the tomb of the Great Marabout, east of Tripoli to 'Receive absolution and assurances of victory'. They were led by Hassan Bey, whose family with those of several other of the Bashaw's senior officers, were kept under guard in a house in Tripoli as hostages for the fidelity of their husbands.

The fall of Derna had been reported to the Bashaw by a fast dromedary on May 22nd, and it was probably this, combined with the reappearance of more powerful American frigates off the coast of Tripoli, that turned his mind at last to the question of peace negotiations. It had already been seen how American officials, such as Tobias Lear and Bainbridge, regarded Eaton's expedition. They were convinced that the Bashaw would not easily yield to force, and that to try to supplant him by his despised elder brother would only strengthen him in his obstinacy and determination. Anyone with a knowledge of the Arab mentality would know that in this they were right and that any scheme by Christians of whatever nation, to attempt to overthrow a Moslem ruler and supplant him, would be doomed to failure. But while the loss of Derna in no way threatened his throne, it was a grave blow to his prestige and, combined with the constant pressure of the American blockade off his shores, led him to consider a return to diplomacy as probably his best way out of the situation.

The Bashaw opened his approach for peace negotiations in his usual tortuous way. During an audience with the Spanish ambassador on December 17th 1804, in which Spanish affairs were discussed, he made a passing reference to the fact that he might be willing to discuss peace proposals with the Americans, provided this could be done on honourable terms. The Spanish ambassador sent this information to Tobias Lear, who had temporarily left his consular post at Algiers and was hopefully cruising in the vicinity of Tripoli, perhaps waiting for just such a move on the Bashaw's part.

Lear wisely made no reply to this *tentative*. He calculated that a time nearer the Spring cruising season in the Mediterranean, when American bomb vessels could appear off the coast of Tripoli, and the blockade could be tightened, would be more suitable to exert pressure on the Bashaw. He waited until March, when a small neutral ship, freighted with clothing and supplies for the American prisoners, was despatched to Tripoli. By the Captain of this ship, Lear sent a reply to the Spanish consul, in which he stated that the

Spring season for operations by the American squadron was now approaching, and it was determined to act against Tripoli with vigour. To this letter he added a short postscript saying that, before the cruising season began, he would be prepared 'to receive and consider any propositions which might come from the Bashaw . . . provided such propositions were compatible with the dignity and rising Character of our Nation, and tending to an honorable and permanent peace'.

The Bashaw accepted this statement as a further encouragement to treat, though still not directly, with the Americans. He now offered, through the mediation of the Spanish consul, to relinquish all demands for a down payment for a peace treaty, and to accept the sum of 130,000 dollars for the ransom of the American prisoners; his own prisoners in American hands to be repatriated free.

Lear refused this, and in return offered to repatriate the Tripoli prisoners in exchange for the American captives, with the sum of 60,000 dollars as an *ex gratia* payment. Negotiations were further suspended for a while as the frigate *Constitution* was driven offshore by gales.

On May 31st the Bashaw, presumably now in possession of the details of the *débacle* of his troops at Derna, suddenly agreed to Lear's terms. On June 1st the captive Captain Bainbridge, under the guarantee of the Danish consul M. Nissen, and accompanied by the Bashaw's foreign minister, went aboard *Constitution* for a few hours, and in an interview with Lear explained that the Bashaw was now more interested in peace and a permanent settlement than in money.

The following day Nissen boarded *Constitution* once more, carrying a written commission from the Bashaw to negotiate. The Bashaw accepted the Articles drafted by Lear, but added that there must be a supplementary agreement to withdraw American forces from Derna, and oblige his brother Ahmed to leave his dominions. This Lear agreed to saying 'it would be a natural consequence of peace', but he stipulated that if Ahmed Karamanli were removed, his wife and children, who had for long been hostages in Tripoli, should be allowed to return to him. This the Bashaw agreed to though he asked for time to carry it out.[1]

At 4 p.m. on June 3rd, Nissen came aboard *Constitution* again with the agreed copy of the Articles of Peace, bearing the Bashaw's seal. *Constitution* now drew inshore and Lear disembarked.

When we were close to the Town, we fired a gun and hauled down the white flag. A salute of 21 guns was fired from the batteries and answered by *Constitution*. I went into the harbour in *Constitution*'s barge, with the flag of the United States displayed, and was received at the landing place by the American officer who had been in captivity, with a sensibility more easily to be conceived than described. An immense concourse of people crowded the shore and filled the streets, all signifying their pleasure on the conclusion of peace.

The next day Tobias Lear had his first audience with the Bashaw:

He paid me many compliments and expressed himself on the peace with much manliness. He is a man of very good presence, manly and dignified, and has not in his appearance so much of the *Tyrant* as he has been represented to be.

The flag of the United States was now raised at the American consulate, the doors of the Castle *bagnios* were opened, while the joyful American officers emerged. But Cowdery the surgeon went straight to see the worn-out, emaciated American seamen, whom he had not been allowed to care for during their many months of hard labour, beating and semi-starvation. When he read the news to these weary ragged men, 'many of them shed tears'.

It was over at last. After nineteen months and three days, 308 American officers and men were freed. Cowdery went to take

[1] There was a secret protocol attached to this document, which was not forwarded to Washington by Lear. In this it was agreed that the Bashaw should be allowed a period of four years before releasing Ahmed Karamanli's family. The reasons for this are not known, but when the news of the protocol at length reached Washington, Lear received a severe reprimand from the Secretary of State for agreeing to such a callous request.

leave of the Bashaw and that curiously emotional tyrant was much affected. He had grown fond of the young American whose medical skill had saved the life of one of the royal Princes.

By June 6th, *Constitution*, with the crew of *Philadelphia* aboard, had left Tripoli for Malta. Two Americans remained behind: Tobias Lear to clear up outstanding business with the Bashaw, and a member of *Philadelphia*'s crew who had agreed to remain temporarily as American agent in the Regency.

The few kindnesses the officers and men of *Philadelphia* had received during captivity from friends in Tripoli were not forgotten. To M. Nissen, the courageous Danish consul who had supported them through all their troubles with food, clothing and moral encouragement, the officers subscribed money for an inscribed silver urn 'as a pledge of our grateful sense of your humane and friendly attention to us, while captives in Tripoli. . . .'

A more evocative gesture was made by the seamen of *Philadelphia*'s crew. Among the slave overseers, who had daily driven them to hard labour with whips and abuse, was one, himself a Neopolitan slave, who had secretly endeavoured to ease their lot and soften the severity of their Moslem overseers. In gratitude to him, the American ratings and Marines subscribed the sum of 300 dollars from their pay to purchase his release from slavery and his return to his native land.

More trouble with the consuls

Peace with America now enabled the Bashaw to turn his attention fully to his policy towards Britain and France, the two great powers on whose benevolence he relied for his freedom to continue his profitable piracy against the smaller maritime powers in the Mediterranean. Nelson's resounding victory over the French fleet at Trafalgar, which occurred only three months after peace was signed between Tripoli and America, brought an immediate change in the thinking of the Bashaw and his *taiffa* of sea captains. Britain was now installed at Malta, threatening his coastline and his outlets to the Mediterranean, and the French fleet, recently so active, had been virtually driven from the seas. With that curious twisted logic which characterised his tortuous nature, he now remembered the encouragement he had received from the French to continue his war with America, and he blamed them for the rather humiliating end to that adventure.

The change in the attitude towards France was soon apparent and the French Consul, Beaussier gloomily summed up the situation: '*Tout le pays, d'ailleurs, en général est dévoué aux Anglais, et avides de nouvelles qui nous sont contraires.*'

It was but another swing in the eternal pendulum of Franco-British influences in North Africa, and an opportunity for Britain to profit from it.

Alas, Britain was now unfortunately represented by a consular incumbent who, though truly worthy and conscientious in himself, was utterly incapable of adapting himself to the strains and unpredictabilities of oriental temperament and political intrigue.

William Wass Langford had first appeared as a secretary to Consul Lucas in 1793. He was painstaking in consular affairs and, when Lucas died was instructed to take over the consulate *ad interim*. This was despite efforts on the part of Lucas's adopted son, Bryan McDonough, to have the post for himself.

Langford's instructions from London were fairly precise. The primary object of his Mission was to ensure that regular supplies of food and livestock reached the British garrisons in the Mediterranean. His reports show that during his tenure of office this was carried out punctiliously, and large quantities of bullocks and sheep for food, and mules and horses for transport, were shipped regularly to Malta for redistribution.

But his instruction also contained the proviso that he must not let himself get involved in palace affairs. What was not realised in London was that, to avoid such involvement in the close, constricted atmosphere of Tripoli was impossible, especially so since Bryan McDonough, who had the Bashaw's ear, was constantly intriguing to get Langford displaced.

Ample opportunities for trouble soon presented themselves

without any special effort on McDonough's part. With the occupation of Malta by Britain, Langford now became responsible for the protection of the large Maltese community in Tripoli and it seems clear that he took this responsibility very seriously.

A consular representative, in the semi-diplomatic position of Langford, is in a particular difficulty in an autocratic Moslem country. If he pursues the interests of his Christian nationals as his prior concern, he is certain at some point to come up against the prejudices, customs, or religious intolerance of the Ruler and the population of the country to which he is accredited. At what point should he put diplomatic necessity before consular responsibility; at what moment should he drop the interests of his Christian client for the continued good relations with the Ruler or his Ministers, whatever the merits of the case?

To steer a middle course with success requires some diplomatic skill. It seems as if this higher diplomatic duty was never clear to Langford. He could not see that, in spite of instructions to the contrary, his prior task was to keep the goodwill and, if possible, secure the friendship of the Bashaw, upon whose whim the supply of necessary foodstuffs to Malta in the main depended. To do this, he must of necessity from time to time disregard the rights of some Christian suppliant.

Instead of this, Langford allowed himself to get involved in a series of squabbles with the Palace which, sedulously fanned by McDonough and possibly Beaussier the French consul, soon led to trouble. In all cases this trouble arose from Langford's too zealous insistence on the rights of the Maltese community.

A really serious dispute broke out between Langford and the Palace in April 1807. On Easter Sunday of that year, the Maltese of Tripoli celebrated an annual feast during which they publicly burned an effigy of Judas Iscariot. In the fanatic atmosphere of Tripoli, this was highly dangerous, and argues the possibility that the Maltese, now under British protection, imagined that they could defy the religious prejudices of the Moslem inhabitants. It seems unlikely that Langford was not informed of this; and that he did not take steps to stop it at once seems incredible.

It was almost inevitable that the inflammable Moslem population believed what was immediately spread amongst them, that the burning effigy was not that of Judas Iscariot, but of a Moslem saint.

Trouble soon started in the streets. The Bashaw's troops were sent out to arrest the Maltese ringleaders, and some of the Maltese immediately rushed to Langford with the story that every British subject was being arrested.

Langford went to the Bashaw to protest, but was informed that the French, Spanish and Portuguese consuls, (the last named being McDonough) reported that the effigy was certainly that of a Moslem saint.

Langford did not wait to press the matter but left the audience chamber and wrote directly to London: 'I am not wholly at a loss to account for this sudden alteration in the Bashaw, and am sorry to observe that he is at present so much under the influence of bad advisers.'

A month later a new dispute broke out over some Maltese vessels in Tripoli harbour. Langford demanded an apology from the Bashaw in public Divan, which was naturally refused. He thereupon left the audience chamber and took the extreme course of striking his flag and departing for Syracuse believing as he reported in a despatch to London of June 20 1807 'it prudent to follow the steps of my Predecessor [Lucas] . . . and repair to Malta'.

He left the despatch of consular affairs in the hands of George Davis, the newly arrived American consul.

Langford had scarcely left port, when an English brig, the *Hirondelle*, arrived under the command of a Captain Skinner. McDonough hurried down to meet the Captain and, accompanied by Davis, dragged him to an audience with the Bashaw who was persuaded to make several charges against Langford, including disrespect to the Bashaw, and peculation. Skinner was now induced to send a letter of complaint against Langford to Admiral Collingwood, who had succeeded Nelson as Commander-in-Chief in the Mediterranean.

Langford was summoned by Collingwood to explain his behaviour, and had several interviews with the Admiral, during which his explanations and general demeanour so convinced the latter that he immediately wrote to the Bashaw direct.

In his Note dated July 21st 1807, he stated:

I have found nothing in the Consul's conduct that ought, in justice and truth to have given to Your Highness dissatisfaction. . . . But it has appeared to me that some Persons at Tripoli whose interest leads them to oppose the harmony which ought, and which my sovereign wishes to maintain, with the States of Barbary. . . .

Armed with a copy of this Note, Langford sent a despatch to Lord Castlereagh on July 26th in which he concludes:

I am satisfied the Bashaw heartily repents of having allowed himself to have been the dupe of a set of unworthy, designing people. I shall leave no means untried to restore a perfect good understanding between H.M.G. and the Bashaw, and I doubt not of being completely successful therein.

He was unduly optimistic.

Langford returned to Tripoli on August 9th in *H.M.S. Bittern*, and, with Davis the American consul, called on the Bashaw in audience. The audience was a disaster, as Davis in a letter to his own Secretary of State reported:

I accompanied the English Consul and the Commander of the Sloop at their audience with the Bashaw. He received them with much coolness, refused to communicate directly with the Consul, and requested him to address me and receive my answers as from himself. The audience was too mortifying to be continued for any length of time.

Four days later Langford tried again, and this time Davis could report 'A private audience with the Bashaw on British affairs, when all difficulties between his Excellency and the Consul were settled.'

Langford reported this settlement to London in a despatch which curiously seems dated as the same day as the 'mortifying' interview. Optimistically, he wrote 'I have no doubt but that the

Bashaw will remember his lesson, and that the service will be ultimately much benefited thereby.'

For a while all seemed quiet, and Langford's reports describe only the internal affairs of the Regency. Possibly as the Bashaw's temper cooled, the pro-British counsels of his Divan and *taiffa* began to prevail. At all events, Langford now begins to report a deterioration of relations between the Bashaw and the French consul. He was quick to take credit for this. In December he writes 'I flatter myself to be able to excite His Highness to a declaration of War against the French and their Dependants.'

Three weeks later, in a despatch of December 29th, he announced the offer by the Bashaw of a secret offensive and defensive alliance, and suggests the immediate sending to Tripoli of a warship, so that the treaty may be signed. He adds that the strictest secrecy must be observed as the Bashaw was surrounded 'by Domesticks in the French interest'. Turning to the wider interests which would be served by such a treaty, Langford observed:

> It will not escape your Lordship's penetration, the many Political benefits likely to result to our Country from the alliance of this Regency, either as it regards the facility of communications with Egypt, the probabilities of exciting the Regencies of Tunis and Algiers to a similar hostile declaration, or the abundant means we shall then possess of supplying Malta with cattle. . . .

It did not, however, escape his Lordship's penetration also that possibly the Bashaw was up to his old game of playing off the various consuls against each other, and no move was made by London to take advantage of the Bashaw's offer. Even when, at the suggestion of the Bashaw, Langford wrote to request the removal of the French consul and his nationals by a British frigate, as had been carried out under Nelson's orders several years earlier, London made no answer.

But Langford's days were running out. He seemed to have some defect of behaviour which put him at odds with all his colleagues. He quarrelled with the American consul: 'Circumstances have arisen to cause me to suspend all communications with this

Gentleman', while the American consul complained to the Governor General in Malta of Langford's 'disrespect'.

On December 1st 1810, there was a final and conclusive scene at an audience with the Bashaw which spelled the end of Langford as British consul.

If Langford had few qualities which distinguished him as a diplomat, he possessed some skill, rare in the officials of his day, in narrative description, and his explanatory despatch written on December 3rd 1810 to Lord Liverpool, portrays a scene which gives us a sudden and rare glimpse of the dramatics which must have been of not infrequent occurrence in the Divan of the volatile Bashaw:

I am truly concerned to acquaint Your Lordship that at my audience on the 1st inst., with the Bashaw to interfere in the matter of a controversy between a Maltese and a Tripoline Jew, His Highness, before a full Divan, so grossly insulted me, that I deem it expedient, for the honor of our Country, to decline hoisting the Flag over the Consulary house until satisfaction is granted. . . .

During this dispute the Bashaw had ordered the offending Maltese to leave the Regency, and Langford, who had had some difficulty in getting this audience, had protested and finally stated that he would report the affair to his King:

The Bashaw looked hard at me; and when, on retiring, I had reached the middle of the Hall, he roared out, '*Tu Minaccia me*?' and, clapping his hand on his pistol, he descended from his throne and ran at me, repeating the words, '*Tu minaccia me*?'. When near my Person, he stopped and knocking the Turban half off his head, he seized hold of his right ear, exclaiming, '*Chi sta te*!' The Bashaw, at this moment, both in voice and gesture demonstrated madness, and I am convinced that the timely interference of the Divan alone prevented the offering of further insult. . . .

That Yusef Karamanli suffered from sudden fits of rage and a sort of seizure had already been noted by the American surgeon Cowdery, who had seen him in what he described as an epileptic fit. It later transpired that only the evening before Langford's audience, the Bashaw in a fit of rage, had struck off the head of one of his Sicilian slaves[1] with a scimitar. He had also made two recorded attempts to kill Peter Lyle, his chief corsair and son-in-law, but had relented at the last moment.

A row of major proportions now developed. The Bashaw asserted that Langford had threatened him with his cane but, as usual, cooling down, attempted to resolve the affair privately. Langford, if he had had any knowledge of oriental psychology, would have gone to him, shaken his hand, and so ended the affair, of which the Bashaw was now probably ashamed, thus leaving the Bashaw in his debt. Instead, Langford insisted that an apology should be given to him in full Divan, with all those present who had seen the original insult. He further demanded that on his leaving the audience chamber, he should have a salute of twenty-one guns.

No Arab ruler could accept such a public humiliation. On receiving these demands the Bashaw became further enraged. He now withdrew all consular privileges from Langford stating that he would himself take British shipping under his protection. Finally, he summoned the Spanish consul and ordered him to take on the conduct of British affairs. Incoming British ships were now instructed by the Rais of the Marine to report to the Spanish and not the British consulate, and when Langford attempted to send off his wife and her maid in a ship in port, the Bashaw sent him a terse message to say that if they left the consular building they would be arrested and taken to the Castle.

In this posture Langford was rescued by the arrival of the British schooner, *Hortensia* in March 1811. She was commanded by Lieutenant Blaquière, an intelligent young man, later to be the author of *Letters from the Mediterranean*, an interesting account of a survey of the Mediterranean coastline carried out by him in 1810.[2]

Blaquière tried to heal the breach between the Bashaw and Langford but without success. He did, however, in the usage of the

[1] Blaquière gives his name as Michele Scotta.

[2] Edward Blaquière. He was later to be associated with Byron and Hobhouse in the affairs of the Greek Committee.

time, write an official letter to Langford which the latter could use in his explanations to London: 'I am induced to believe His Highness the Bashaw, with his Minister, as being extremely inimical to the Interest of H.M.G., and that the extraordinary conduct manifested towards His Majesty in your person on December 1st last, was precisely as you have described it to have been.'

Blaquière dutifully carried his views to Malta, and two months later, the frigate *Topaz*, arrived off Tripoli. Her commander Captain Hope, and Blaquière demanded an audience with the Bashaw and took Langford with them. The Bashaw, as ever relieved for a distinguished intermediary to settle a tiresome affair, was induced to relent. All was cleared up and ceremonial swords and attar of roses were given to the visitors.

But H.M.G. had had enough of Langford. He received orders to prepare to leave Tripoli and to hand over to a new Consul, Wilkie. As usual, he did not arrive, and Langford lingered on until January 1812, his relations with the Bashaw remaining cool and distant as before.

In January he received a curt letter from the Secretary of State ordering him to leave at once, and stating that his conduct in remaining was 'highly censurable'.

Wilkie, who it transpired was only coming *ad interim* as a pro-consul, arrived on January 3rd 1812, accompanied by a private secretary called Somerville. Langford left for Malta and London where he arrived on May 12th. He was not, in fact, censured on arrival, and later was used by the government to write some useful papers on Tripoli affairs for the Secretary of State's information.

Wilkie remained only a few months in Tripoli, during which his only recorded work was to initiate, under instructions from London, a peace treaty between Tripoli and the Kingdom of the Two Sicilies. He left Tripoli towards the end of 1812, and his post was occupied, again *ad interim*, by his secretary, Somerville.

The arrival of Consul Warrington

Langford's departure from Tripoli coincided with a rise in the fortunes of Yusef Karamanli. Britain's state of war with France, and her relations with America, left the Mediterranean in that state of partial anarchy which most suited his corsair fleet.

With no Great Power in a condition to despatch warships to protect the smaller maritime States, the Bashaw's admiral Peter Lyle could seize on vessels with comparative immunity, and he now did so, using all sorts of transparent pretexts, such as wrong passports, mistaken flags, passengers carried from enemy States, etc.

To dispute any attack from the sea, the Bashaw could now afford to strengthen his land defences, and Tripoli port was soon ringed with a series of defensive forts, with a total of 136 cannon.

For internal security, he had an army of about 30,000 infantry, 15,000 *Kuloghli* cavalry, and 30 mobile guns. With these forces he could easily control the provincial towns, patrol the caravan routes, and extract the tributary payments from the tribes of the interior and the Fezzan.

Meanwhile, the slave markets in Tripoli were filled with Danish and Sicilian slaves, the result of his captures, (500 Italian slaves alone were installed in the Castle *bagnios*), and a tributary stream of black slaves from south of the Sahara, came along the cleared caravan routes to swell the wealth of the Castle coffers. Profitable deals with slave merchants from Cairo and Constantinople were made, and the bazaars of Tripoli were filled with gold dust, ivory, ostrich feathers and spices. British and French travellers, noting the stocked caravanserais near the Marine Gate of the city, began to report in their letters the great wealth which might await explorers and merchants in the lands of central Africa.

A new sense of security reigned in Tripoli. 'In point of tranquillity and cleanliness,' wrote Blaquière, 'Tripoli might be taken as a model by some European towns in the Mediterranean . . .

you never see acts of violence being committed in the streets, and robberies are altogether unknown. . . .'

With increasing revenues, Yusef Karamanli was able further to indulge in one of the more admirable qualities of his dynasty. Extensive building and improvements went on in the Castle, and large numbers of Italian workmen, both slaves and free, bringing their skills in masonry, stucco carving and coloured marbles, worked in the State apartments and the Karamanli quarters. He created an audience chamber which astonished foreign visitors. The American consul Lear noted that the Bashaw now received his guests with a pomp exceeding by far that of Algiers—the richest of the Regencies.

Within his beautified *harim* he maintained one white wife, called the Padrona Grande, and two black concubines. By the former, he had five children—three sons, Mohammed, Ahmed and Ali and two daughters. The daughters, according to the Karamanli system of personal control, were married, one to an Italian renegade, the *Khasnadar*, his Treasurer, the other to the Scottish Admiral of his fleet, Peter Lyle.

While from the audience chamber he dispensed a severe, but relatively impartial justice, and the security of the State was his overruling concern, his policy both internally and externally, was to stimulate national and tribal divisions. The hereditary feud between the two great tribes, the Magarha and the Wuld Sleiman, was discreetly encouraged, thus preventing their uniting. His dependants were also allowed to intrigue against each other for his favour, and their mutual suspicions and jealousy were artfully stimulated.

A similar tactic was employed in his foreign relations. Blaquière, probably on information from Langford, wrote:

> Whenever the consuls, no matter of what nation, betray a disposition to be on terms of friendship, recourse is immediately made to calumnies of every sort, to separate them, and excite mutual digust. . . . The system of intrigue and calumny pursued here especially by the agents of France, is truly diabolical. . . .

The consuls, who were frequently trading rivals, and worried about their prestige and their precedence, and their influence with the Bashaw, as well as their constant financial difficulties and entanglements with their nationals, already tended to regard each other with suspicion, and this was a fertile soil to be exploited by the Bashaw.

Meanwhile, the British consulate continued to be maintained by Somerville, and the question had arisen in the Colonial Office of a suitable replacement. A series of factors were now emerging which were combining to make the Regency of Tripoli a place of growing importance to London. Britain, after Trafalgar, had taken on heavy responsibilities in the Mediterranean. Her troops were stationed in Malta and Sicily, her fleet still operated from Port Mahon and, with the continental ports closed to her as a result of war with France, she was increasingly turning to the North African ports for supplies. For these, Tripoli with its proximity to the British base at Malta, was becoming the most important.

There was a further reason for a growing interest in Tripoli, British merchants with the continental markets closed to them, were taking a closer look at new markets for trade, and were beginning to assess the reports of consuls and travellers on the opportunities awaiting them in the scarcely known markets of Africa. This combined to stimulate afresh an interest in the geography of this part of Africa, which had already begun in 1788 with the formation in London of the so-called African Association, whose object was to provide funds for the exploration of the interior of Africa.

Central Africa was still a dark enigma to the British geographers and hopeful merchants. What really lay beyond the Sahara? Did the Niger river, that vast watercourse which debouched on the west African coast, flow eventually into the Nile and thus connect west Africa with Egypt? And, far up the reaches of the Niger, was there a great central mart of trade, from whence came the caravans of black slaves, ivory and gold-dust, which travelled along the ancient trade routes, through Bornu, Kawar and the Fezzan, to Tripoli? There was a growing belief among geographers and financiers in London that expeditions to the interior of Africa would have the best success if sent via Tripoli. Furthermore, Yusef Karamanli had been favourable to the attempt by the traveller Lucas in 1788 when he had attempted to travel into the interior via Misurata. Yusef had also stated to several British travellers that he was prepared to favour any further efforts. There was a growing feeling that now was the time to make the attempt again.

There was a final question. The conscience of Britain, already aroused and active about a slave trade which yearly carried thousands of negroes from west Africa into slavery in the Americas, had begun to realize that slaves in their hundreds, white and Christian, were still drawing out their unhappy days on the shores of the Mediterranean and the Bosphorus, subject to sale and resale, the humiliations of chains and the lash and doomed to perpetual hard labour unless redeemed. To study this disturbing state of affairs, to report, and indeed, if necessary to act as an agent for redemption, might well be regarded as within the purview of a new British consul.

A change was taking place also in the government attitude towards the consular service. Although another ten years were to pass before the terms of service and, more important, the payment of consuls were to be properly established, it was realised that the day of the trading consul, underpaid, neglected and unsupported, were over. No longer would this unfortunate individual, starting his service in debt, paid, if at all, a small pittance at irregular intervals, and reliant for most of his subsistence on his own commercial efforts though nearly always doomed for lack of funds, be expected to represent his government abroad. Though, as in other government service, influence and political interest were still to be deciding factors in appointment, at least the prestige, the conditions and emoluments could draw better claimants.

For all these reasons it was now possible to make of the offer of the Tripoli post a more agreeable appointment. A man was wanted of intelligence, vigour, personality and courage. And now one with at least three of these qualities, was found. He was residing in Gibraltar, and his name was Colonel Hanmer Warrington.

Some odd British consuls have appeared in this narrative during the early years of the Karamanli regime. There was now to step on the stage of Tripoli a character who might well have emerged from the pages of Dickens or Surtees.

Since, for the next thirty-two years, this unusual Englishman was to play a leading and controversial rôle in Tripolitan affairs, and was at times to dominate the Bashaw, infuriate his colleagues particularly the French, and exasperate the Colonial Office yet, at the same time maintain British prestige and give a warm welcome and loyal assistance to all the British explorers passing through his hands, it will be useful to say something of his early life and character.

The bare facts of Colonel Hanmer Warrington's private life are on record, and of his official life, there is not only the vast volume of his letters and despatches—his melodramatic effusions, excuses, self—praise, and not infrequently intelligent suggestions which streamed from him to the Colonial and Foreign Offices during his tenure in Tripoli—but there are the accounts of him given by the visitors to Tripoli, the naval officers, and the North African travellers, who were to owe him a considerable debt in their explorations. Other sources, if they may properly be so called, are the various statements he put out at times about his own past history, and the curious footnotes to his history given by French historians of Tripoli—Féraud, Bernard, and Pellissier de Reynaud. A strange, disconnected picture emerges, for, while neither his own versions nor those of the French commentators quite tally with the known facts, they are not completely invalidated.

Hanmer Warrington was born of an old Welsh family in a village near Wrexham in North Wales, the son of a clergyman. (And here, by parenthesis, is the first mystery: his pedigree exists; he is not in it, but his children are!)[1] At the age of sixteen a cornetcy was purchased for him in the Dragoon Guards, and he remained

[1] Warrington's pedigree was obtained and kindly given to me by Lord Rennell.

in army service until 1802, when he sold out with the rank of Major. All his service, except for about six months in 1795 when he was on the Continent, was spent in Britain. In 1798, he married Jane Eliza Pryce from the Isle of Wight, by whom he had ten children. Little is known of how he spent the years between 1802 and 1810. In 1812, after short service in Spain during the Peninsula War, he was serving in Gibraltar, in some small official capacity.

So much for the official record. But from here, we wander into a world of conjecture, rumour and untruth, with gaps, opposing versions, exaggerations, and aposiopeses.

It must for example, have been nonsense, when he told an Arab sheikh in a letter of 1826, that he had 'once stood in the breaches at the siege of Acre', which took place in 1799. On the other hand, it may be true though elsewhere unconfirmed, when he told the Secretary of State, in a certificate of character in 1826, that he had raised a troop of volunteer cavalry and gone to the Peninsular War with the rank of Lieut. Colonel, where, in the charge for the retaking of the English guns at Malaga, he had two musket balls through his coat, and his horse shot under him, which, he added with characteristic bravado, 'although unfortunate to others, was highly creditable to me'.

The fact that the troops he alleged he commanded were volunteer cavalry may explain the absence of any mention of him in the official reports on the Malaga engagement. But is it true? At the battle of Malaga in 1810, the French captured most of the British troops with their commanding officer General Lord Blayney. In 1814, when Lord Blayney was released, he wrote what he called 'A Narrative' of his experiences. In this he lays some blame for the defeat on the lack of information and assistance he received from the local Spanish guerillas. For this he censures certain British officers, including Colonels Bosset and Warrington, who were recruited haphazardly in London where they were languishing without jobs, and sent to the Malaga area to organise an intelligence service among the peasant guerillas, and lamentably failed in their task, learning nothing of either the language or the character of the Spaniards. This latter criticism so accords with Hanmer Warrington's character that it must be to him the reference points. It is unlikely anyway, that there were two officers named Warrington of the rank of Colonel on special operations in the Malaga area at this date. It was subsequently noted that Warrington avoided all reference to these years in Spain in any later discussion with friends.

But now enter the French commentators. What are we to think of the statement of Charles Féraud, the historian of Tripoli that in Spain, Warrington was so badly treated by General Soult that he had '*une rancune instinctive a tous les Français*'? Or that he had quarrelled in the Peninsula with the Duke of Wellington, for whom he had '*une haine mortelle*'. And, stranger still, what are we to think about Féraud's equally positive statement, based he says, on information from Warrington's descendants, that Warrington's wife Jane Eliza, a retiring female about whom we learn virtually nothing else, was really '*une fille naturelle du roi, George IV*', which marriage, Féraud darkly points out, '*explique les millions qu'il gaspille à Tripoli, et le menagement que le Cabinet de Saint James avait pour lui, malgré ses fautes, ses violences, et ces excentricités compromettantes. . . .*'

We are well in the region of speculation. There were, of course, no millions for Warrington to spend in Tripoli; his entire salary was £930 a year, plus extraordinaries and whatever small private means he had. Yet if this statement about money is clearly Latin exaggeration, one cannot entirely discount Féraud's assertion about some connection between Warrington and the Royal Family. Recent research has shewn that, although his name does not appear anywhere in the papers of the Royal Household at Windsor, there is in the files of the Royal Geographical Society, a letter referring to a night of gambling, in which Warrington lost a large sum of money to the Prince Regent.[1] There is also indirect evidence that it was through the Duke of York that he obtained his appointment to the Peninsula, and subsequently to Gibraltar, where he was when he got the Tripoli appointment. He was later

[1] *Missions to the Niger*. Edited by E. W. Bovill.

to be in touch with the Duke about the purchase of horses in Tripoli, and he obliged the Bashaw to let him have some antiquities from Leptis Magna for despatch to the Prince Regent.

The rest is silence except for one other authority, who makes Warrington's comparison with a character from Surtees not seem too inapposite. In 1832, the great sporting journalist Nimrod who, under his real name of W. C. Apperley, was the snobbish critic of the English hunting field, wrote his memoirs, and here, on the Welsh hunting field, appears Warrington, 'a great ally of mine, being just my own age, and equally fond of horseflesh as myself'.

Gambling, horseflesh, drink; it may well be, as with so many of his class and period, that it was heavy debts which drove Warrington to leave England and accept a life in the insalubrious climate of North Africa.

From all this, it will be seen that he was a man of a very different quality and temper from the previous run of British consuls in Tripoli. That he was bombastic, violent, hard-drinking, and a tyrant to his colleagues and his family, will only too evidently be seen; but that he was also honest in his convictions, courageous and patriotic will also be made clear. Above all, with all his faults, eccentricities, exaggerations, tactlessness and garrulity, he was devoted to the cause of British expansion in Africa and never wavered in his help and encouragement to the mixed, and often difficult band, of English travellers, who now were about to arrive on the shores of North Africa.

Hanmer Warrington with his wife and eight children and their English governess, arrived in a naval storeship from Gibraltar on November 30th 1814, and were saluted with the courtesy of twenty-seven guns from the Castle as they entered the harbour. As the ship's boat brought the Warrington family slowly towards the shore where Mr. Somerville with some officials from the Castle awaited them, Jane Eliza Warrington, once more pregnant, must have gazed at the scene in front of her with varying emotions.

That is, perhaps, a suitable moment to look at Tripoli as it seemed to the eyes of a well-bred woman coming from Europe for the first time. It is possible to do so through the eyes of the wife of the Dutch consul M. de Breughel, who arrived shortly after the Warringtons and stayed with them in their house. She has left a rare manuscript of her impressions:

A closer acquaintance with the town gave van Breughel a sad feeling of deception. The reality appeared far different from the appearance at a distance. Near the disembarking place, a troupe of musicians awaited to give them a welcome on landing. This was a troupe of Maltese, furnished with old instruments, the only band available, which, as the boat approached, began a *pitoyable tapage*, which dolourously assailed their ears, and made a noise like a set of devils. . . . They entered the town. But what streets! Of pavements, no trace. Nor were the facades of the buildings either welcoming or picturesque; long rows of walls whitened with lime, narrowly facing each other, with a perspective of stone arches—this was all that one could see. In these walls could be seen doors leading to the houses, which were hidden behind them. These gave light to the dark courts within. No windows were visible on the street; everything seemed to be dead. And what a disagreeable sensation reached their nostrils, an unpleasant odour which seemed to surround them. Presently, they had an explanation for this phenomenon, an unhappy augury of the streets themselves. Imagine, I beg you, a footway fairly wide, sometimes watered but never properly swept, covered with all sorts of dirt, vegetables, egg shells, old bones, remains of meals, the middle of the way comparable to a gutter or small ditch. When it rains, these roads are transformed into rivers, which carry down the muck to the sea. Otherwise the dogs, which circulate freely, are the only street cleaners, seeking and gnawing the discarded bones. For the population, a single mulatto, some negroes, some veiled women, some naked children, playing and rolling on the ground. . . .

At last we reached the British consulate. It was not, like most of the other consulates, in a special Quarter. This was not the case in Tripoli; here the consulates were spread all over the town. Arriving at the Warrington house, one entered a porch, which gave on to a large interior court. At the rear, a large stairway led to a long, narrow room, with two small windows which opened on to the court. Of the darkness of this reception room, one could have no idea. At the end of the room, a door opened on to several small rooms, furnished as bedrooms, each one more dark and tomb-like than the others.

Madame de Breughel inspected the place. Her depression did not lift, and the idea that she would be obliged to pass a large part of her life, in a similar house and atmosphere, brought tears to her eyes. . . .

She soon recovered herself and rang the bell. A servant appeared. She asked him to bring some tea and a little supper for the children. How revealing was the reply she received! There was scarcely anything but a little tea available. Night had fallen, and it was scarcely 5 o'clcock in the afternoon. At first, Madame thought the man was teasing her, but it soon appeared that he spoke the truth and with just cause. In this country, there is no dusk; with the setting of the sun, the night falls suddenly and without transition. A little tea was brought with some sugar and some bread. 'And milk?' asked Madame. One must not think of it. It was an article of luxury and impossible to procure. The hungry children had no other resource than to soak the bread in the tea and swallow it. Meanwhile, the bread also had a disagreeable taste. It made the family think involuntarily of the disgusting odour in the streets.

It is easy to imagine that the couple at length went to bed in a sad mood, and passed the night almost without sleep. The raucous cries of camels and braying donkeys, to which they were unaccustomed, made them start up in fright, every time they closed their eyes. Early next morning, Madame left the bed, on which she had rested her tired body, only a little refreshed by sleep. And now, how horrified she was to find her clothing dotted with a hideous sort of insect, which she was unaccustomed to. It was one of those odious creatures, which only breed in the heat, and attack human beings by sucking their blood. Endemic on the North African coast, they still to this day, contaminate the best and cleanest houses. In order not to worry his wife, M. de Breughel had kept silent about this insect, which he already knew. It was necessary to pursue it and drown it in water. . . . This chase was the painful beginning of a new day, which was yet to bring experiences more painful. . . .

Such was the country and such the life, to which Eliza Warrington, her brood of children, and her eccentric husband came. In all the years the Warrington family were to reside in Tripoli, and through all the vicissitudes they were to undergo, Mrs. Warrington remains a shadowy figure. 'Striking and dignified,' Madame de Breughel remembered her; 'at first rather reserved, but most charming when one knew her.' It is the only epitaph of this most long-suffering woman of possibly royal blood which remains: the only testimony to a woman who, for twenty years, in the unwholesome climate of Tripoli, strove to bring up a large family and sustain an autocratic and highly eccentric husband.

Warrington found the consular building in a state of deplorable repair. A series of impecunious consuls had inhabited it for years, and the whole building and its trappings seemed to him both unrepresentative of his country, and of his own prestige. He immediately sat down and reported to London that he was buying a new flagstaff and a new flag:

> The Moors estimate the Flags by the freshness of their Bunting, and if that were a Criterion to judge by, the British Flag at this Consulate would be precipitated from the highest pitch of Glory and Greatness to a State lower than any nation having a consular representative residing here. . . .

He put his dragoman and servants into new livery, and purchased a stout six-oared boat to row him from the *menshia* to the Castle, for having taken one look at the consular building, he had decided to reside there as little as necessary. He would build himself a house in the *menshia*. He acquired some land there, and arranged to build on it a small five-bedroom house. Round it he made his famous garden, for gardening was one of the loves of this strange man. It was a hobby he shared with one other person in Tripoli who loved flowers—the renegade Scots pirate, Peter Lyle.[1]

By the pen of the historian Féraud, the six-oared boat in which Warrington could be seen from the town rowing to the Castle becomes '*un grand canot pavoise, monté pas les matelots indigenes*', and the house in the *menshia*, of which a crude drawing exists in the

[1] According to Féraud: 'This renegade, child of some Scottish seaport, died in Tripoli. He lies buried, under his Arab name of Rais Mourad, in an honoured place in the mosque of Dragut.'

Public Record Office, becomes a legendary '*résidence somptueuse, tout de marbre et de faiences vernies, aportées d'Italie a grand frais*'.

Here, also according to Féraud, the British Consul-General and the Scottish pirate held drinking parties and pottered in the garden among the flowers. It is a picture worth preserving, and may even be truc.

On December 1st 1814, Warrington made his first official call on the Bashaw accompanied by Somerville and the consular dragoman. At that time there was still only one entrance from the town to the huge, rambling complex of buildings, and this was by a drawbridge across a dry moat opposite the Karamanli mosque, which led through a low and narrow gate into a wide courtyard, filled with soldiers and with stabling for the Bashaw's famous stud of grey horses. At the end of this, in his habitual chair, sat the striking figure of the Chamberlain, or Grand Kehya, a Russian renegade, dressed in coloured silks under a vast turban. He now rose, the guard presented arms and, with the Grand Kehya leading, the party dived into the labyrinth of dark tunnels and passages, so broken underfoot that the visitor could only grope and stumble in the gloom. At intervals in these noisome passages, lit only by occasional holes in the roof, the party passed groups of soldiers, slaves, and vast, negro *hampas*, armed to the teeth, so that forward movement was a constant scuffle with barely discernible forms.

Eventually, the lilting sound of the Bashaw's *nubar*, or band of timbrel, drum and reed, could be heard, and the party arrived in a large courtyard outside the audience chamber, filled with more soldiers, Palace officials, bedraggled Christian slaves, suppliants for justice, and criminals awaiting judgment. From here, a small flight of steps led to the audience chamber itself, its doors guarded by two huge, black guards armed with matchlocks and scimitars.

As the British Consul-General stooped and entered the doors, a scene of splendour met his eyes. The Bashaw's recent building programme had lined the walls with bright Chinese tiles, along which were ranged black *hampas*, armed with blunderbusses, forming a background to the assembled members of the Bashaw's

Divan, *taiffa*, religious dignitaries, and Sheikhs, all in a colourful variety of clothes and uniforms.

At the far end of the chamber stood a raised dais with a throne, backed by a large gilt canopy in the French manner, a trophy of spears, cannon and flags, all gilded, and surrounding a large silver hand, tipped with rubies and hanging there to avert the evil eye. To the right of the throne, sitting in a semi-circle of gilt chairs, were the Bashaw's sons, and standing beside the throne was another black slave, holding at the ready on a silk cushion, the Bashaw's pair of pistols. On the other side of the throne stood two other black slaves, magnificently dressed and bearing in their turbans, the Bashaw's official sign of the silver hand.

Upon the throne sat Yusef Bashaw, now about fifty years old, a short, plump, fair-skinned figure, dressed in a many-coloured silk cloak glittering with diamonds, baggy silk trousers supported by a belt with a huge diamond buckle, and pink silk stockings. Beneath him, from silken cushions, protruded a jewelled scimitar.

If Warrington was impressed by his first view of the Bashaw of Tripoli and his Court, the Bashaw himself may have been no less overawed. For Warrington, a man as Féraud grudgingly admits, '*d'une taille superbe*', had designed his own consular uniform, and there now approached the throne a figure wearing the plumed hat of a field marshal, the red and blue coat of an ambassador, the epaulettes of an admiral, and the trousers, boots and spurs of a huzzar.[1]

Some gilt chairs stood to the Bashaw's left and to these, after salutations, the British Consul-General's party was escorted and the audience began. And now, if anything further were required to maintain an atmosphere of *opéra bouffe*, there stepped forward the magnificently dressed figure of the Bashaw's Admiral of the Fleet, who addressed Warrington in broad Scots. It was Peter Lyle offering his services as interpreter.

Back in his consulate, Warrington wrote his first despatch, dated October 10th. His reception had far exceeded his expectations.

[1] So Lord Grosvenor found him dressed on a visit to Tripoli in 1830.

His Highness asked me whether H.R.H., the Prince Regent, would shew him an extra mark of Friendship by presenting him with a Brace of Pistols for his own use, a Brace for his Minister, four Silver Watches and two Guns. All of which I immediately assured His Highness the Prince Regent would acceed to. . . . I communicated that the British Flag had been planted on the Walls of Washington, and every circumstance relating to that most Brilliant Achievement. The Bashaw received it with the most visible marks of joy. . . .

Unusual perhaps in tenor, this was an auspicious beginning. Warrington's appearance, his soldierly bearing, declamatory style of address, haughty but polite manner, all were impressive to an oriental, but there was something more. The engaging, but wily and ruthless Prince, and the almost theatrical Welshman, both judges of good horses and strong brandy, felt an immediate bond of understanding, which was to endure, with many rifts, for over twenty years. Both recognised strength when they saw it; both were realists in love of power. 'I am certain', wrote Warrington to the Secretary of State, 'that Firmness is the only Line of Policy to be observed in the Barbary States.'

He was soon to give ample evidence of this policy.

Warrington's first clash with his colleagues in Tripoli was, characteristically, with the French representative. This humble and unfortunate official, M. Delaporte, was only *gérant* of the consulate, after the departure of the former consul M. Guys, and he was in an extremely delicate situation. From an almost complete lack of communications with France, with the virtual clearance of French shipping from the Mediterranean, he had only rumours of Napoleon's break-out from Elba and return to power in France to inform him. He was accredited by Louis XVIII and flew the Bourbon flag above his consulate. But what, if Napoleon should succeed in regaining power, should he do; and when? He may have consulted his archives and found that a French consul at the time of the French revolution, unaware of events in France, and still flying the Bourbon flag, had been insulted and almost manhandled by a ship-load of marine *sans culottes*, who had suddenly appeared off Tripoli, after the fall of the Bastille.

In such a situation, it might have been a kindness in his European colleagues to have realised his predicament, and to have supported him, at least on a personal level. Not so for Warrington.

In March 1815, Napoleon, after flight from Elba, in which he eluded the British guard-ships and reached Toulon, began his 100 days. The news reached Tripoli by the end of the month, throwing Delaporte into such confusion, that he had the temerity to call for advice from his colleagues.

The Spanish consul, at least a fellow Latin, was first visited for advice, and he hurried to Warrington with the news. '*The chargé d'affaires* of France', reported Warrington, in a letter to London of March 22nd, 'is already at work, in favour of his old Friend. . . . He is a dangerous and Improper Character to represent the Bourbons. . . .'

Two days later, in an outburst to the Governor of Malta, Sir Thomas Maitland, he let fly the first shots in his long and bitter feud with the French. On April 1st, he wrote:

Sir,

We have heard of Buonaparte's having quitted Elba and arrived in France—a circumstance fraught with evil, and, in consequence, conjecture is all alive. The French *chargé d'affaires* here has already shewn the *Cloven* foot—M. Delaporte was an adherent, Friend and Protege of Buonaparte, and as it is Impossible to serve two Masters, that circumstance only renders him a Dangerous and Improper Character to represent the Bourbons. Last night, to My utter astonishment, M. Delaporte came to the Consulate and to my Amazement Commenced the subject alluded to, which I find it necessary to submit to the consideration of Your Excellency; as, should Buonaparte make any Head—it would be advisible to put an Extinguisher upon any Republican faction here *immediately*, by sending M. Delaporte to answer for his Treachery to His Legitimate King. M. Delaporte began the Conversation by asking if I had any news relative to Buonaparte. I immediately answered him by saying that nothing could be apprehended from such a Tour, which must have arose from *amusement*, or from a bewildered Brain.

A dispute now broke out with the bewildered Delaporte. Warrington pointed out that all Napoleon's former ministers had sworn an oath of allegiance to the King. Delaporte replied that, according to the Proclamation of the mayor of Elba, Napoleon had been called back by 'the voice of the people'; and he was unwise enough to add that such an occurrence might happen in England.

This final remark was enough to send Warrington to the rostrum:

> I replied that Hell itself never could shake the Throne of England, that in that Happy Country there was too much Honor in every Class of Society to make them Swerve from those Feelings of Affection towards the best of Fathers and of Kings. . . .

The interview almost broke up in disorder. Warrington concluded:

> My own private feelings were nearly overcoming the regulation of my Official Conduct. However, I shall take care in future that my walls shall not be contaminated with such expressions. . . . My Eye is upon the Conduct of that Gentleman and I shall take great care that the tri-coloured Flag is not Hoisted here, in case of Buonaparte's gaining ground.

Napoleon did gain ground and this led to further trouble. On June 29th, a courier arrived in Tripoli with news that the Republican flag had been hoisted in Tunis and Algiers, and a message arrived at the British consulate that Delaporte intended to lower the Bourbon flag and hoist the tricolour in its place.

Warrington immediately called on the Spanish consul and the two hurried to an audience with the Bashaw. They found that Delaporte had preceded them with a request for an audience in which he was to deliver a letter from Napoleon's first Minister, and to request permission to take this as evidence of an official change of government, and therefore to fly the tricolour at the French consulate.

Warrington succeeded in getting first to the Bashaw, and in one of his declamatory interviews, protested against this permission being given. Napoleon, he told the bewildered Bashaw, was now an outlaw.

'If the Bashaw wished to respect the good friendship and Faith of England and Spain he would not suffer such a Step to take place till we heard from our respective governments,' Warrington wrote in his account of the affair, 'I am happy to say that he has promised not to permit the Tricoloured flag to be hoisted till we hear from London and Madrid.' As to Delaporte: 'The *chargé d'affaires* of Lewes the eighteenth, has shown the cloven foot, and I now beg leave to say that the full figure of the Old Gentleman is personified in the Conduct, Character and Disposition of M. Delaporte.'

To Delaporte, he now wrote, addressing the letter to 'The Chargé d'Affaires to His Majesty Lewes the 18th, or Napoleon Bonaparte':

Sir,

Consistency is the grand Bais [*sic*] for all Public Characters to act upon.... I have the Honor to inform you that, as a Public Character, as well as a Private one, it will be incompatible with me to hold any sort of intercourse with you, and as I regret the loss of your Society, tenfold do I lament the circumstances which cause this avowal.

Delaporte, in some anxiety, since he did not wish a rupture of relations, sent a reply, pointing out that events were forced upon him, and reiterating that he must now regard Napoleon as the representative of the established government of France. This brought an immediate riposte.

Sir,

The receipt of your letter, and the contents therein conveyed, cannot be viewed in any other light than an Intentional Insult to his Britannic Majesty's Consul General here. As a Private Gentleman, it is also considered in the same light. Therefore, the undersigned, will take the most laconic and explicit manner to express His Heartfelt abhorrence at the Vile, Base and Truly detestable career of Napoleon Bonaparte; and His having been proclaimed an *Outlaw*, and outcast from Society, will stamp his present adherents with the same degree of Infamy.... Thank God, the Principles of England are pure and unsullied....

Copies of these effusions went off punctually to London, though Warrington had so far received no instructions on the official attitude he should adopt. By the end of June it was known that Britain was again at war with France. Warrington then set up a second flagpole at his consulate and raised the Bourbon flag. He also put a white cockade in his hat, and when, either with or without Delaporte's connivance, three French sailors appeared outside the British consulate wearing republican cockades and singing revolutionary songs, he acted with vigour.

'I immediately acquainted the Bashaw with the circumstances,' he informed Lord Bathurst, the Secretary of State, 'and He instantly sent me a guard, and I caused the three Men in question to be lodged in the Common Prison, and next day shipped off from this Regency.'

At this juncture M. Delaporte's difficulties were resolved by the arrival of a newly appointed French Consul-General, this time a professional diplomat, called M. Mure, described by Féraud, as '*un homme déjà avancé en âge, grave et ferme, quoique très prudent*'. M. Mure needed all these qualities, for he found on his arrival in Tripoli a most extraordinary state of affairs.

Delaporte, as the result of pressure from Warrington on the Bashaw, had been declared *persona non grata*, and was closely contained in the French consular building, from which he stoutly flew the tricoloured flag. A French merchant had been ordered by the Bashaw to conduct French consular affairs. From the roof of the British consulate, the Bourbon flag was flying, side by side with the Union Jack.

Mure's first action was to send a polite Note to Warrington, pointing out what appeared to him an unfortunate situation, in which, a Foreign Power seemed to be interfering in French affairs.

Warrington was shocked by the suggestion of interference, and indeed, by the general tenor of Mure's Note. He had expected Mure to have had Delaporte arrested and shipped off to France: now he learned that Mure had received Delaporte in the most kindly manner, and indeed was to be accompanied by him on his round of official consular visits.

Warrington's guns were now turned on Mure, and the

Secretary of State was again sent details of the correspondence. He complained on October 17th:

The French consul general having taken M. Delaporte (altho' being made acquainted of his Diabolical Treachery) by the hand, has caused a Coolness between M. Mure and myself. . . . I am certain both the French Consul general as well as Delaporte are real and sworn friends of Buonaparte . . . and I believe I may class the American consul as the third. . . .

How this imbroglio eventually was resolved the State Papers do not relate. Probably, with Napoleon's exile, tempers simmered down. In any case, at the end of 1815, Warrington was involved in issues of more immediate moment. Even in private matters concerning his own family the Foreign Office had to be dragged in. Perhaps some of these irrelevant letters may have illumined a dull hour in the daily round of business at Downing Street:

Your Excellency is aware that on my arrival in this Regency, I relieved Mr. Somerville, who was an utter Stranger to me, and from that circumstance, availed himself of a Project of carrying into effect the Seduction of an Amiable and accomplished young Lady, Miss Stuart, at that time Governess to my children, under the *Promise of Marriage*, and had it not been for the honorable feelings of the Spanish consul and His Lady (who informed me of the circumstance of His being already married) I verily believe the marriage would have taken place and of course the Lady doomed to perpetual Misery.

On my taking Mr. Somerville to task, He acknowledged He had been married, but believed His Wife was dead, but from which ground it was necessary to shift, by saying everything Injurious to the Character of His Wife and that he was about to be divorced, and finding that Position not tenable, He resorted to the plan of saying that his marriage was illegal being only married in the Greek Church, on which I informed him that in the eyes of God and Honest Men it was equally binding, and told Him that His conduct had been so Base that I must decline all communication except on Official business, and that on no account whatever was he ever again to appear in the presence of Miss Stuart.

Mr. Somerville was shipped off to Malta. What happened to poor Miss Stuart is not recorded and Warrington turned to other things.

However his high moral tone in this affair, must have made its impression on the consular corps for in June the Danish consul came to him for help. Among the slaves recently brought in by the Tripoli corsairs were two Danish boys. They had been imprisoned while their case was being examined, and while in prison had been sexually molested by the *janissary* guards.

Warrington summoned the whole consular corps, and then sat down and drafted a Note to the Bashaw, which he obliged every consul to sign. It was a letter in his finest style:

> Whereas it has been represented to us that some of the Guardiana, having taken those liberties with the Boys, taken in the Danish vessels, which ought to be confined to the Female Sex, and as we view the same with the utmost horror and disgust, and which is not only a disgrace to Human Nature, but renders the Persons concerned worse and more contemptible than the Beasts of the Field. . . . We, the undersigned, therefore solemnly protest, in the name of our respective Nations, against any such abominable and disgraceful Practices, and trust that His Highness, the Bashaw, will immediately Inflict the most exemplary Punishment against anyone so offering to offend on the Body of any Slave, whether Man or Boy. . . .

Impressed with this document the Bashaw called a full Divan and sat in judgment. Warrington, the Danish consul, the two Danish boys, and the accused *janissaries*, were then called to attend. There follows, from Warrington's brief account of the affair sent to Sir Thomas Maitland, a glimpse of the sudden dramas of life and death in the Bashaw's courts. The boys were called to identify the culprits:

> On this being done, the Bashaw offered to take off their heads on the spot, but, as the act was an attempt, we considered about 1000 Bastinado sufficient, and in our Presence that Punishment was Inflicted, with that severity that there is but small hopes of the Wretches surviving.

Trouble with the Bashaw

Inevitably during 1815, there arose further difficulties between the Bashaw and Warrington which served to indicate the gradually increasing ascendancy of the British Consul-General over the Ruler. These difficulties came mostly from the complicated system under which the accepted laws of piracy operated. Ships were regularly issued with passports by consuls which exempted the vessels from capture. But, organised from Malta by some enterprising Maltese, a system of forging passports had begun to operate. Corsair captains, finding in some cases that they had been duped in the capture of legitimate prizes, began to take a firmer line with captured vessels and this led to frequent mistakes. One such mistake occurred in October 1815, when a vessel with a legitimate passport from a British consul was brought as a prize into Tripoli.

To a thundering complaint from Warrington, the Bashaw offered to execute the pirate captain.

> His Highness, [wrote Warrington to the Commander in Chief in Malta,] offered me the Head of the *Reis*, but not conceiving myself authorised nor justified in depriving a fellow creature of Life in such a delicate affair, I demanded he shall remain in Irons till the sentiments of your Excellency are known. . . .

His Excellency in Malta was quick to reply that he

> . . . should wish to encourage His Highness in that humanity, with which justice should always be tempered.

In fact, the ship and stolen cargo were returned, and the corsair captain—no doubt much relieved—sent to Malta to pay a fine of 500 francs to the British Tribunal.

This would have been all right, and matters between Castle and Consulate returned to their normal state of friendship, if, a few days later during some internal *fracas* at the Castle, a Christian slave had not, in a moment of fury, tried to murder the Bashaw with an English pistol. He failed and was executed on the spot, but the fact that the pistol was English aroused the Bashaw's never completely dormant suspicions. In a Divan the following day, he wondered aloud if the British Consul-General had been aware of the plot. Though there was no other evidence of this except the pistol, a period of coolness between the Bashaw and Warrington ensued. This was enough to encourage one of the corsair captains, *Rais el Maghrebi*, to seize a British merchant vessel in the Malta roads.

News of this capture reached the Bashaw before the arrival of the vessel, and such was his nervousness of Warrington, that he sent orders that the vessel should be brought in secretly, without the customary salutes from the port. He then hastened to send his expressions of regret and disassociation.

This time Warrington was pitiless. He saw the Bashaw in full Divan, demanded an apology, and insisted that *Rais el Maghrebi* should be hanged from the yard-arm of the captured British vessel by the British sailors themselves, in full view of the shore.

Both the Bashaw and Peter Lyle, the Bashaw's admiral, pleaded with Warrington to allow the *Rais* to be forgiven, or if not, at least to be hanged by fellow Moslems according to their rites, and not by Christians, which would only excite the townspeople.

Warrington refused. On leaving the consulate, he had struck his flag, and he refused to fly it again until sentence had been carried out:

> I was firm in not Interfering or impeding the execution of the Mandate of His Highness, and nothing can prove more forcibly the Vicissitude of Human Affairs, that in half an hour, the very Rope which bore in Triumph and exaltation the British Flag, should have suspended on it the *Rais*. . . . As the British Flag went up, it received 21 Guns, and on the last Gun being fired, and one from the corsair, the *Rais* was run up, and, after hanging two hours, was taken down and buried. This, I trust, will be an awful and permanent example, to these People.

Warrington could now, with satisfaction, report to London: 'The Bashaw and myself are on the best of terms, and as long as he is kept in Subjection, we shall remain so. . . .'

That Warrington by these abrupt and hectoring tactics, had succeeded in achieving an ascendancy over the Bashaw, was now clearly apparent, and this fact resulted in his being asked by a number of foreign countries to act for them in Tripoli. In all cases, he accepted, and by the end of the year 1815, he was acting consul for the Kingdom of the Two Sicilies, Neapolitan Dominions, Portugal, Holland, Austria, Hanover, Tuscany and Russia.

It was in this year also that he accepted the appointment as Agent of the Africa Institution for the Release of Slaves. These were, of course, black slaves who still thronged the markets of the East, of the Caribbean, and of the Americas. The fact that white slaves still languished in the *bagnios* of Algiers, Tripoli and Tunis, aroused less compassion in the reformers. Their redemption was a national concern, and funds for it had to be raised with difficulty, from governments and private institutions. Christian slaves—now almost entirely Italian, Spanish, or Greek—were nearly always sold in the countries whose corsairs had captured them, and retained, for ransom, or for perpetuity, in the same countries. This meant that they could be relatively easily traced for redemption. But now, with the growing shortage of Christian slaves, a new traffic had sprung up in the sale of these slaves from one African country to another. Warrington tried to oppose this. With a fine collision of metaphors he reported to the Governor of Malta in October 1815:

Sir,

A Christian slave this morning threw himself into the arms and Protection of the British Flag, having been sold to African Traffic, to end his days in God knows what Climate. . . . It has hitherto been the custom of this Barbary Power to capture Christians for the sake of Ransom from the Respective Nations they may belong to, but if once it is permitted that these unfortunates are sold and doomed to misery in an unexplored part of Africa, it would, in the End, be establishing, by this Bashaw, of white for Black men. . . .

The Bashaw had sent his Chief Minister to demand the man's return. An altercation had ensured, in which Warrington had demanded the Bashaw's promise that the man would not be sold to any African Power. The Minister had the temerity to ask what England had to do with the Bashaw's private concerns. Warrington almost threw him out: 'I was obliged to desire him to walk from under the Flag, which he endeavoured to Pollute and Insult.'

Faced with this stern refusal the Bashaw again relented, and gave the required promise that the slave would neither be sent abroad for sale, nor punished for seeking refuge in the British consulate-general. But Warrington wanted confirmation from his superiors:

I am well aware of the full Force and Meaning of our Glorious act of Parliament for the abolition of the Slave Trade, and altho' it is confined, to prevent the Extraction of the wild African from his native soil, still I should conceive that the British Government never would allow a system of Traffic to be carried on by this Barbary Power, as Inhuman as Unprecedented . . . I simply ask Your Excellency whether or not England will Interfere to prevent such a Traffic being established from this Regency.

One more glimpse of the terrors of Christian slavery, appear, among many others from this period, in a letter from Warrington to the Governor of Malta, of October 9th 1815:

A Cruiser belonging to this Regency returned yesterday with ten poor creatures taken from under their own Roofs on the coast of Calabria. Last night, the Bashaw sent an Infant of the Age of Eighteen Months to this Consulate, and I have to assure your Lordship that he shall remain in safety, and every possible care shall be taken of him till I hear from His Excellency, His Neapolitan Majesty's Minister, or the child is claimed by his relations. My Vice Consul, with his Accustomed Humanity, has taken Charge of the Infant.

It draws Tears of Blood from my Heart in relating the Melancholy Circumstance that the Mother was murdered when in the act of shewing the most endearing and Maternal tenderness to Her Infant. Human Nature shudders at such foul and diabolical Conduct, and I trust ere long the Regency may experience the just vengeance of both Heaven and Earth. . . .

P.S. I have further ascertained that more people were assassinated in the diabolical attempts of the Pirates, and, among these, probably

Consul Warrington's house in the *menshia*, from a contemporary sketch, showing him planting trees

The scene of the murder of Hassan Karamanli by his brother Yusef

Captain William Eaton

A Kuloghli in uniform

the father of the Infant. The poor woman, who died of her wounds, was violated by nearly the whole Crew, and expired under such Atrocity....

It was doubtless reports such as these from the consuls which helped to foster the agreement made at the Congress of Vienna in 1815 by the European powers, to order the release of all Christian captives in the Barbary States. The task of enforcing this order was given to Britain and in 1816, a powerful naval squadron under the command of Lord Exmouth sailed for Algiers, Tunis and Tripoli. By April 27th, the Squadron was in Tripoli roads, and the Admiral in the name of the European powers, imposed the following conditions on the Bashaw.

(I) No more Christian slaves were to be made. Persons captured in vessels with whom the Bashaw was at war were to be treated as prisoners-of-war, i.e. could not be bought and sold.

(II) Tripoli was to recognise both the State of the Ionian Isles, and Hanover, as being under British protection.

(III) A state of perpetual peace must be agreed with the State of Sardinia, and, for ten years with the Kingdom of the Two Sicilies.

(IV) 144 Sardinian and Genoese slaves must be released, without compensation; and 420 Neopolitan slaves, for a payment of 50,000 piastres. Sardinia, however, must pay the Bashaw an annual subsidy for her peace terms.

Tunis had already captiulated, and, with some eighteen British men-of-war riding off the Tripoli roads, the Bashaw had no recourse but to accept. Under the threat of Exmouth's guns, which were later to pound Algiers into submission, 500 Christian slaves trooped out of the stinking Castle *bagnios*, and were shipped off to their respective countries.

The moment Exmouth's top-masts were out of sight, the Tripoli corsairs continued their cruises, and mockingly told their new captures that they were not slaves but called 'prisoners-of-war'. In the early 19th century the difference between the two categories in terms of work and conditions can have been little. There were however, no more open sales of Christians in the slave markets. Prisoners-of-war, on the other hand, might be put to work anywhere.

This state of affairs lasted for a further three years while large numbers of 'prisoners-of-war' continued to slave in Tripoli. Then in 1819, a combined Anglo-French squadron, under the joint command of Commodore Fremantle and Admiral Jurien de la Gravière, appeared off the Barbary shores. This time the Barbary rulers were obliged to give up all attacks on Mediterranean shipping, under whatever pretext. It was the end at last of a menace that for nearly five hundred years had stalked the Mediterranean.

It was the death blow to the rulers of the Barbary States. No more could their expensive treasuries be supported by big ransoms, rich subsidies and the sale of ships and booty. Subsidies under the 1816 Agreements continued to be paid for a few years, but one by one they dried up. The Bashaw made some attempts to capture shipping of smaller powers, but the threat of Anglo-French reaction was too great, and they were only really empty gestures of defiance. Britain and France, the policemen of the Mediterranean, were themselves at peace. By 1825, all sources of revenue from the old trade of piracy and Christian slavery had dried up.

The enigma of the Niger

With a large part of his revenues cut, the Bashaw of Tripoli was obliged to turn elsewhere for finance. The source to which he now turned was the sale of negro slaves. With this in mind, he started to reorganise slave caravans, and strike, if possible, deeper into central Africa. This was a move that was to coincide fortunately with the arrival of the first British travellers to explore the trade routes southwards from Tripoli.

The African Association, that body of private gentlemen who had formed themselves in 1788 to 'Promote the discovery of the interior parts of Africa' had already sent several explorers to try to explore these areas, to discover the source and exit of the great

Niger river and whether in fact, as many believed, it flowed out of, or into, the Nile.

Simon Lucas from Tripoli in 1788, and Ledyard from Cairo in the same year, had both failed; the first had been turned back at Misurata, and the second had died in Cairo of plague. They had been followed by the German traveller Hornemann, who in 1799, had reached Murzuk in the Fezzan, travelling from Cairo along the Siwa route. But he had also died later in the year at Bokani, not far from the Niger. Most of his geographical notes however had been preserved, and they were sufficient to support the belief that along this great river, far in the depths of Africa, there flourished a civilisation possibly of great importance as a source for trade.

With Hornemann's death, the task of promoting the exploration of the Niger region had fallen to the British government which, now free from war commitments, was becoming aware of the possibilities of these important markets and equally, of the danger of letting the French get into them first.

In 1805, the British government had mounted a large expedition headed by the famous traveller Mungo Park, and consisting of forty-six Europeans, to attack the problem of the Niger from the west coast of Africa. Every single member of this expedition had perished before any concrete results could be obtained. Two further attempts made in 1816, also from the insalubrious west coast, resulted in deaths of the leaders and had to be abandoned.

The African Association, though they had passed over the task to the Government, continued to maintain that the discovery of the Niger regions would be best attempted from the north rather than the west coast. Their view was strengthened in 1816 by the report of a naval officer, Commander Smyth, who visited Tripoli to collect the antiquities promised by the Bashaw to the Prince Regent.

Commander Smyth, impressed first by Warrington's close relations with the Bashaw, by the latter's control of the trade routes, and his statements, frequently repeated, that he would be glad to assist any British travellers in their exploration in his territories, wrote in an important letter to John Barrow, Second

Secretary at the Admiralty, and a man deeply concerned with African exploration, 'By striking due south of Tripoli, a traveller will reach Bornu before he is out of Yusef's influence.'

Smyth's report was passed by Barrow to the Colonial Office, who were now the department responsible for government Missions to Africa, and the report carried with it a strong endorsement of the proposition to send a Mission from Tripoli. The Colonial Office agreed to be responsible for a new Mission, and to Smyth's idea that the route to be followed should be the old Garamantian trade route through Murzuk and Kawar. This was still the main slave route from the Sudan, and used by the armed caravans bringing merchandise to the Mediterranean.

Approval for the plan of a Mission starting from Tripoli reached Warrington in February 1818, and he replied enthusiastically in a letter to Barrow of March 7th: 'The plan is fraught with innumerable advantages to geographical science, to the commercial interests of the civilized world, and, ultimately, I hope, it may rescue millions of our fellow-creatures from an abyss of ignorance and superstition.'

A few weeks later Warrington was sent the names of the two men whom the Colonial Office had selected to undertake the first Mission. They were Joseph Ritchie, a Scots surgeon of about thirty-five, and Captain George Lyon, a twenty-three year old naval officer. It was emphasised that the funds available for this exploration were small, and it was therefore proposed that, after acclimatising themselves for a period in Tripoli, they should proceed to Murzuk. Here Ritchie should establish himself in an official nature, as vice-consul, and set himself to learn the local dialect and gather information on the prospects of safely continuing a journey to Timbuktu. On arrival at Timbuktu the Mission was charged 'to collect all information as to the further course of the Niger, and of the probability of your being able to trace the stream of that river, with safety, to its termination'.

Warrington approved this plan in principle, but he had sufficient knowledge to realise that Commodore Smyth's enthusiasm for the safety of the trade routes, which had inspired the plan, was rather too optimistic. He believed that, rather than travelling alone under a promise of the Bashaw's protection, it would be safer to make any excursions in the Fezzan in company with the Bashaw's slave-raiding troops.

Joseph Ritchie, leader of the Mission arrived in Tripoli in October and George Lyon a month later. They were joined by John Belford, a shipwright from the Malta dockyard who was supposed to be able to build them a boat should they ever reach the Niger river. In character, the two senior members of the Mission were very different. Ritchie proved to be a quiet, uncommunicative, self-contained man; Lyon was a hard working young naval officer, of considerable charm, who rapidly made himself liked.

From the moment of their arrival Ritchie found he was short of funds. He had already spent a considerable part of the original financial grant from the Colonial Office on what were believed to be articles for trade in the Fezzan, and much of the rest was set aside for expensive presents for the Bashaw and the guide whom they were to accompany to the Fezzan. Lyon, who had some private means of his own, generously offered to supplement their resources although Ritchie told him very little about their finances. It was clear, however, to the worried Warrington that they were woefully short of funds on which to start a highly speculative journey into the heart of Africa.

Nevertheless, introduced by Warrington, the Bashaw welcomed them pleasantly, accepted his present, and suggested that they should travel to the Fezzan in the company of el Mukni the newly-appointed Bey of Fezzan, who had already been of some assistance to the traveller Hornemann, and who was then in Tripoli collecting a strong force of guards with which to make a slaving expedition from Murzuk. By accompanying the Bey, Ritchie and Lyon would have adequate protection for the journey and a guarantee of further assistance when they reached Murzuk. Meanwhile, they had a useful period of five months to stay in Tripoli since the slaving party did not expect to leave before March of the next year.

Ritchie at first stayed with Warrington at the latter's house in the *menshia*, but when Lyon arrived, they moved into the empty Portuguese consulate, (Warrington was now acting consul for Portugal) and settled down to study the manner and customs of the Moors.

It was, most possibly, on the unwise advice of the Bashaw that they now tried to diguise themselves as Moors. They engaged a *fighi*, or learned religious, to teach them the language and the manners of the local Moslems, and even went so far as to have themselves circumcised, and adopted Moorish dress.

Warrington, with that practical commonsense he could so often show where English travellers were concerned, regarded these affectations as both unwise and even ridiculous. 'If we send a vice-consul to Fezzan,' he wrote in a letter to a friend in Malta, 'let him go in his real Character, which is more respectable, and more to be respected, than the adoption of the Moorish costume, or disfiguring the Person by circumcision. The result will prove whether it is a childish game and whether the lookers-on are imposed on. . . .'

This was sound advice, and accepted as such by all subsequent travellers. To complete the imposture, which can have deceived no one Ritchie now assumed the name of 'Yusef el Ritchie,' the dockyard worker Belford became 'Ali', and Lyon 'Said bin Abdulla'. It was further announced that they were Mamelukes, or mercenary Moslem soldiers from Cairo.

Lyon and Ritchie

On March 22nd 1819 the Mission started from Tripoli in the company of Mohammed el Mukni. The travellers had by now spent nearly all their funds, and even the small supplementary sums provided from Lyon's own pocket were swallowed up in purchases for the journey. Nor did Ritchie seem clear about what additional funds might be received from the Colonial Office, nor even how, if any were received, they were to be paid. The problem of how they were going to set up a vice-consulate and live for a considerable period in Murzuk, does not seem seriously to have occurred to either of them. Ritchie communicated the financial details of the Mission to no one, and Lyon's belief in his leader and his extreme diffidence about questioning him, prevented him from learning the truth. If he had had a sight of the trade goods which Ritchie kept locked up, and which Lyon believed could be sold to defray their expenses in the Fezzan, he would have been deservedly perturbed.

In the company of el Mukni and a strong guard of Tripoli, soldiers, the journey across the Sahel, the mountains of Gharian the stony surface of the *hammada el hamra*, the great basalt hills of the *jebel es soda*, the sand slopes of the *ramle el kebir*, and finally the flat plain leading to Murzuk, was made without incident.

On May 4th they reached the outskirts of the capital, where, according to custom, a ceremonial entrance was made through the gates.

> Having shaved, washed and adorned ourselves in the finest clothes which we had at hand, we started [wrote Lyon]. Mukni, however, unwilling that his new Mamelukes should be less fine than his own people, sent for two splendid *bournouses*, which he lent to Mr. Ritchie and myself, for this grand occasion, making us ride on the right and left of him. . . .

In this manner, preceded by drummers, pipers and dancers, they entered Murzuk.

Murzuk in 1818, in spite of its importance as a trading centre and administrative capital, was a town of no more than 2,500 inhabitants, mostly negro. It lay in the flat plain surrounded by a girdle of crumbling mud walls with gates, its low buildings clustering round the high Sultan's palace. One main street only divided the town, and this wide open space served as market place, storehouse, and *mukef*, or tethering place for slaves and animals. Beyond the gates lay a few oases of date palms, crowded round pools of brackish water, from which at nightfall rose clouds of anopheles mosquitos the carriers of malarial fever. In the town also, there were several similar pools of rather salty water, which as Lyon no doubt correctly guessed, 'promote the advance of summer fevers and agues'. Of such fevers, twenty years earlier the traveller Hornemann's German companion had died.

The lack of foresight and preparation which characterised this expedition, soon began to show itself. They were barely settled in the house provided for them by Mukni when Lyon, probably from water impregnated with gypsum, was attacked with severe dysentery which confined him to bed for twenty-two days and, as he wrote, 'reduced me to the last extremity'. He had no sooner begun to recover when 'Mr. Ritchie fell ill, and was confined to his bed with an attack of bilious fever, accompanied with delirium and great pain in his back and kidneys. . . . When a little recovered, he got up for two days, but his disorder soon returned with redoubled and alarming violence. He rejected everything but water and, excepting for about three hours in the afternoon, remained either constantly asleep or in a delirious state.'

In these conditions, their remaining money soon ran out, and they found they could get no credit, for Mukni, who had expected further presents and money from them, on seeing their true predicament, deserted them and they could barely subsist. 'For six entire weeks', wrote Lyon, 'we were without animal food, subsisting on a very scanty portion of corn and dates. Our horses were mere skeletons, added to which, Belford became totally deaf, and so emaciated as to be unable to walk.'

The goods Ritchie had brought from England for sale, but which he still refused to be allowed to be sold for food, now proved on being opened, to be of the most extraordinary nature. In one chest there was 600 pounds of lead, in another a camel-load of corks for mounting insects, in a third a quantity of arsenic for killing the insects. Of trade goods there were very little. In his moments of lucidity, Ritchie still insisted that nothing, not even gunpowder of which they had a quantity, should be sold for food. They must await the arrival of the funds from London for which, as far as now can be ascertained, he had made no proper provision.

In this state, neglected by the Fezzanese, and treated with an indifference only occasionally lightened by those flashes of pure altruism and kindness which all travellers have found to lurk in the recesses of the oriental character, they suffered through the hot summer, concerned only with the struggle to keep alive. In July, Mukni's great slave-raiding party left for the South without them. The cooler weather brought some relief, and Lyon was able to get about and make notes on the language and customs of the country. A little more food now became available, for Mukni, who had returned, began to fear that reports of his behaviour might reach Tripoli. Although Lyon and Belford were frequently prostrated by fever, Ritchie it was clear, was slowly dying. Even in his extremity he would not allow Lyon to sell a few trifles to get him some comforts. By November 20th he was now desperately ill, and his two emaciated companions strove endlessly to keep him alive.

'On the 20th', wrote Lyon, 'we got a fowl, of which we made a little soup for him. The broth which Mr. Ritchie drank was the first nourishment he had taken for ten days, though we used all our endeavours to prevail on him to eat. He said he felt much revived by it, and turned round to go to sleep. I placed my bed at the entrance of the room and remained watching him. He seemed to breathe with difficulty; but as I had often observed this during his former maladies, I was not so much alarmed as I should otherwise have been. At about 9 o'clock, Belford, on looking at him, exclaimed in a loud voice, "He is dying!" I begged him to be more cautious, lest he should be overheard, and immediately examined Mr. Ritchie, who appeared to be still in a sound sleep; I therefore lay down on my bed and continued listening. At 10, I rose again, and found him lying in an easy posture and breathing more freely; five minutes, however, had scarcely elapsed before his respiration appeared entirely to cease; and on examination I found that he had actually expired, without a pang or groan, in the same position in which he had fallen asleep.'

Ritchie died as he had lived, silent, withdrawn, uncommunicative. He had been a bad choice as leader to an expedition of this nature. Since reaching Murzuk he had made no attempt to make contact with the Fezzanese, had kept no notes of his observations, and clearly, while ill, had been obstinate and unco-operative. Yet no word of this escaped from Lyon. Indeed it is probable that only the loyal, courteous and obedient nature of Lyon had kept the Mission from exploding into the acrimony and personal quarrels which bedevilled all subsequent African travellers.

That night, Lyon and Belford who still posed as Mamelukes, secretly read the Protestant burial service over Ritchie's body. The next morning this curious, secretive man was given a Moslem burial in the graveyard outside the town. Almost as the last spadefuls of sand were being smoothed over the grave, a messenger arrived from Tripoli with a letter announcing the grant of another £1000 to the Mission.

Lyon's character on his chief's death shines forth as one of the most unselfish, gallant and determined of the African travellers. He was unable to touch the £1000 grant which lay in Ritchie's name, and since Warrington had never been informed by Ritchie how any moneys received for the Mission were to be forwarded, there was no means anyway of collecting the actual sum which lay at Malta. Warrington had offered Ritchie monetary facilities for use in Murzuk when the latter had first arrived in Tripoli, but that secretive man told the consul bluntly that he had made his own arrangements. Whatever these were he took them with him to the grave.

Penniless as he was, and constantly sick with malaria, Lyon was determined not to return to Tripoli without some information, on the unknown country to the south of Murzuk. He managed, by selling Ritchie's horse and other personal effects, to pay off the Mission's few debts, and collect enough supplies for a journey of a few weeks. Fever again struck them before they set out, and for ten days both lay in bed, tended with devotion by one little Arab girl. Then, armed with a *teskera*, or official pass from Mukni, they set out on horseback accompanied by a small camel-boy who knew the route. 'We more resembled two men going to the grave, than fit persons to travel over strange countries,' wrote Lyon.

In this debilitated state they reached Tegheri, a town about 100 miles south of Murzuk, where for the first time they saw members of the Tebu tribe, parties of whom had descended from the Tibesti mountains to lurk along the caravan routes for plunder. This handsome race, veiled like the Tuareg, were carefully studied by Lyon, who succeeded with his undeniable charm in becoming so intimate with them that he both did drawings of their features and made a rough vocabulary of their language.

At Tegheri however, Belford had become so ill and weak that it was clearly impossible to continue any further, and the small party turned back for Murzuk.

Lyon, freed from Ritchie's unfriendly manner, had by now won several friends in Murzuk, and his journey back to Tripoli was lightened by several gifts from new friends, among whom was a Tuareg merchant, Hatita ag Khuden, from the Ghat region of the Sahara, who was later to become so well known as a friend to African travellers. On February 9th Lyon and Belford, joining company with a slaving caravan, set out on the journey back to Tripoli.

Day after day, as Lyon rode alongside the caravan dragging its painful way across desert and mountain, driving about 1200 slaves, most of them women and children, he watched the wretched creatures flogged or left to die by the mounted overseers, and took notes of what he saw with a view to publication:

> These poor, oppressed beings were, many of them, so exhausted as to be scarcely able to walk; their legs and feet were much swelled, and by their enormous size, formed a striking contrast with their emaciated bodies. They were all borne down with loads of firewood; and even poor little children, worn to skeletons by fatigue and hardship, were obliged to bear their burthen, while many of their inhuman masters rode on camels, with the dreaded whip suspended from their wrists. . . .

At length on Friday March 24th, the caravan had its first glimpse of the sea, and the same day Lyon and Belford discerned

Warrington and some of his family riding out to meet them from Tajura. So changed with privation and sickness were the two travellers that at first Warrington did not recognise them.

In Tripoli Warrington had anxiously awaited news of the first African Mission. Through the hot summer months, no couriers went between Tripoli and Murzuk, and it was not until late in December that Lyon's letters with the news of Ritchie's death and the bad treatment they had received from Mukni, reached him. His letter of reply to Lyon contains the usual mixture of overripe sentiment, with streaks of commonsense:

With tears of sorrow did I peruse the sad and ever to be lamented news contained in your letter of the 22nd November. Poor, poor Ritchie, what would thy Country gain, could we recall thy Vital animation. Alas, we cannot, we have therefore only to accept the only Consolation for the Death of such a Man and of such a Friend. He died in the Service of His Country and for the Benefit of Mankind and such a death every Man must be ambitious of. Let God's will be done, and without arraigning the Power of the Almighty, we may regret that his Earthly career was of that short duration. . . . [Of Mukni, he added, coming down to earth solidly]. They are all damned rascals, and all that low trick and subterfuge is so deeply ingrafted in them that it cannot be eradicated. Imposition is practised from the highest to the lowest, and we must submit, and when done, with a good grace, we gain on points of greater moment. . . .

This last sentence, which contains a cardinal proposition in dealing with orientals, shows Warrington's fundamental shrewdness, a shrewdness not always present in his behaviour.

A more sober letter went off the same day to Lord Bathurst in which he gave generous praise to Lyon's behaviour:

That Gentleman has had a Painful Duty to perform and he has executed it with that unremitting and kind attention to the dictates of Friendship during Ritchie's long Illness, and which is only to be equalled by the Indefatigable Zeal which he has manifested in his Public situation. . . . You must not, for one moment, attribute my Gloom to any despondency in the success of the undertaking. The object certainly is to be accomplished from this Quarter, and I am proud to add that Ritchie's opinion confirms my sentiments that it is that Infernal Traffic, the Barter of Human Flesh, that shuts the avenue to communication. . . . [He concluded] In my humble opinion, it is from September to May which is the time to prosecute the Research, and if the Bashaw gives that facility which I expect and which I am certain He will, the Travellers may penetrate as far as it is necessary, and we have full time to make every arrangement with His Highness. . . .

The weary travellers were cared for with great devotion and with some skill by Warrington and a newly arrived Englishman, Dr. Dickson.[1] Although sick and exhausted from his hardships and the long journey from Murzuk, the memory of the many days and nights spent in the company of the unhappy slaves of the caravan, moved Lyon to go down and bid them farewell in the slave market. The poor creatures waiting for their sale and despatch to unknown destinations, greeted him with smiles and tears.

Notwithstanding my happiness at once more rejoining my Christian friends, [wrote Lyon] I really felt no small regret at taking leave of our poor fellow travellers, many of whom, I knew, were destined to proceed to Tunis and Turkey. Their good humoured gaiety and songs had lightened to me many hours of pain and fatigue, and their gratitude for any little benefits I had it in my power to confer, quite warmed my heart towards them.

Of all the English travellers who were now to come to Tripoli, George Lyon should be remembered by posterity as the most honest, loyal and warm hearted. He paid a last visit to the Bashaw, who was delighted with his Arabic and his knowledge of the Fezzanese dialect, and who promised to give any assistance to Lyon in his travels should he ever return to Tripoli.

On May 14th Lyon and Belford left to return home, and Lyon

[1] Dr. Dickson was the progenitor of an English family who remained for several generations in Arab countries. His grandson, was the late Colonel H. H. R. Dickson, formerly a Political Officer in Irak and author of *The Arab of the Desert* (1949).

in his subsequent book *Travels in North Africa*, was to remember Warrington with gratitude:

> I cannot omit the opportunity, here offered me, of expressing my sense of the kindness invariably shown me by Colonel Warrington, the British Consul, from whom, as well as from his family, I received the most unremitting attention. I can only sincerely lament my total inability to do justice to his friendship, evinced towards me, not only in his official capacity, but individually, and on all occasions when he had the power of serving me. . . .

Oudney, Denham and Clapperton

Lyon's account of his journeys and his observations on the geography, the peoples and the character of the country between Tripoli and Murzuk, had been studied with interest both at the Colonial Office and the Admiralty. Although he had got no further south than Tegheri, the Mission had found no insuperable difficulties in getting there. It seemed therefore that Consul Warrington's statement about the writ of the Bashaw running far into the Sahara might be true. Lyon's notes also contained the information that, according to many Arab travellers, the mysterious Niger river, whose source and head were partly the objects of the exploration, flowed both into Lake Chad and into the Nile, as some English geographers supposed. In making his report, Lyon maintained the hope that he would be allowed to lead a new expedition, this time to Bornu, which would form the centre for exploration along the river Niger on its supposed eastern course.

But, even while Lyon was on his way home, that energetic African expert John Barrow of the Admiralty, had projected and obtained support for a new expedition, which was to be launched with more funds available for its support. And before Lyon had reached London, two members of this expedition had already been chosen.

One of these was Dr. Walter Oudney, a thirty-one year old ex-naval surgeon who was at that time practising medicine in Edinburgh. He was a small man, of not very strong constitution, and his chief interests seemed to be chemistry and natural history, but his main claim on Barrow's support was that he was an ex-sailor with a very good record at the Admiralty. In the same Edinburgh street as Oudney, lived a friend, Hugh Clapperton, a Scots doctor's son, who, after serving for a time in the merchant marine, had entered the navy where he had seen much active service. He was the other choice, a tall, strong man aged about thirty-three, and Barrow described him to Goulburn of the Colonial Office as 'posessed of resources of a superior kind'.

It was at first planned that these two, Scotsmen and friends, should form the new Mission to Bornu. But, presently, through outside influence another member was added, Lieutenant Dixon Denham, a half-pay officer of the Military College at Sandhurst. He had met Lyon just after the latter's arrival in London, and determined to join the expedition, using, it is thought, an acquaintanceship with the Duke of Wellington to do so.

As soon as Denham's appointment was announced his true character began to show itself. Intelligent and courageous, with a good record in the Peninsular War and some superior skill, both as draughtsman and writer, he was also a snob, domineering, jealous, and with a tortuous streak of real meanness in his nature. He assumed from the first, because of his superior connections, that he was to lead the Mission, and wrote haughtily to Barrow that his instructions should place him 'independant of the Governor of Malta and the consul at Tripoli, except as concerns my interviews with the Bashaw'.

Whether it was Denham's aggressive personality, or his shadowy backer, the character of the expedition was now reviewed. Oudney was to accompany the Mission to Bornu, where, like Ritchie at Murzuk, he was to set up a vice-consulate and study the trading possibilities of the area. Meanwhile, Denham, accompanied by Clapperton, was to carry out the exploration to the Niger.

Oudney and Clapperton, who may have had some qualms about the new arrangements, but fortunately had no idea what they were to undergo with their new companion, left England in September 1820 and reached Tripoli on October 20th where Warrington welcomed them. It was still not clear from the Colonial Office instructions to the Mission who was the leader of the whole party, and Oudney wisely induced Warrington to set out in writing the fact that he, Oudney, was in general charge. This document contained the phrase: 'You are charged by His Majesty's Government to Conduct this Interesting and Important Mission into the interior of Africa.'

At Tripoli the two travellers were joined, at Warrington's request, by the son of a friend of his in Malta, John Tyrrwhit, who the consul decided should replace the dead Ritchie as a vice-consul at Murzuk. Contemplating this pleasant trio round his dinner table, Warrington enthusiastically told the Colonial Secretary: 'I never saw Men better calculated for the Undertaking'.

Denham arrived in Tripoli on November 19th carrying a copy of his instructions from the Colonial Office. These, based on those already given to Oudney and Clapperton, after stating that Oudney was to remain at Bornu, where he was nominated 'His Majesty's Vice-Consul to the Sultan of Bornu', instructed that Denham and Clapperton were to 'explore the Country to the Southward and Eastward of Bornu, principally with a view of tracing the course of the Niger and ascertaining its Embouchure'. Although Clapperton was to travel as Denham's assistant, it was to be 'without any reference to his Relative Rank in His Majesty's Service'. Finally, Oudney was to make all arrangements, hold all funds, and be responsible for obtaining the permission of the Sultan of Bornu for the journeys in his territory.

Thus from the start, it was not clearly stated whether Oudney or Denham was the real leader of the Mission. There was a confusion here that was to provide Warrington with much trouble in the days to come.

Denham had scarcely been one month in Tripoli when Warrington was obliged to act as peacemaker in a dispute between him

Captain Hugh Clapperton by G. Manton

Dixon Denham by T. Phillips

Captain Alexander Gordon Laing

Captain Lyon by John Jackson R.A.

and the other two. Denham showed his feelings for his companions in a letter he sent to his brother in London on April 11th. He had already annoyed Oudney by setting out in writing a march discipline for the travellers, presumably based on that used in the British army, and containing such irrelevancies for African travellers as, guard duties, ration issues, posting of sentries, punishment of defaulters, etc., and handed a copy each to Oudney and Clapperton. Oudney had rejected the document as an impertinence, which, in the circumstances, it was. Annoyed, Denham told his brother:

In the choice of my companions, I do not think His Majesty's government have shewn their usual sagacity; we are not well classed, and I have scarcely a fair chance. They are both Scotchmen and Friends, and as one of them is under my orders, and the Consul Dr. Oudney, and myself, independant of each other, no small jealousy exists on their part, and to push me off the stage altogether would be exactly what they wish. [Clapperton he described as] vulgar, conceited and quarrelsome, [Oudney as] this son of War, or rather of Bluster, completely rules, therefore any proposition from me is generally negatived by the majority.

He did not add that any proposition from him was usually couched in such domineering and objectionable tones as to incense his companions.

There were the inevitable delays in the departure of the Mission, and constant visits to the Bashaw. The Colonial Office had provided Warrington with a substantial sum of money as a gift to the Bashaw, in the mistaken belief that he would use it to collect a party of soldiers to escort the Mission to Bornu. Warrington, wisely knowing his Bashaw, only handed over a part of this sum, and his foresight proved correct, for as the weeks passed with renewed but empty promises from the Bashaw, it became obvious that he had no intention of spending the money in recruiting escorts for the Mission, but was awaiting the annual visit of the Bey of Fezzan, with whom, on his return, they might go free of cost. But the new Bey, el Ahmar, showed no sign of appearing, and in March, the Mission feeling that the summer months might be frittered away in Tripoli while their funds gradually diminished, decided to take the risk and travel to Murzuk alone.

They had now another addition to the party, a shipwright from Malta called Hillman, who was to construct the boat in which to navigate the Niger. When they left Tripoli therefore, in the second week of March, they consisted of five Europeans. Travelling as Christians and in their own clothes, and bearing a *teskera* from the Bashaw, they made the journey without difficulty reaching Murzuk early in April.

Here to their chagrin, they found that the Bey, al Ahmar, had still not left for Tripoli, and that therefore he would be absent for some months, gathering supplies and forces for the slaving expedition they had hoped to accompany to Bornu. This was disastrous news, for Lyon had stressed to Denham the danger to health of a long stay in Murzuk, with its noxious pools of stagnant water, breeding fever.

Denham, who seems to have had a greater fear of illness than the others, now proposed that he should return to Tripoli to see whether he could not bring pressure to the Bashaw to provide the escort so they could proceed on their journey. This had become even more urgent, since the Bey of Fezzan who was just about to start on his journey to Tripoli, had forbidden them to leave the Fezzan during his absence and withdrawn all travelling facilities from them, including camels.

Oudney and Clapperton fell in with Denham's idea enthusiastically. They may even have encouraged his fears of illness, in the hope that he would not return. 'His absence', wrote the sailor, Clapperton, to Barrow, 'will be no loss to the Mission, and a saving to his country, for Major Denham could not read his sextant, knew not a star in the heavens, and could not take the altitude of the sun.'

After Denham's departure Oudney and Clapperton set off on an exploration to the west of Murzuk. A fortunate occurrence helped them in this enterprise, which was of some danger, since the country round Ghat west of Murzuk was the *dira* of the Ajjer

Tuareg, through whose territory no writ of either Bashaw or Bey was able to run. It will be recollected that Lyon in his last days in Murzuk, had been befriended by a Tuareg chief called Hatita ag Khuden. Lyon had promised this man an English sword and had given it to Denham. Just before his departure for Tripoli, Denham had observed a tall man veiled like a Tuareg, and with large brilliant eyes, watching the British house from a distance. Denham had hailed him, only to find that he was, in fact, Hatita. The Tuareg had been delighted with the sword, and it was his company as guide and protector, or *dalil*, on the way to Ghat that had made possible the journey to Oudney and Clapperton.

Denham returned to Tripoli to find no change in the situation. The Bashaw still insisted that the Mission must not make any attempt to reach Bornu without the Bey's assistance. The Bey had not yet reached Tripoli himself, and would be at least six months there when he did arrive. This meant that no move could be made from Murzuk for a long period.

This news determined Denham to hurry back to London, ostensibly to report on the situation to the Colonial Office, but in reality, as a letter to his brother shows, to get his own military rank raised to Lieutenant-Colonel, and to obtain a new instruction clearly appointing him as leader of the Mission. He found a small French ship starting for Marseilles, and this, in spite of Warrington's protests, he sailed in.

The Bashaw now had one of his characteristic changes of heart. A Fezzanese notable and merchant, Abu Bakr Bu Khallum, (invariably called by Warrington and the others 'Buckaloom') with an escort of about three hundred men, was about to return to the Fezzan, and from there continue on to Bornu. He was leaving Tripoli shortly, and agreed for a sum of money, shared with the Bashaw, to escort the Mission from Murzuk to Bornu.

Warrington, who was ready to find the money, wrote in haste to Denham then in quarantine at Marseilles:

> This morning the Bashaw has offered to send Buckaloom, with One hundred Horse and One hundred Infantry to convey the Travellers to Bornou etc., provided we give Him Ten thousand Dollars. The

escort to leave Tripoli in fifteen days after the Payment of the Money, and Mourzouk in Two Months from the same date. It is a most material and certainly most Important point gained. . . . Therefore, the moment you receive this, I suppose you will return from Marseilles immediately, and with your usual activity and zeal, will join them at Mourzouk.

Denham now realised that he must return, but before doing so fired off a couple of vicious letters to Bathurst at the Colonial Office, and to his brother Charles Denham.

If he had hoped by these letters to denigrate Oudney and Clapperton, and so get the appointment to command the Mission with a rise in rank, he failed. The Colonial Office was quick to send back a reprimand expressing Lord Bathurst's surprise:

that you should have felt yourself warranted in leaving Tripoli at a time when you could most usefully have assisted H.M.'s Consul General in completing the final arrangements for your departure into the interior of Africa; nor can his Lordship understand the grounds upon which you seem to have imagined that your presence in this country would have advanced the interests confided to your charge. . . . [As to Denham's unpleasant remarks about his companions,] Lord Bathurst has felt considerable regret at the general tone of your observations; and, although his Lordship will be willing to make some allowance for the feeling of irritation which prompted you to leave Tripoli, and for the haste in which your letter was written, yet he feels himself called upon to caution you most earnestly in future not to allow yourself to yield to angry feelings and impressions which, if not restrained, must have the effect of disturbing the harmony of your party and of extinguishing the mutual disposition to amicable co-operation, without which the wishes and expectations of H.M.'s Government must be frustrated.

With this flea in his ear Denham hastened back to Tripoli to join Bu Khallum's caravan. Meanwhile, doubtless from Warrington, the news of his attempted journey to England reached his companions now back in Murzuk. Both Oudney and Clapperton and even the simple Hillman, were astonished. 'What', enquired Oudney, in reply to Warrington's news, 'has taken Major Denham to England. He has not written a word on the subject to Murzuk . . . I do not know how he can exculpate himself, or look us in the face, for leaving the Mission at a time when its objects were so near being accomplished.'

Denham felt no such qualms, and by the end of September was on his way back to Murzuk with Abu Bakr Bu Khallum. A letter from Warrington to Oudney preceded him, and Oudney, sick with the endemic Murzuk fever, and weakened by the incipient consumption from which he was later to die, wrote back in a mood of resentment:

For my part, I have never borne so much from any Man as from him, and all for the sake of Peace—it is not my disposition to be quarrelsome, on the contrary, to live in harmony with all men, and thank God, I have always been able in a great degree to do it, except with him. Had I known the Man, I would have refused my appointment . . . [Then, with a change of heart—for he was an honest and kindly man—he concluded] Destroy this, it may be considered spleen, Envy, or some of the evil passions proceeding from a mind weakened by weakness. Take no notice of it, I beg, but always have in Mind that 'a Snake often lies concealed under the Grass'.

Warrington watched Denham's departure for Murzuk, with a misgiving that he later enlarged on to the Colonial Office in an anxious letter sent off in November:

The Hostile disposition existing in the Southern Mission, [he explained] was due to the jealousy existing between Oudney and Dehnam. Probably the Breach has been widened by various paragraphs in the News Papers, saying that the Mission is under the Immediate direction and auspices of the latter. [He added, gloomily] impossible to reconcile these Gentlemen, and I should strongly recommend that Lt. Clapperton should be attached to Dr. Oudney. They are Countrymen, very Old Friends, and Dr. Oudney has undoubtedly the most commanding Influence over Lieut. Clapperton. Major Denham is of a difficult cast oʒ character, and is more a Man of the World.

In a further letter in December, he added:

The Great Bone of Contention appears to me a jealousy as to whom the Mission is confided to. I think the Orders and Instructions speak for themselves, which clearly shew that Oudney and Denham are distinct and Separate, it being the duty of the Former from his Official Appointment to afford every facility and to give every assistance to the latter. . . .

The Colonial Office, perhaps torn between Oudney's prior claim to leadership, in point of time, and Denham's, in point of influence, now suggested that a change should be made in the composition of the expedition. Clapperton was to come under Oudney and his place, as Denham's aide, was to be taken by the young Tyrrwhit, and Warrington wrote hopefully to Denham in March 1823 to say that the Colonial Office had made these changes, authorising Tyrrwhit to join him. It was typical of Denham that he accused Tyrrwhit of being only attached to him as a spy for Warrington.

In this unhappy atmosphere of dissension, the Bornu Mission left Murzuk in November with Bu Khallum's caravan, to which were attached a number of merchants from Tripoli and Socne under the protection of the armed escort.

Clapperton, whose naval skill in map-making was abundantly praised by later travellers, was soon at loggerheads again with Denham who seemed incapable of even the smallest courtesy to his companions. The new dispute resolved itself into a series of written notes passed between the tents of the party during their nightly halts. Denham in peremptory terms, had demanded that Clapperton should pass over to him the daily results of his observations on longtitude and latitude. Clapperton, who, under the stress of the journey was becoming increasingly obstinate and difficult, wrote in reply:

You take upon yourself a great deal to issue such orders, which could not be more imperative, were they from the Horse Guards or Admiralty, you must not introduce Martial system into what is civil and scientific, neither must you expect from me what it is your duty to execute. . . .

This must have infuriated Denham whose knowledge of the use of sextants and compass was very limited, and whose own observations on areas which he covered alone, were found by later travellers to be wildly inaccurate. The trouble about all these constant disputes, many of them trivial in the extreme, is that the persons involved insisted on sending copies to Warrington in Tripoli, who was expected to forward them to the Colonial Office.

By mid-February when the caravan had reached Kukuwa, relations between Denham and Clapperton had reached breaking point. On April 11th Denham addressed a long letter to Clapperton, in which he rehearsed a series of accusations about Clapperton's bad behaviour, both to the servants of the Mission, to whom he was alleged to have been rude and violent, using 'offensive abuse and degrading epithets', and to Bu Khallum, 'in my presence insulted, his Officers abused', etc. It is quite possible that Clapperton, an ex-merchant sailor, used to the hard discipline and violent epithets of the sea, did swear and curse more than was normal, especially under the strain of travel. But in the opening paragraph of Denham's complaint, there occurred a curious sentence, referring to Clapperton's 'impropriety of conduct, both public and private'.

At a loss as to what this reference could mean, Clapperton handed it to Oudney and asked for his written opinion of its contents. Oudney instantly sprang to his friend's aid and next day wrote in reply:

> You have requested my opinion on a letter from Major Denham, containing accusations highly prejudicial to your character. I feel glad I have witnessed most of them and can place them in a light totally different from him. How your conduct, public or private, has or will tend to injure the interests of the Mission, I am at a loss to conceive. . . . In concluding, I cannot but express my indignation at the vileness of the letter. . . . It indicates a mind void of every drop of the milk of human kindness, a mind that hordes [*sic*] its venom to sting when it may find an opportunity.

The venom stored up by Denham was now about to appear. He had arranged at Kukuwa to go with Bu Khallum on a slaving expedition to Mandara, although this was against orders from the Colonial Office. Before he left, he explained somewhat hurriedly that what he meant by Clapperton's impropriety of conduct . . . private was the fact that it was known that Clapperton had committed buggery with one of the Arab servants. Oudney and Clapperton were aghast, and Clapperton asked Oudney to make an immediate investigation, while Denham, having planted his poison, disappeared westwards in the wake of the slaving party.

The result of Oudney's investigation, in which he was helped by Hillman, was almost foregone. The evidence of everyone in the party was that the rumour had been put about by an Arab servant whom Clapperton had dismissed for inefficiency. Most of the camp servants, including Hillman, had heard the rumour and dismissed it as absurd rubbish. Denham had heard it and stored it up. A shower of letters now descended on Warrington:

No one [wrote Oudney,] that knows Clapperton, will ever listen to such a charge against him . . . the whole has so much improbability that the most disinterested would pronounce it a Vile, Malicious report. . . . Your judgement will direct what is necessary to be done, whether to investigate more into the business, or let the matter rest.

Warrington was equally appalled and felt it incumbent on him not to let the matter rest. He forwarded copies of all the letters to the Colonial Office, with a covering letter, written November 4th 1823, in his accustomed style:

It is indeed painful to be under the necessity of referring to a Subject which must be as disgusting to you to read, as it is to me to write. . . . A more Infamous, diabolical Insinuation was never before resorted to, and I have not the smallest hesitation, in the Presence of my God, to say that it is false, malicious, and conspiring against the future Happiness of an Individual. . . . Lieutenent Clapperton, I know little of, but in that little, I would with my life answer for Him that he would never disgrace Human nature by such foul and damnable Conduct. Dr. Oudney acquits him, the Examination acquits, and Mr. Hillman acquits him. . . .

The Colonial Office was quick to reply that after a careful study of the documents provided, no suspicion whatever attached to Clapperton's character. On the other hand, if Denham had evidence of any other nature, it was his duty to give it immediately.

He must either explain the insinuations he had made against Clapperton, and substantiate them, or return at once to England. If, on the other hand, Denham would disassociate himself from the charges, 'Lord Bathurst has only to express his hope that the whole of the discussion may be buried in oblivion.'

A copy of Warrington's letter to the Colonial Office about the affair had now reached Denham, who, realising he had gone too far, made a quick move to extricate himself. In a letter to Warrington of May 10th 1824, he wrote that he himself had always believed the accusation to be 'a very wicked and malicious falsehood', but, characteristically, he could not help adding that the report arose from Clapperton's 'constantly associating with the lowest Arabs'.

He concealed from both Oudney and Clapperton the fact that he had made this official disavowal, thus leaving Clapperton unaware that he had been cleared of the accusation, and labouring under a continual burden of uncertainty. Warrington was soon to notice this omission, and he administered a rebuke to him in a letter of August 18th: '*You acquit him*, and being persuaded of his Innocence, it is to be lamented that you did not communicate that opinion to Dr. Oudney and Lieut. Clapperton. It would have saved them much unhappiness. . . .'

But Clapperton's unhappiness was Denham's revenge; and even after receiving this reprimand from Warrington he made no attempt to apologise and relieve Clapperton's mind. Even after Oudney's death, when the two men continued for months in the close relationship of solitary travel on their return route to Tripoli, he kept silent. It was an unforgivable act of cruelty and meanness.

But meanwhile, amid all these personal strains and stresses, the work of the Mission had to go forward. From Murzuk, accompanied by the Bashaw's escort, they had followed the old Garamantes road, now lined with the bleached skeletons of slaves. It was not long before they had found what Oudney had always suspected, that the escort was of more trouble than use, and that without it, they would have been much better off. The people of the oases, the *harateen*, or freed slaves who were implanted to keep the wells working, were friendly to the caravan provided the dues on which they lived were paid. The main trouble arose from the proclivity of the escort for leaving the line of march, and dashing off on excursions to capture slaves.

As has been shown, it was at Kukuwa that the incident between Denham and Clapperton occurred, and Denham had left on the slaving expedition with Bu Khallum. The Sultan of Bornu, Mohammed el Kanemi, in whose territory they now were, was friendly, but he did not want to take the responsibility of allowing them to continue on into the dangerous territory further south. He did however, give a reluctant permission for Oudney to turn westwards and take the five-hundred mile route to Sokoto.

In December, having spent some months in the Kukuwa region where they explored a part of Lake Chad, Oudney and Clapperton with some Arab merchants, took the road to Sokoto. Oudney had caught a severe cold, and had noted in a letter home that he had a 'disagreeable and suspicious affection of the chest'. As a surgeon he probably suspected what this was, and as his weakness daily increased, he seemed to become resigned to the inevitable. With indomitable strength he kept on his feet until almost the last moment. Clapperton, his old friend and Scots neighbour, was fortunately with him at the last. On the morning of January 12th 1824, at a town called Murmur, Clapperton helped Oudney to dress and later wrote:

> He ordered the Camels to be loaded at Daylight and drank a Cup of Coffee. . . . When the Camels were loaded, with the assistance of His Servant and I, he came out of his Tent. I saw then that the hand of Death was upon Him and that he had not an hour to live. I begged Him to return to his Tent and lay down, which He did and I sat down beside him—he expired in about half an hour after.

Clapperton, much grieved, buried his companion at Murmur and resumed his march to Sokoto, which he reached in mid-March. He could proceed no further without the Sultan's permission, and after drawing a map of the area he returned to Kukuwa. There he found Denham returned from his slaving expedition, and, though now almost alone, they still did not meet but exchanged information by letter.

Clapperton arrived back in Tripoli in February 1825. On arrival he immediately wrote a formal letter to Warrington asking him to open an examination of the charges Denham had made against him of homosexuality. His comments on hearing from Warrington that Denham had, months earlier, withdrawn the charge without informing him, are not on record.

Denham now returned, and with Oudney dead, went to London to write the official account of their Mission for publication. In this he not only attempted to cut out all of Oudney's interesting and useful report of the journey made to Ghat, but he watered down the contributions of both Oudney and Clapperton so that anyone reading the report would surmise that the whole expedition had been carried out by himself. Here and there he interlarded the narrative with severe and unjust criticism of his companions.

It was fortunate that John Barrow of the Admiralty, and the publisher of the book, John Murray, read the manuscript carefully before publication. They soon discovered the interpolations and excisions. Barrow thereupon not only reinserted the valuable contributions of both Oudney and Clapperton, but cut out all Denham's criticism. Readers were thus enabled to assess the true worth of the travels carried out by this first Mission to Bornu.

Within a space of the next seven years, both Denham and Clapperton were to follow Oudney to African graves; the former at Sierra Leone, the latter at Sokoto. In dismissing Denham from this narrative, it is difficult to dissent from the verdict of a noted historian of African travel:[1] 'It remains difficult, in the checkered history of geographical discovery to find a more odious man than Dixon Denham.'

Nevertheless, in spite of sickness, personal dissensions and death, this ill-assorted party which formed the first Bornu Mission had made a considerable addition to knowledge of central Africa.

[1] E.W. Bovill, Ed. *Missions to the Niger.*

Though they had failed to trace the source of the Niger, they had filled in some blank spaces on the map, chiefly owing to the accuracy of Clapperton's surveys. They had also shown that the writ of the Bashaw of Tripoli did indeed run to Bornu, though not beyond; that the long and difficult Sahara caravan route was passable by Europeans without much danger, and that beyond it lay important towns, advanced civilisations of Africans, and great entrepôts of trade.

In attaining this knowledge, Denham in his book paid Warrington a compliment that later travellers were to repeat:

> Of this gentleman it is not too much to say that by his cheerful and good-humoured disposition, his zeal, perseverance and extraordinary good management, we owe, in a great degree, that influence which England possesses with this government, far beyond that of any other of the Barbary powers. . . . He stated broadly to the government at home, that the road from Tripoli to Bornu was as open as that from London to Edinburgh; which, with a small allowance for Oriental hyperbole, was found to be true.

Gordon Laing and Emma Warrington

Even while the surviving members of the Bornu Mission were making their way back to Tripoli, a new project for exploration of the Niger regions was already being mounted in London. The Bornu Mission had clearly shown that the western caravan route through Murzuk, Bilma and Kukuwa, was open, though the Sultan of Bornu was not anxious to promote further travel beyond his territories, for reasons of security. But there was a second caravan route from Tripoli further west, which passed through the markets of Ghadames and Insalah, and led to that supposed great entrepôt of trade, Timbuktu. Lord Bathurst had now reverted to the plan, first put forward by the African Association, to promote a search for the source of the Niger from this route, using Timbuktu as the centre of exploration. This was a much more dangerous route than the Murzuk—Kukuwa route; water was scarce, fodder for horses and camels almost non-existent, and the caravan track passed through areas of desert continually being raided by tribes of the uncontrolled Tuareg nomads. But it was remembered that the Tuareg chief Hatita, the friend of Lyon to whom Denham had carried the elaborate sword, had once made a promise to take Oudney in complete safety to Timbuktu. It was hoped that the new traveller could make contact with Hatita, who came periodically to Tripoli, and use him as a guide through the dangerous area of the route.

Another Scotsman, Gordon Laing, a young and ambitious soldier from Edinburgh, had been selected to make this journey. He had already, while serving as a regimental officer in Sierra Leone, made several useful journeys into the interior of west Africa, during which, to quote his biographer,[1] 'he had shown himself to have all the essential qualities of an explorer'. In fact during these journeys, he had proved conclusively that the Niger was not a part of the Nile. It was a discovery that had brought him to the notice of the Colonial Office, and led to his present selection to make the hazardous journey to Timbuktu.

Gordon Laing arrived in Tripoli in August 1825. Young, good-looking, with a distinguished record and a distinct charm of manner, he was made warmly welcome by the large Warrington family at their house in the *menshia*, now, on account of its beauty, known as the English Garden.

Warrington's family at this date consisted of Mrs. Warrington, seven sons and three daughters, a fourth daughter had died in 1815. How this large family crammed into the five bedrooms of the house in the *menshia*, is not explained by Madame de Breughel, who during this period was a frequent visitor there, but somehow, the young Gordon Laing was given room. It was a wild household; though it was stern and puritanical in some things, Warrington allowed an unusual freedom in others. The benevolent, but sharp, eye of Madame de Breughel noted this: 'There was no question of discipline, order or rules. Everyone did what he

[1] Robert Chambers. *Biographical Dictionary of Eminent Scotsmen.*

wanted, and, like the proverb, "every horseman wanted to be Captain. . . ."'

In this atmosphere Gordon Laing met the three Warrington daughters—to quote Madame de Breughel again—'Jenny, a big, strong girl of about twenty-five . . . Emma, thin and of medium height, and Louisa.' It is regrettable that so little is known about Emma, for her short, sad life was to be filled with romance. Perhaps on rides over the rolling sands of the *sahel* and the cool green lanes of the *menshia*; or perhaps in the lovely surroundings of the six acre English Garden, where peach, pomegrante, lemon, almond and jasmine trees wound among the ruined marbles of Roman and Greek goddesses brought from Leptis Magna, Gordon Laing fell in love with Emma Warrington.

While, for reasons which will be seen, the arrangements for Laing's journey hung fire in Tripoli, Laing at length approached Warrington and asked for the hand of Emma. Warrington liked Laing. He had written in a letter in May: 'I am quite delighted with Major Laing—His talents are conspicuous, his zeal unbounded, his gentlemanly manners and honorable conduct I am certain will be duly estimated in any quarter of the world.'

But to approve a hasty marriage for his daughter to one who was shortly leaving on a very hazardous journey did not coincide with his ideas, either of commonsense, or for some curious reason, the proprieties. Under pressure he agreed that they might plight their troth, but must wait to marry until Laing had returned from Timbuktu.

Did the young people, in their precious moments together, have some prescience of the short days to be allotted to them? Did Emma feel, that with this gallant, amusing and lovable man gone from her, with only their troth plighted, she might lose everything about him for ever? Did she, in fact, hope for a child? One cannot now know.

But, let Madame de Breughel take up the tale:

> Emma fell ill, and all the family were plunged into despair. The Doctor was immediately called, and, after an examination, he concluded that it was a case of poisoning. Tortured by violent cramps,

Emma admitted that she had wished to finish her life, since her father had refused his consent to her marriage with Laing. She had therefore poisoned herself. She was immediately offered an antidote, but in spite of her agonies, she refused it until her father had given his consent to the marriage.

How true this statement was it is now impossible to say.[1] It seems clear, however, that Emma put on some sort of hysterical performance to frighten her father. In this she succeeded, but only partly. Warrington agreed to marry them in his capacity as Consul-General, but would only do so on their agreement not to cohabit until Laing returned.

As usual, he brought the Colonial Office into the affair, and one of the most extraordinary letters to lie in their files was sent off to Lord Bathurst a few hours after the marriage ceremony:

I have the honor to Inform your Lordship that Major Laing was this morning married to my Second Daughter. Although I am aware that Major Laing is a very Gentlemanly, honorable and good Man, I must allow a more Wild, Enthusiastic, and Romantic attachment never before existed, and consequently every Remonstrance, every Argument, and every feeling of disapprobation was resorted to by me to prevent even an Engagement under the existing circumstances. . . . After a Voluminous correspondence, I found my wishes, exertions, Entreaties, and displeasure, quite futile and of no avail, and under all circumstances, both for the Public good, as well as their Mutual happiness, I was obliged to consent to perform the Ceremony, under the most Sacred and most Solemn Obligation, that they are not to cohabit till the Marriage is duly performed by a Clergyman of the Established Church of England, and, as my honor is so much involved, that I shall take due care they never be for one second from under the observation of myself or Mrs. Warrington. Now, my Lord, I do not conceive a Father can possibly be placed in a more delicate situation, as long as doubts may arise as to the Power and Legality invested in me as His Majesty's Consul General to unite two of His Majesty's

[1] Madame de Breughel's memoirs, published in 1875, long after the events described, may well be confused on some points. She did however keep up her friendship with the Warringtons until long after she had left Tripoli, and Mrs. Warrington left her some keepsakes in her will.

Subjects, as Man and Wife and till that doubt is completely removed, I will take good care my Daughter remains as pure and chaste as snow.

The last fleeting hours, therefore, were passed by the young lovers under the stern eyes of Warrington and the timid eye of his wife, and 'pure and chaste' poor Emma remained, when, four days after the wedding, Gordon Laing left on his hazardous journey.

The two months delay which Gordon Laing was forced to undergo in Tripoli by the Bashaw's procrastinations sprang from two causes. The first of these was money. The Bashaw had begun to feel that in government subsidies for European travel in his territories there was a useful remuneration to offset his losses in other fields. Laing had already noted this when he wrote, after several inconclusive interviews with the Bashaw, and informed the Colonial Office:

His Highness informed me in the most unequivocal language that the door was shut to me unless I opened it with money, that without some pecuniary *douceur* he would continue to detain me in Tripoli upon the most frivolous pretences.

It was only after protracted haggling that the Bashaw at length agreed that for an immediate payment of £500, a further £500 when Laing reached Ghadames, another similar payment from Tuat, and a final sum of £1000 on his return from Timbuktu, that Laing would be permitted to depart with assistance on his journey. These sums proved to be far above the amount allotted by the Colonial Office for the Mission, and Warrington was to have a difficult time eventually explaining them to his paymasters.

The second reason for the Bashaw's delays can only be explained by the gradual decay of British influence in the Regency. It was perhaps only natural that, after ten years, during which Warrington had virtually reigned supreme among the European consuls in Tripoli, having an influence over the Bashaw part psychological, part due to the logistics of the British presence at Malta and Gibraltar, there should be a change of attitude. The Bashaw was looking for an escape from this oppressive pressure.

He was to find it, as so often before in Karamanli politics, by turning to Britain's rival, France, now reviving her interests in Africa and in particular, the Barbary States. This was first to show itself in 1824 by the appointment by the Bashaw of a new Chief Minister, Hassuna d'Ghies, educated in France and a strong Francophil.

Warrington was quick to feel this change in his relations with the Bashaw, and, with his usual honesty, reported it immediately to Lord Bathurst about the time of Laing's arrival:

> I am sorry to inform your Lordship that for several Months past I have perceived that British Influence has been on the decline with this Government; and having been constantly at work to ascertain the true cause, I fear it may be attributed to the appointment of Hassuna d'Ghies as Minister.

Warrington's personal prestige received a further blow with the appointment in 1825 of a new French Consul-General to Tripoli, Baron Rousseau. Rousseau was an official of a quality much superior to most previous French consuls. He was an orientalist, a writer speaking good Arabic, and with a facility for ingratiating himself with the oriental character. His history, which is of some relevance to later events, is interesting. He was the son of the French Consul-General in Baghdad by an Armenian mother, and grew up with a knowledge of Armenian, Persian and Arabic. In 1807 he had been appointed a consul in Basra, and subsequently served in Teheran, Aleppo and Baghdad. By nature he was a publicist and wrote copiously for the Paris news-sheets, but he was accused of plagiarism, by using the reports received by him in his official capacity from French travellers, and sending them to Paris as his own. He was an acquaintance, and soon became a close colleague of, Hassuna d'Ghies.

Warrington, hospitable as ever even to French colleagues, had been among the first of the consular corps to welcome Rousseau on his arrival, and had invited Rousseau, his wife and son, to stay at his house in the *menshia*. Alas the visit did not go down well. Féraud is alert to point out why:

M. Rousseau accepta cordialment une première invitation de son colleague. Les quelques heures passées chez son hôte l'initièrent a un genre d'existence bruyant, accompagné de libations à outrance, qui était loin d'offrir le moindre attrait à son caractère studieux et reflechi, pas plus qu'a celui de Madame Rousseau, laquelle, originaire de Corfou, et conservant le costume grec, etait de moeurs très casanières.

Surely, the chronicler's pen may pause for a moment here, while his imagination inevitably roves to scenes with Madame Rousseau in her Greek costume, sitting down at Warrington's table with Peter Lyle the Scots pirate, a frequent visitor to the English Garden, where according to Féraud, he and Warrington 'cultivent la bouteille et les fleurs'. But Féraud soon puts us right: 'Les deux consuls des lors se virent peu'.

Relations were soon not far from straining point. Warrington was naturally jealous at his loss of influence at the Castle, and particularly at the fact that Rousseau could see the Bashaw alone without an intermediary to interpret. He was afraid also, as was the Spanish consul, that Rousseau might try to assert France's traditional rôle as protector of the Christians, and so gain an influence over Warrington's Maltese nationals who were all Catholics. Most of all, he suspected rightly, that the French were trying to obtain the geographical and trade information on Central Africa which British travellers were gathering at such heavy cost.

In fairness to Rousseau, who was soon to go through a trying ordeal with Warrington, there is nothing to show that he was anything more than a rather Byzantine character and certainly a ruthless and tireless collector of facts for the press, though otherwise a normal consul carrying out the ordinary functions for his country. That Rousseau wished to keep on good terms with Warrington is evidenced by the fact that he was to ask Warrington—probably before Laing's arrival in Tripoli—for the hand of Emma Warrington for his son Timoléon Rousseau. Warrington, of course, refused.[1]

[1] Nevertheless, Timoléon Rousseau continued to love the tragic Emma Warrington. In the French embassy in Tripoli is preserved a tombstone. It is that of the unhappy Timoléon, and is inscribed: '*Alexandre Timoléon Rousseau; Mort à Tripoli, Victime d'un amour insensé. 6 Mars 1829.*'

Laing's journey to Timbuktu

Laing, with his personal African servant Jack le Bore, a Jewish interpreter named Nahum, and two African boat builders, Rogers and Harris, left Tripoli on July 18th 1825 on the first stage of their journey to Beni Ulid. Laing had changed his mind about travelling in European dress and the party were dressed in Arab clothes. To keep up the proprieties as recognised by this Edinburgh dominie's son, Laing informed Warrington that every Sunday he would oblige his party to put on European clothes while he read to them from the Scriptures.

The Bashaw had provided Laing with a *teskera*, clearing him with the authorities on the route, and supplied him with an escort of *Kuloghli* cavalry as far as Beni Ulid—in fact for the safest part of the journey.

They reached Beni Ulid on August 1st without incident, and here Laing met the Sheikh Babani, a rich merchant from Ghadames who had arranged, for payment, to travel with him to Tuat where the Tuareg Hatita ag Khuden, friend of Lyon, would meet him and escort him through the dangerous Tuareg country to Timbuktu.

At Beni Ulid a letter from Warrington reached him. It was to inform him that Clapperton was making a journey eastwards from the Guinea coast and hoped to reach Sokoto. Warrington expected that Laing would make his way thither from Timbuktu, and that there the travellers might meet. Included in Warrington's letter was one from the Colonial Office carrying advice from Clapperton to Laing.

Clapperton, who as has been seen, though efficient and honest, had a streak of jealous secrecy in his nature which made him dislike giving information to others, had been called upon by the Colonial Office to supply information to Laing for use on his travels. It was only under considerable pressure that Clapperton had done this. Laing, who, because of Warrington's obtuseness in praising Clapperton so continually to him, now cordially disliked the man, wrote back to Warrington a sarcastic reply, which since he knew Africa much better than Clapperton, was understandable:

I have received hints from the Colonial Office, furnished by Clapperton, evidently wrung from him for my guidance. They amount to this:

'I must cordially co-operate with you.' Bono!

'I must wear Turkish dress' just as 'I must be kind and patient with the natives.' 'Tis not my nature to be otherwise.

'I must not take observations secretly.'

The sun does not shine in sly corners!

'I must not speak disrespectfully of the women.'

I wonder how he found this out. I might have been a century in Africa and never made such a discovery!

'I must not meddle with the females of the country.'

Prodigious!

'I must have presents to give away.'

We need not ghosts to rise from their graves to tell us this!

Having posted these sarcasms back to Tripoli, Laing and his small party, now deprived of the escort of cavalry,[1] struck off alone across the desert. The temperature at midday was 120°F. and there was a great shortage of water on the route, which was due south instead of west to Ghadames. The desert to the west of Beni Ulid was reported to be full of plundering tribes, and it was thus necessary for the small caravan, now carrying merchandise for the Ghadames merchant Babani, to make a dog's leg of the route, going south to Tamsawa, then west to Bir Mraia, and almost due north again to Ghadames, thus circling the danger area. It was well they did so, for when he reached Ghadames he learned that a party of raiding Beduin, having news of the caravan, had waited for some days at one of the wells on the Northern route.

At Ghadames, which they reached on September 13th, they found a warm welcome awaiting them, and, more important,

[1] On August 13th, Laing's last direct contact with the Bashaw was severed when the last three of the Bashaw's horsemen left him.

Hatita the Tuareg, who was to be Laing's future guide on the road to Timbuktu. From Ghadames a series of entertaining letters were sent back to Tripoli, and to his 'Dear Emma' he wrote regularly a few lines every day.

Warrington had by now received a severe reprimand from the Colonial Office for the sums which had been advanced to the Bashaw over and above the agreed subsidy. The Colonial Office clearly had not realised the changed climate in Tripoli between the Bashaw and the British, or Warrington's difficulties in getting Laing's Mission off the ground. Some of this news he must have communicated to Laing, for the tone of the latter's correspondence began to change:

I am agitated by a thousand opposite feelings; love and tenderness one one side; disappointment and indignation, on the other. . . . No one can regret more than I do, the unhandsome rebuke which you have received from Downing Street, after all your exertions, your honourable exertions, to assist in promoting the honour and credit of the British nation. . . . Had I thought it possible that such mean, such sordid, illiberal ideas could have existed in the fabric of Downing Street, I shou'd have dropped the Mission after the first interview with the Bashaw: Wou'd to God I had—I might now be enjoying the happiness which I hope I deserve with my dearest Emma in England. . . . I have not yet opened the letter which I find addressed to me from Downing Street, so fearful am I of having my feelings wounded, so tenacious of an insult—for if they had not thought it necessary, or have not been delicate enough to spare you, an old and distinguished servant of Government—what am I to expect, I who am hardly yet known to the world. . . .

Warrington had sent with the packet of correspondence, a miniature of Emma painted by the Spanish consul, Herrador. Gazing at it, in his hot little room in distant Ghadames, Laing was seized again with foreboding—rare in his apparently ebullient character:

My heart throbs with sad pulsating on account of my dearest, most beloved Emma—you say she is well and happy—but I fear, I feel, she is not—Good God, where is the colour of her lovely cheek, where the vermilion of her dear lip—tell me, has Mr. Herrador, or has he not, made a faithful likeness?—if he has, My Emma is ill, is melancholy—her sunken eye, her pale cheek and colourless lip haunt my imagination, and adieu to resolution—Was I within a day's march of Tombuctoo and to hear My Emma was ill—I wou'd turn about, and retrace my steps to Tripoli—What is Tombuctoo? What the Niger? What, the world to me without my Emma? Shou'd anything befall my Emma, which God forbid, I no more wish to see the face of man; my course will be run—a few short days of misery, and I shou'd follow her to Heaven. . . .

But the mood of depression passed. He put away the sad little miniature, and the same evening took up his pen again and addressed himself to the dangerous task ahead: 'Excuse my agitation of this morning, my dear Consul—I often feel in that way, but thank God, I have not always a pen in my hand at the time. . . .'

In this long letter dealing with his plans, there occurs an ominous phase: 'The Bashaw's authority finishes at Ghadames'.

But he is optimistic about his future, and now saw in view the end of his journey:

I expect to go through in the following order with regard to time—Tuat, October 28th—Tombuctoo, December 10th—where I shall remain till the 1st January, when I shall cross the river, and traverse a desert of Ten Journeys, which will bring me to Wangara, and the Lake where I presume the Niger terminates—a month more, the middle of February, and I am on the coast, where, if I find a man of War, I shall instantly embark, calling at Sierra Leone and Gibralter on my return, for letters. . . .

The source of the Niger, and the non-consummation of his marriage—these were the opposing thoughts which continued to trouble his head during that long wait in Ghadames, and in another long letter about money, camel-loads for the caravan, presents for the sheikhs on the route, he pauses to ask once more if, when he returns to Tripoli, he may at last consummate his marriage with his beloved Emma:

Will you still consider it necessary to keep me to the promise which you have from me in *writing* (and which wou'd be sacred was it merely verbal) or will you absolve me from it? Do not be offended at my putting such a question—As I merely do it to prevent a disappointment which might take place was I to return to Tripoli without being so liberated; for I made a solemn promise to my Dear Emma, the night of our separation, (that melancholy night which you will well remember) never again to part from her when it shou'd please God to restore us to one another. . . . I therefore trust that you will understand me, that I ask for the sake of information and to prevent an awkward dilemma hereafter.

With these thoughts turning in his head Laing left hospitable Ghadames on November 3rd. 'At length, my dear Consul,' he wrote on that day, hastily, while a messenger waited,

I have it in my power to say that I am on the road to Tombuctoo—The camels are all loaded, and only wait for me while I give you notice of the event.

Then, after a few lines about his plans for the journey, with a poignancy which later events were to make more sharp, he added:

My mind forebodes nothing ill—I have a strong presentiment that my Dear Emma is well, but it is truly painful to remain so long in the dark. Had I but a single line from her dear hand, I shou'd mount my camel satisfied.

In that month, as evening fell over the wide wastes of the great Sahara, a large comet could be seen moving southwards across the heavens. Laing nightly watched its silver tresses as it moved slowly down the sky: 'I regard it as a happy omen,' he wrote. 'It beckons me on & binds me to the Termination of the Niger'.

Laing was now traversing the desert in areas well beyond the controlling influence of the Bashaw of Tripoli; areas controlled by raiding tribes who lived almost entirely on the plunder of travellers and caravans. Nevertheless, he succeeded in crossing it without incident in four weeks in spite of frequent pauses to plot the route on his map. On December 3rd he arrived at Insalah, with nearly half his journey finished.

News of the coming of a Christian traveller had preceded him, and large crowds were assembled to meet him—the first Christian to have been seen in that territory. It was dangerous publicity for an unprotected traveller in that fanatic place, but proved temporarily useful, for he found that a caravan was already assembled whose leaders had the strange impression that the company of a Christian would give them added protection on the long road to Timbuktu.

This was what he had hoped for, as the road on to Timbuktu was extremely dangerous for a lonely traveller, but he had scarcely unsaddled to give his animals a few hours rest, when news was brought of a sudden outbreak of fighting between the tribes of Ahaggar and Ulad Dleim across the Timbuktu route. Immediately the experienced caravan merchants decided that the journey would be too hazardous and decided not to go. Laing was thus faced with the decision whether to turn back to Ghadames and call off the expedition, or go on alone.

As he waited for better news of the road, he was besieged by sightseers, particularly women, who tried to force their way into the room in which he was quartered in the Sheikh's house. 'The women', he told Warrington, 'neither appear to labour under much restraint, nor to possess a great deal of delicacy.'

This region of the Sahara was known as Tuat, and Laing could not resist sending George Warrington his brother-in-law, a few lines telling him that from the amorous proclivities of the women, 'Tuat' was a good name for the area. Temporarily, at least, his spirits were high.

But time and money were running out. As the days passed at Insalah, with no news of any clearance of the caravan route ahead, he had to make a great decision. Should he take the extreme risk of going on alone, with the news already ahead of him that a Christian was in the area or should he turn back to Ghadames? His decision—a decision described by the historian of African travel, E. W. Bovill, as 'so splendidly courageous that in the stirring annals of geographical discovery, it is hard to find a parallel' was announced to a friend in London, in a letter of January 1st 1826: 'I have been rather taken aback and for a day or two did not exactly know what I shou'd do; but I have at length determined upon setting out, solus, in four days more. Come what will, come what may.'

On January 10th, Laing and his little party consisting of the Jewish interpreter Nahum, Jack le Bore his personal servant, the two negro boatbuilders Rogers and Harris, and a guide,[1] left Tuat, Insalah, and struck off across the encircling sand dunes towards the terrible desert of Tanezrouft (land of thirst). Their departure so shamed the caravan of Sheikh Babani still lurking fearfully at Insalah, that they decided to join Laing. For the next two weeks Laing travelled in the company of some 150 armed men and 300 camels.

He should now have felt reasonably secure, even though the Tuareg on this route must have known he was traversing it. He was apparently unperturbed when, after sixteen days of travel, the party halted at a watering place, the Wadi Ahennet.

Here, a party of twenty Hoggar Tuareg rode in and joined them their black veiled faces showing no sign of recognition of the European party. Although the Ghadames merchants were suspicious of these visitors, no warning seems to have been given to Laing who lay down to sleep in his tent, with his servants near by, on the night of either February 2nd or 3rd.

A vivid and probably fairly accurate account of what then occurred, was given many months later by Laing's camel-driver Mohammed. Laing's own version of the events was characteristically short and unemotional.

At 3 a.m. in the morning, the twenty Tuareg rose and, leaving the rest of the caravan untouched, attacked Laing's party. Mohammed reported:

They surrounded Laing's Tents and, without saying a word, fired into them, one ball striking Laing, while asleep in the side; they then rushed on the tents, cutting the canvas and cords, on which I raised myself, I received a sabre wound on the head which brought me to the ground. They entered Laing's Tent, and before he could arm himself, He was cut down by a sword on the thigh, He jumped up again and received

[1] Hatita ag Khuden, the Tuareg guide, had returned to Ghat.

one cut on the Cheek and Ear, and the other on the right arm above the wrist which broke the arm, he then fell to the ground where he received seven cuts, the last being on his neck . . . .

Thinking Laing and his party were dead, the Tuareg now rode off without disturbing the rest of the caravan.

Laing's wounds were terrible. He was later to describe them as five sabre cuts on the crown of the head, and three on the left temple from which much bone came away, one on the left cheek which fractured the jawbone and divided the ear, one over the right temple and a dreadful gash on the back of the neck, a musket ball in the hip, five sabre cuts on the right arm and hand, three fingers broken and wrist bones cut through, the hand cut three quarters across, three cuts on the left arm, the bone of which was broken, and a deep gash on the left leg.

Of his party, the interpreter Nahum was killed as was Rogers, one of the boatbuilders. The other man, Harris, was wounded and Jack le Bore, who had managed to run off in the darkness and hide, was untouched.

Grievously wounded, Laing was now set upon his camel and, relying on that iron constitution of his, was supported by his few remaining servants, not back homewards to Ghadames, but forward again on the road to Timbuktu. The caravan deserted him, for he could, on account of the nature of his wounds, only proceed slowly. Thus, surviving appalling wounds, thirst and loss of blood, he crawled slowly onwards, undisturbed by the Tuareg who thought him dead, until some time in April, he reached the shelter of a friendly Arab Sheikh, Mohammed el Mukhtar, of the Kunta Arab tribe, who gave him succour and gradually restored him to health, though warning him against continuing on to Timbuktu, since the tribes were raiding each other on the road, and would be merciless against a Christian once they found out he was still alive.

Such was Laing's constitution that, in spite of attacks of dysentery which killed both Jack le Bore and his other servant Harris, he slowly returned to health, though his right hand was virtually useless and he had to write with his left. As his health returned so did his indomitable spirit. He determined to push on to Timbuktu as soon as possible. In a letter to Warrington, sent back by messenger, in which he characteristically played down his wounds, he added 'I am nevertheless doing well, and hope yet to return to England with much important Geographical information'.

Seeing that he was determined to push on, the kindly Sheikh el Mukhtar provided him with a strong escort and this enabled him without further trouble to cover the last hundred miles to Timbuktu, which he entered—the first Christian to do so—on August 13th 1826, an historic date in the records of North African travel.

Laing remained in Timbuktu for five weeks, doing much of his researches into the Niger river after dark when it was safer for him to go out. He was received with much kindness by the townspeople, but he was constantly warned that he must not stay long, for his own safety. An order against him had already gone out from Mohammed Bello, the Sultan of the area, that he was a Christian who had come to spy out the country and must be disposed of if found.

It was this news, and his bad health, permanently weakened by his wounds, that made him send a letter to Warrington, his last, from Timbuktu, dated September 23rd:

> A very short epistle must serve to apprise you, as well as my dearest Emma, of my arrival and departure from the great Capital of Central Africa.... I have abandoned all thought of retracing my steps to Tripoli . . . , my situation in Tinbuctu [*sic*] is rendered exceedingly unsafe by the unfriendly disposition of the Foolahs of Massina, whose Sultan has expressed his hostility to me in no unequivocal terms.... He has now got intelligence of my being in Tinbuctu, and as a party of Foolahs are hourly expected, Al Kaid Bouboker, who is an excellent good man and who trembles for my safety, has urged my immediate departure.... My destination is Sego, whither I hope to arrive in fifteen days, but I regret to say that the road is a vile one, and my perils are not yet at an end....
>
> Again, may God bless you all. My dear Emma must excuse my writing . . . she is ever uppermost in my thoughts.

His plan now was to escape from this dangerous territory as soon as possible across the surrounding deserts where his enemy were watching for him. He determined that his best route was to follow the Niger river westwards, through Sansanding and Segu to the French areas of the Senegal beyond, where he would be safe. When this change of plan was known in Timbuktu, he was approached by a certain Sheikh Mohammed el Abeyd of the Berabich tribe, who controlled this route, to offer his services as guide and protector. Laing accepted, feeling that this was the least dangerous route by which to escape his approaching enemies.

Was it Emma that was uppermost in his thoughts as he left Timbuktu on September 22nd 1826, and struck westwards to where Death awaited him on the road, veiled and menacing as a Tuareg. He was accompanied only by an Arab boy, a black slave called Bongola, and members of the Berabich tribe and their Sheikh.

About two days out from Timbuktu, it is believed at a lonely well called Sahab, Laing was attacked at night by his host and protector, the Berabich. He and the Arab boy were killed as they slept and Laing's head was cut off. It is believed that some passers-by found the bodies and buried them under a tree. His belongings were seized and scattered, and his papers, his maps, the journals and valuable records of months of meticulous observation of the geography and ethnology of the countries through which he had passed, disappeared, either scattered and destroyed, or stolen.

By a curious irony the only letter from Laing's beloved Emma to survive, was written in ignorance two months after his death, and should have been sent like the others by messenger to await him at Ghadames. Let it stand as the epilogue to this poignant little story.

Tripoli 10th November 1826.

Yesterday, my beloved Laing, I had the pleasure of closing my letters and delivering them to the Maraboot and Jacob, who are now on the road to meet my own adored husband. I now begin to feel some ray of comfort. The departure of these people shews me that there is some prospect of my again being restored to happiness which for many a long month has been a stranger to my bosom. I have, this moment, by the Consul's desire taken a duplicate of a letter, which he has already sent by the Maraboot, and by that letter I see that I have been kept in perfect ignorance of all the dreadful, cruel reports in circulation about you. I do not know whether so doing was cruelty or kindness. Why let me deceive myself with the hopes of your speedy return. The month I first expected you to return in passed away, and disappointed and sickened, I looked forward to the next, but to be disappointed again. At last the dreadful truth was revealed to me and without being at all prepared for it, the blow was most severe. I heard of your wounds, of your sickness—the chill of death appeared to pass over me, not a word, not a complaint could I utter, not a tear would fall from my eyes to relieve the agonising oppression of my heart. I spent the whole night in a state of stupefaction, not understanding anything I heard. The morning dawned, the first object that presented itself to my eyes was your dear picture which hung from my neck. At the sight, my recollection returned to me, and I wept over it almost heartbroken.

Oh, my beloved, dearest Laing, alas, alas, what have you been exposed to, what danger, what suffering. To have saved you one pang, I would with joy have shed every drop of blood that warms this heart. Had I been with you in that fearful moment, my arms would have encircled you, might for some time have shielded you from the swords of those Daemons, and, at last, we might have fallen, pierced by the same weapon, our souls might have taken their flight together to that land where sorrow can never come. My beloved Laing, sorrow has laid a heavy hand on your Emma's head, and so it has on yours. Alas, Laing, how cruel, how sad has been our fate. Are we destined to endure more misery, or will a kind providence at length pity our unhappiness and restore us to each other. Will you, my own idolised husband, return to your Emma's fond arms, will you come and repose on her faithful bosom. Will you restore happiness to her torn heart?

Never for a Moment, my beloved Laing, have you been absent for my thoughts. You have always been present to my imagination, waking and sleeping. You will find your Emma the same in heart and soul, as when you last embraced her, entirely and forever devoted to her Laing. God of Heaven protect you, dearer to me than life. May he guide you in health and safety and may your own dear Emma be cold in death ere she shall again hear tidings of any evil or unhappiness having befallen her idolised husband.

Adieu, my dear beloved, May Heaven soon restore you to the arms of your adoring, devoted wife,

Emma Gordon Laing.[1]

Laing's missing papers: Rousseau flees

The Sahara has few secrets; every man is a messenger, every report, every story, passes with the speed of camels across the huge empty spaces. Gordon Laing was murdered in the third week of September 1826, and by March 1827, the first convincing report of his death reached the Bashaw in a letter from Ghadames, which he immediately communicated to Warrington. Anxiety had already been growing in Warrington's mind about Laing's whereabouts and possible fate, and he had put increasing pressure on the Bashaw to send for information. The delay in getting positive news, which in reality was caused by the Bashaw's inability to control the areas of the desert beyond Ghadames, was blamed by Warrington on the Bashaw's dilatoriness, and his suspicions of what he had earlier called: 'some foul and Underhand work' began to grow.

His suspicions as to the reason for this delay were shared by the Colonial Office, to whom, of greater importance than Laing's death, was the whereabouts of his valuable papers and journals, and it was indirectly to aid Warrington to put pressure on the Bashaw to discover where these documents had disappeared, that during this uncertain time, three British frigates separately called in Tripoli harbour.

The suspicion was now growing in Warrington's mind that the journals, far from disappearing, had been abstracted from Laing's effects and sent by secret messenger to Tripoli, and that, through

[1] Since the messenger who was carrying this letter was recalled, the letter must have been handed back to Warrington with other mail. Instead of returning it to Emma, this extraordinary man filed it with the consular archives, where it remained, the sole testimony of Emma's side of this pathetic story.

the agency of Hassuna d'Ghies, they had been passed to his friend, Baron Rousseau, the French consul. These suspicions, which were supported by several rumours about Rousseau that were common knowledge, such as his known history of a previous abstraction of geographical material from another Frenchman, and his keen interest in getting for France any information on matters dealing with central Africa, were strengthened when, in May 1827, while reports of Laing's death were still only surmise, an article traced to Rousseau, had appeared in the French journal, *L'Etoile*, confirming Laing's death and the disappearance of his journals.

In August 1828, nearly two years after Laing's murder, the negro slave Bungola, who had been with him on that last march, arrived in Tripoli, and what must be considered as the story nearest to the truth of Laing's end, was got from him by Warrington. Why he himself was spared from the swords of the Berabich can only possibly be explained by the fact that he was a slave, and therefore of no importance. His story, obviously adapted to exonerate himself from any accusation of cowardice or negligence, was that he was wounded in the attack, and so stunned that he did not see what happened to Laing's papers and other effects.

Warrington, on hearing this, was thrown back on his nascent suspicions that the valuable journals had been abstracted under orders sent by the pro-French Hassuna d'Ghies. By October of that year he was committing these thoughts to paper in a letter to R. W. Hay at the Colonial Office:

> You are aware of the Miserable Intrigue carried on here, and I have cause to suspect the French consul may have purloined the Papers of Major Laing. . . . If His Majesty attaches any importance to the Papers, and is pleased to demand their Production, we shall obtain them, I am fully certain.

The reference to the King was, of course, an attempt to get a reply which would increase the pressure he was putting on the Bashaw to extract the truth about the papers from Hassuna d'Ghies.

By now, with rumour, counter-rumour, accusation and denial, the whole consular corps in Tripoli was aware of, and drawn into, the wrangle. Warrington was supported by the Dutch consul de Breughel, the Spanish consul Herrador, and the British community. Rousseau and Hassuna d'Ghies had one strange supporter, the U.S. consul.

The Bashaw was in an unfortunate position. It is clear he had not the slightest notion of what had happened to Laing's papers, and could not understand the international importance which was attached to them. If he proved dilatory in helping Warrington it is because he did not know what to do. Warrington suspected otherwise and, convinced that the Bashaw, once a close friend of Hassuna d'Ghies, was concealing something, decided in June 1829 to do something further. He struck his flag and refused any further contact with the Castle, removing himself to his house in the *menshia*.

This now really alarmed the Bashaw, since he feared the loss of Britain's help at this moment when disturbing reports were reaching him from agents in Cairo that the French, now preparing their plans for the conquest of Algiers,[1] were proposing to the ruler of Egypt, Mohammed Ali, that he should occupy Libya in concert with their invasion.

The situation was ripe for the sort of intrigues so natural to the oriental temperament. Warrington waited in the garden while various messengers with news from Tripoli inspired by the Castle, and repeated in the bazaars, reached him. It seemed that the Bashaw had at last discovered the truth about Laing's murder. An amazing and completely fictitious story now emerged. From this, Warrington reported to Hay on August 10th, that Laing's lost papers had been 'brought down last March twelve months, sold by Hassuna d'Ghies to the French consul for a deduction of 40% on a large claim he had of 6000 francs against Hassuna'.

Added credence had now been given to this report by the actions of Hassuna d'Ghies himself. After an initial attempt to brazen out the charge against him, he suddenly fled to the sanctu-

[1] The French invaded Algiers in 1830.

ary of the American consulate, and on August 8th was smuggled aboard an American corvette, disguised as an American sailor, and left the country. Warrington dashed off a note to Hay: 'I am apprehensive, Mr. Rousseau will fly to America also, as soon as he hears his Infamous Villainy is detected.'

This seemed proof conclusive of some collusion on the part of Hassuna d'Ghies in the theft of the Laing papers. In fact, though the wrangle continued for some years, nothing was ever proved against d'Ghies or Rousseau. The Bashaw, sick of the whole affair, and nervous of the British attitude, had decided to settle it in the only manner a Karamanli understood. Summoning Mohammed d'Ghies, the elder brother of Hassan and a former minister, Yusef drew his sword, and in a melodramatic scene, threatened the old man with death if he did not confess to Hassuna's guilt. Thus threatened, Mohammed, who was aware that his brother was safe with the Americans, confessed. The Bashaw could now sheathe his sword, and summon Warrington, de Breughel and the British vice-consul Rossoni, to an audience. At this, Mohammed d'Ghies was confronted with the consuls and ordered to repeat his statement. The result was a completely vague document drawn up by the consuls and dated August 12th 1829 stating 'We, the Undersigned, declare that when, in the presence of His Highness, this 12th day of August 1829, His Highness said: "Now I think that Hassuna d'Ghies and the French consul were the cause of the murder of Major Laing." '

Apparently accepting this clearly trumped-up document, Warrington declared himself satisfied, and, as the Bashaw no doubt expected, returned to his consulate, and rehoisted his flag, which was duly saluted from the Castle with thirty-three guns. Diplomatic relations were now resumed.

Baron Rousseau lurking in his consulate, must have felt himself entangled in a web of misunderstanding, intrigue and falsehood from which he looked in vain for relief. Hassuna d'Ghies, his alleged conspirator, had fled the country with all the appearance of guilt, and no doubt it was not long before he himself was apprised of the contents of the Bashaw's declaration about

Laing's murder. He was the accredited French diplomatic representative in Tripoli and entitled thereby to all the courtesies and protection of his position. But he had lived too long in the East, among oriental potentates, to feel secure. The Bashaw in his present mood, might do anything to please the British and the rumours and reports coming out of Egypt of the French proposed plan for the conquest of Algiers must have left him intensely uneasy.

At this juncture he received a message from Warrington which rapidly concentrated his faculties:

Sir,

I shall not disgrace my pen by addressing such a Convicted Villain, and with Infamy will I brand your name to the extremity of this World. I will, however, Glory in giving you satisfaction, and, please God, sending you before a Tribunal, where Treachery and Falsehood will avail you nought, and where you will answer for your unparalleled Iniquity.

This could be nothing less than a challenge to a duel, and the persecuted Rousseau realised there was only one thing left for him to do. He stole away to the American consulate where the obliging Mr. Coxe, the consul, smuggled him aboard an American merchant ship bound for America.

The Bashaw's supposition—for it was nothing more—about Laing's murder was at once forwarded to London, where, owing to the climate of the times, it was accepted, and stirred the British government to make an official request to the Quai d'Orsay that an enquiry into the allegations against Baron Rousseau should be carried out by a French commission. The matter now reached international dimensions. Opinions in England became divided on the matter, and sections of both the English and French press repeated Warrington's charges against Hassuna and Rousseau.

The French government set up a Commission of Enquiry under Baron Monnier an experienced orientalist, and the result was included in a reply addressed to Lord Aberdeen, the Prime

Minister from the Duc de Laval, dated February 8th 1830, completely exonerating Rousseau and d'Ghies from the charges.

Nevertheless the wrangle went on, for the French Commission's findings were not acceptable everywhere. The *Quarterly Review*[1] summed up a large body of British, and some French, opinion when it wrote:

Our conclusion, we must confess, is very different as regards both these persons. So far from its being improbable, we think that it is morally certain, that Hassuna d'Ghies, by fraud and perfidy, did obtain possession of Major Laing's papers. . . . But, admitting Hassuna to be guilty, what object, it may be asked, could make Baron Rousseau so anxious about getting possession of Major Laing's journals? The ambition of publishing the contents of the said papers in his own name. It seems he had already been dabbling in oriental literature, chiefly Arabic, and has been charged, with what truth we know not, of appropriating the labours of a young man in Syria, to himself.

The Monnier Report was, however, regarded by Hassuna d'Ghies as a complete exoneration of himself, and he now turned up in England, where he had friends, and approached the Colonial Office, backed by some of the more influential of these, with a series of vague charges against Warrington. The result of these charges was the production of an official Blue Book which incorporated long statements by Hassuna criticising Warrington for many misdemeanours and for exerting an evil influence over the Bashaw. The Blue Book was never published since Hassuna, who hoped to return to Tripoli, refused to authorise what, in the events, was a strong criticism of the Bashaw himself.

After dragging on for a further two years, the matter of Warrington's behaviour was summed up and left, in the words of Lord Goderich, now Secretary of State for Colonies, to one of Warrington's most influential critics:

I am by no means prepared to say our Consul of Tripoli may not, from excess of zeal, for the service of the government, and from a very natural eagerness in the pursuit of those persons who have been the

[1] No. xlii, 1830.

cause of his Son-In-Law's death, and of the abstraction of his papers, have possibly adopted some erroneous conclusions and have occasionally acted with precipitation, although I must state that after attentive perusal of the various papers which I have received from Mr. D'Ghies, I am wholly unable to discover what is the actual offence of which the Consul is asserted to be guilty. . . .

And there the matter of Gordon Laing's lost papers and journals rests, although there have been many since who believed that the papers reached Tripoli some time in 1827. No evidence adduced by later research has confirmed or denied the judgment of the French Commission of 1830. It is most probable that Laing's murderers, the superstitious Berabich, destroyed all his papers for fear of their containing magical formula inimical to themselves.[1]

[1] The French, when they occupied Timbuktu, made various attempts to discover the truth of Laing's murder. In 1910, from information received from an old member of the Berabich tribe, a French officer dug up the skeletons of a European and an Arab boy, under a tree at Sahab. These were later buried in the cemetery at Timbuktu. Various belongings allegedly from Laing's baggage were reported to be scattered among the tribes in the area: but none was seen. Among these was a small gold trinket in the shape of a cock—perhaps a gift from Emma. No trace of his papers was ever found.

5

ALI, THE LAST OF THE KARAMANLIS

The Turks return to Tripoli

Italian historians have ascribed the quarrel between Britain, France and Tripoli, over the vanished papers of Gordon Laing, as the beginning of the final decline of the Regency of Tripoli, and the dissolution of the dynasty of the Karamanlis. But earlier, and more potent factors, were slowly and surely bringing a grinding pressure to bear on the regime. The cost of maintaining troops whose constant presence was the ultimate guarantee of security, the cumbersome and uneconomic system of government, and the high standard of pomp and luxury which the Karamanli court demanded, could not be met only from the legitimate sources of taxation and customs revenue. The traffic in Christian slaves, the rich prizes from piracy at sea, the large annual subsidies drawn from some of the maritime powers for security of their commerce—all these had slowly and inexorably been withdrawn under the pressure of European political events; and without these sources of revenue the Regency, so long as it maintained its high expenses, must have inevitably foundered. The economics of 'robbing Peter to pay Paul' must always, in the end, collapse.

Old, infirm, and now growing daily more beset by that fatal indolence which characterised his family, the Bashaw began to let the control of affairs slip from his fingers. Of his children—he had had three by his white wife—Mohammed, Ahmed, and Ali, the first had died in Egypt in 1828 having fled there from his father; the second Ahmed, who on his brother's flight had been nominated Bey du Camp or commander of the troops (and had so appalled the Italian physician, Della Cella, who had accompanied him on one of his tours of the interior to collect tribute, by his unspeakable cruelties), had fortunately perhaps, died later in the same year. This left Ali, to whom the people of Tripoli should look when they began to consider the question of a successor to the throne. On the other hand there were five mulatto sons by the negresses, and the eldest, Mohammed, was considered by the *Kuloghlis* as a possible heir to the throne. Of the Bashaw's five daughters, three, in the Karamanli tradition, were married to his chief Ministers. The closely related Palace circle was completed by the fact that the Bashaw's cousin was the Grand Kehya, the Treasurer was his brother-in-law, and the Sheikh el Beled, or town leader, was his father-in-law; finally, the Captain of the Port and Customs, was another cousin, and the commander of the Fleet was a son-in-law. With the exception of a newly appointed Foreign Minister, Hajj Mohammed Beit el Mal, none of the Ministers had either the intelligence or the will to take stock of the state of the government. All supinely seemed to await the outcome of events.

Meanwhile in the Castle, the Bashaw remained closeted among his *harim*, drinking brandy with three voracious negresses, his concubines who squandered his money on jewellery, drink, and their own dependants. Féraud draws a picture of his state: '*L'état de maison de ces trois femmes, entourées elles-mêmes d'enfants, de clients et d'esclaves, étant uniforme, il en resultait des dépenses énormes!*'

While the Bashaw behind his high walls, sat thus, leaving the control of affairs of State to an inefficient and corrupt Divan, the country began to slip back into its natural anarchy. The powerful Ulad Sleiman tribe, whose large *dira* was in the Socne area bordering on the Fezzan, had thrown up a remarkable leader in the sheikh Abd el Jelil Seif el Nasser. By the end of 1850, Seif el Nasser had succeeded in doing the almost impossible task of uniting his tribe, in a political union with the Gadadfa tribe in the area of Sirte, and the powerful Orfela tribe centred round Beni Ulid. This union of tribes, always the fear of the Karamanlis, was now able to control not only the exits from Tripoli to Cyrenaica through Sirte, but also the caravan routes coming north from the Fezzan. Emboldened by this success, Seif el Nasser despatched his brother with strong Beduin forces, to the Fezzan, where they captured the town and invested the Castle held by only a few of Karamanli's troops. The result was to cut Tripoli off from the markets of Chad and Bornu and the export market to Egypt through Cyrenaica. It was a further blow to the rocky economy.

It was at this moment, August 1830, that a squadron of the French navy, detached after the French occupation of Algiers and commanded by Admiral Rosamel, arrived off Tripoli. Its appearance was a direct result of the events of the *affaire Laing*. French prestige had been badly affected. The French consul, Rousseau, had been publicly humiliated by the actions of the Bashaw and forced ignominiously to flee the country. The Monnier report had cleared Rousseau of all complicity in the disappearance of Laing's papers and now France demanded reparation. Admiral Rosamel's orders were not to negotiate, but to impose the following conditions on the Bashaw:

1. A public retraction of the accusations made by the Bashaw against Rousseau, and a personal apology by either a son or nephew of the Bashaw to Rousseau, on his return to Tripoli.
2. The immediate payment of the large sum of money owed, for a long period, by the Bashaw to French creditors.
3. Complete abolition of piracy and the making of so-called Christian prisoner-of-war.
4. No increase under any pretext of the Bashaw's navy.

Faced by a strong naval force in the harbour, the Bashaw had no other alternative but to accept these crippling conditions. On August 11th, a new Treaty was signed under which France was to be paid the sum of 800,000 francs, part of which sum was to be set aside for the payment of the French creditors. Tripoli was also to accord once more to France her previous place as 'most favoured nation' in precedence, a question that for over a hundred years had agitated French and British consuls.

Rosamel's fleet carrying the Bashaw's submission was scarcely over the horizon, before an infuriated Warrington was demanding an audience at which he indignantly requested an immediate retraction by the Bashaw of his compliance to the French demands about Rousseau's guilt. This the Bashaw was obliged to refuse to do. Warrington, without reference to his superiors in London, immediately struck his flag and retired to the *menshia*.

The Bashaw was now in great trouble. He could not raise the large indemnity required by the French while his economy was in a sad state with interrupted communications and a tribal war. The news of the French capture and occupation of Algiers aroused his fears that the rumours of a Franco-Egyptian plot to take over Libya might be true, and could indeed take place if the English, now his only protectors, deserted him. Fortunately for his peace of mind, Warrington received an admonition from London for striking his flag without orders, and in November, was ordered to resume diplomatic relations. He did so, but, with a grim face, presented a bill for immediate payment by the Bashaw, of 200,000 francs, owing to British creditors. Warrington saw, he told the Bashaw, no reason why French rather than British creditors should be paid.

Sadly, the old man began to divest himself of the only immediate assets remaining to him—his diamonds, his wives' jewellery, his valuabl estud of horses. An additional tax was levied on the Jews and every other means of extortion was used to obtain money.

Meanwhile, Seif el Nasser's revolt was spreading, and the Bashaw's remaining white son Ali, now Bey du Camp, was in the field against him. He was an energetic and fairly successful commander, but cursed like his brother Ahmed, with a streak of ruthlessness that was his undoing. Against the tribesmen of the Ulad Sleiman and the Orfela, he had the hard-fighting and experienced *Kuloghli* levies of the *menshia*, and a few remaining *janissaries* and black guards from the Castle garrison. With these he succeeded in bringing the fighting to a stalemate in which the customary *marabout* was called in to make the peace. But Ali suspected that there had been some collusion between the *Kuloghlis* and the tribesmen in the fighting, and he had one of the *Kuloghli* leaders publicly strangled. The levies returned to the *menshia* in a state of mutiny. Their complaints to the Bashaw were ignored, and they began to fall an easy prey to the intrigues of the Bashaw's grandson, Mohammed (son of the now dead exile in Egypt) who settled in the *menshia* and announced himself as the true heir to the Bashaw.

* * *

The year 1851 opened with the Regency in a parlous state. To meet his debts, the Bashaw had not only sold all his personal assets, but, for a lump sum, had farmed out the customs revenues and, looking even further had, much to the annoyance of the citizens of Tripoli, tried to sell some of the brass guns of the fortifications.

The embarrassments which would generally have been caused by the return of the former French consul Baron Rousseau, upon which the French government had insisted, had been removed by his death in France. The new consul, M. Schwebel arrived in June, and with him, the traditional struggle between Britain and France for influence was resumed. This soon showed itself in the growing estrangement of relations between the town of Tripoli which favoured the *Bey du Camp* Ali, as heir to the throne, and the *menshia*, where the *Kuloghlis*, detesting Ali, preferred the pretender, Mohammed Karamanli, who was now gathering adherents about him in the *menshia*, including representatives of the Ulad bu Seif and other tribes.

In the *menshia*, from his famous garden, Warrington wielded considerable influence, and it was not long before he was in contact with Mohammed Karamanli, with the *Kuloghli* chiefs and with Abd el Jelil Seif el Nasser. Indeed, some of the prisoners captured in the fighting between the Bey du Camp Ali, and the tribes, who were in Tripoli, were helped to escape to the *menshia* by Warrington, and so make their way back to their tribes. The Bashaw was afraid to complain of this breach of diplomatic behaviour for fear that Warrington would press further for payments of the British debt.

How much of all this the Colonial Office in London knew is difficult to discover. The complicated rush of events, the aims and the combinations of the different parties involved, the constant changes in the political scene, must have been beyond the comprehension of the busy officials in Downing Street. Perhaps only one matter really concerned them; the Bashaw had not paid his debts to Britain.

In July 1832, British patience over the debts became exhausted.

Warrington received peremptory orders to demand an immediate payment and in the same month, Commodore Dundas with a squadron of warships based on Malta, arrived off Tripoli to enforce the request. An audience was held with the Bashaw, and an ultimatum delivered to pay the 200,000 francs within forty-eight hours.

Driven to extremity, the Bashaw now carried out an act which broke not only the rule invariably observed by his Karamanli ancestors since the dynasty came to power, but also a rule of the Sultans of the Porte. He put a tax, with a demand for immediate payment, on the *Kuloghli* military levies of the *menshia* and *sahel*. This the *Kuloghlis* naturally refused to pay and, in anticipation of trouble, withdrew themselves from the area round the city behind their walls in the *menshia*. The Bashaw was now obliged to to confess to Warrington that he could not pay the sum required. According to instructions, Warrington struck his flag, handed over the conduct of British affairs to his colleague the Tuscan consul, but instead of embarking on the Commodore's flagship as instructed and leaving the country, he retired to his house in the *menshia* on the plea that his daughter was too ill to be moved. From here he sat down to watch events.

The *Kuloghlis* had now organised themselves into a respectable opposition. The gates of the city were shut and sporadic fighting began. Tripoli, in fact, became besieged by the *menshia* as it had been, forty years ago, by Yusef Karamanli himself. One might indeed wonder as he stood on the ramparts of the Castle and looked across to the green glimmer of the *menshia*, if he remembered those days when he himself was friend of the *Kuloghlis* and of the tribes.

At the end of July, a great concourse of *Kuloghlis* and tribesmen met in a solemn conclave at that sacred spot in the *sahel*, the tomb of the great *marabout*, Sidi el Said, and publicly announced the dethronement of Yusef and the election as Bashaw of his grandson Mohammed, at the same time naming Mohammed's younger brother Ahmed, as the traditional Bey du Camp. Mohammed Karamanli signified his acceptance by occupying the

Bashaw's summer palace in the *menshia*, and simultaneously, the *Kuloghlis* opened up a bombardment of Tripoli with cannon, to which the Bashaw with no heavy armaments left, could not reply.

The position had now become unendurable for the population of Tripoli. The Bashaw's feebleness and incapacity led to a demand in the Divan for his abdication and for the enthronement of their protegé, the heir Ali. The situation was quite extraordinary. While, within the City, the new French consul Schwebel, Ali, the heir to the throne, and a large section of the leading citizens pressed for the Bashaw's abdication, outside in the palm groves, Warrington, Seif el Nasser and the leading *Kuloghlis* publicly supported the pretender Mohammed.

While this was going on, frantic efforts were being made by the Bashaw to come to terms with the *Kuloghli* forces, and various mediators were sent out to them. All these efforts were in vain. In fact, as the Italian historian Micacchi succinctly puts it:

> M. Schwebel, the French consul, and Ali Bey the Prince, both intervened to prevent any attempt at reconciliation; the Prince because he thought such an accord would exclude him from the succession, and the consul because he would regard it as a success for Warrington's policy.

At length, under pressure from Ali Bey and the French consul, a delegation of Ministers and leading citizens appeared before the Bashaw in formal audience, led by his old counsellor Mohammed d'Ghies, now restored to favour. They formally requested his abdication from the throne.

Seated simply on his denuded throne, shorn of his diamonds, his gold chains, his rows of ruby rings and embroidered clothes, Yusef, trembling with age and infirmity, received them and made little attempt to refuse. Indeed, weighed down by the problems of a disintegrating throne, he may have been relieved. The following day, August 12th 1832, a large assembly of Tripoli Ministers, divines, notables and tribal chiefs, met in the tiled audience-chamber of the Castle. Here, before the gathered Ulema, the Mufti and the Qadi, Yusef Bashaw received them, sitting again on his throne, surrounded by the remaining sons, nephews and cousins of his family. In front of him lay some of the sacred books of Islam, the 'Traditions' of Bukhari, the books of Shafi' and *Ibn Jama'ah.*[1] And here, faced by this large concourse, the old man, divested of the habiliments of royalty, pronounced in simple words a formula which, Féraud relates, touched all present, who had known the days of his greatness, with its pathos and simplicity:

> I have called you to hear from me that I am tired and wish to end my days in peace. I desire with all my heart that the Prince, Ali Bey, should succeed me, and that my younger son, Ibrahim, should be appointed his heir.

As he pronounced these words, the once 'proud, beautiful rash youth' of past memory, burst into tears. He recovered himself and approaching the sacred texts, placed his hand on the book of *Ibn Jama'ah*, and pronounced the traditional formula of abdication, following it by an oath of fealty to the new Bashaw. One by one his other sons, nephews and cousins followed him, with one exception, his son Amura who, it is recorded, refused to swear allegiance, persisting even after his father begged him. Oaths of fealty were now sworn by all the Ministers, by the Ulema, and in due order, by the leading citizens and such of the Beduin tribes who were still faithful to the throne.

Ali the new Bashaw, then confirmed all the Ministers in their previous appointments except one. His father's chief Minister, Beit el Mal was dismissed and replaced by Mohammed d'Ghies who was now back in power again.

The abdication of Yusef, and the succession of Ali as Bashaw, was received by the pretender Mohammed in the *menshia*, with a closer blockade of the City, and the consequent complete interruption of supplies. By now, the provincial towns of Zliten, Misellata, Misurata and Tarhuna had joined the *menshia* in pro-

[1] Féraud, in describing this scene, states that the oath was sworn on the book of Abu Jamra. But surely he means Ibn Jama'ah, the 14th century Qadi of Damascus who laid down the rules on Islamic succession?

nouncing in favour of Prince Mohammed as the new and legitimate Bashaw. The consular corps was divided. The consuls of Tuscany, Sweden and Denmark had followed Warrington into the *menshia*, and set up their Missions there, though how they carried out their consular duties while cut off from the capital is not explained. The consul of Portugal had fled to Malta. The French, Spanish, Sardinian and Neapolitan consuls remained in the beleaguered city.

The Bashaw in reply to the blockade from the *menshia*, now declared a blockade of the whole coastline. This was accepted as legal by the consuls residing in the city, but not by those in the *menshia*. Warrington in particular, kept up the important flow of supplies of meat and grain to the British garrisons at Malta, and from his house operated a sort of customs office. To aid him in keeping his sea communications open, the commander-in-chief at Malta sent a British corvette, which lay at anchor just off port Avena.

The new Bashaw had already sent off the usual letters to the foreign powers informing them of the change of succession, and to the Porte requesting the customary *firman* of confirmation from the Sultan. At the same time, a letter was despatched to William IV asking that Warrington be instructed to return to Tripoli and acknowledge the new Bashaw. This brought a non-committal reply from the Colonial Office, dated December 13th, stating that H.M. Consul had been instructed to remain strictly neutral in his attitude. It indicated that His Majesty's government recognised the possible legality, if not the propriety, of Prince Mohammed's claim to the throne.

Meanwhile, the fighting pursued itself in the inconclusive manner of all civil war in Tripoli, where shifts in allegiance, desertions, shortage of powder and shot, and a dozen other factors, rendered no engagement conclusive to either side. The young Bashaw, however, was showing a skill in diplomacy worthy of a better cause. By personal negotiation he managed to come to terms with the Sheikh Gouma of the powerful Mahmid tribe, the traditional ally of the Karamanlis. Gouma, who had fought and captured the town of Zavia as a supporter of Prince Mohammed, changed his allegiance to the Bashaw, and this secured the adhesion of the whole area of Zavia to the throne. A similar diplomatic approach to the Sheikhs of the Cyrenaica region, succeeded in deterring them also from aiding the *Kuloghlis* of the *menshia.*

The Bashaw's agents in Europe had also been busy. The discrediting of the British consul was necessary, to lessen his influence over the *menshia,* where he was almost running a government of his own. To do this, Hassuna d'Ghies, Warrington's old enemy and brother of the Mohammed d'Ghies, now the Bashaw's chief minister, was recruited.[1] He was appointed the European ambassador of the Regency, and some time in 1833, had turned up once more in London, and had immediately begun an attack on Warrington. From all accounts, Hassuna d'Ghies was a personable Arab, whose financial dishonesty was concealed under an attractive and persuasive manner. He already had English friends, and among these he began his campaign of denigration. The result was a series of attacks on Warrington and his alleged maladministration of his consular post, which were repeated in the *Times* newspaper, and by the Attorney General in the House of Commons. How much of the resulting noise was really a criticism of a diplomat, and how much was the result of internal politics between Government and Opposition, is debatable.[2]

It was fortunate that Warrington had friends, including a very active brother. The result of the whole affair was at length set out in a letter which the latter wrote to Warrington on January 1st 1834:

I am happy to learn the step I took in regard to the foul slander and accusations that were brought against you, met with your approbation,

[1] He was also brother-in-law of the new Bashaw.

[2] *The Times* in its issue for July 14th 1834, printed a letter under the signature 'S' (probably Robert Scarlett) which says: 'We shall hope that at last the British Government will become undeceived themselves in regard to the real conduct and integrity of the Agent in whom they have so long reposed confidence to their own prejudice and the ruin of the country to which he was accredited....

and I can assure you I have not been idle since. I have the pleasure of being well acquainted with Mr. Spring Rice, who is now down here [Cambridge] canvassing for his re-election for this Town, and as I am one of his constituents, I have had an opportunity of much conversation with him on your affair, or rather on the accusations brought against you by Hassuna d'Ghies, who, it appears is a friend of Mr. Robert Scarlett, a son of the Attorney General, and under whose sanction the charges were made, and previously mentioned in Parliament by Sir James Scarlett. Mr. Spring Rice, being Colonial Secretary, undertook to inquire into the affair, and, until after the enquiry was made, did not know any relationship existed between us; but he is a most honourable man and was determined to investigate the matter thoroughly and do all Parties Justice. Indeed, it was well for you that so highly honourable a man was in office, as you will be surprised to hear this Hassuna d'Ghies had got access to Court and had found means to persuade the highest person in the Realm that his statement was true and that through your influence as Consul, Ali Pasha had suffered great wrong as legitimate Sovereign. . . . However, I am now delighted to tell you that Mr. S. Rice says that, after a most patient and laborious investigation, he is convinced there is not a *particle of truth* in the allegation.

This news must have been welcome to the old man in the *menshia*, who may have wondered how much more chagrin he was to suffer for his long battle over the papers of his dead son-in-law and the enmity this had aroused. He must have been gratified when, in October of the same year, a private and confidential letter from the Colonial Secretary reached him, saying:

In consequence of the former communications which have taken place between us, I think it at once just and satisfactory to inform you that I have this day had a long conference with Captain Sir George Young,[1] and that he has borne the strongest testimony to your character and conduct. Should any future discussion arise on the affairs of Tripoli, this testimony of a nature so wholly unsuspected, and so highly honorable to you, shall not be forgotten. . . .

Thus encouraged, Warrington could prepare to face out another winter in the *menshia*. But now an emissary of the Sultan

[1] One of the frigate Captains who had visited Tripoli.

of Turkey arrived in Tripoli, bringing the *firman*, the Sultan's official confirmation of Prince Ali's legitimacy as Bashaw. This at once put an end to any dispute on the legality of the succession, and in December Warrington and the other consuls returned to Tripoli and once more flew their flags. Back in the *menshia*, the rejected Prince Mohammed, seeing his friends melt away, committed suicide. His young brother Ahmed flew to Malta.

Attempts were now made to settle the dispute between the *Kuloghlis* and the new Bashaw. A collective letter was sent from the consular corps to the remaining leaders of the revolt, promising that, if peace were made, there would be no reprisals from the Bashaw. This was ignored.

In order to get money for his empty treasury, Ali Bashaw now undertook a series of ruthless measures with his own family. He seized and sold the personal jewellery and effects of considerable value, of Yusef's black wives, and he ordered the Qadi, the Islamic religious judge, to remove Yusef's control over his personal lands and estates, and give them to himself, thus leaving his father practically destitute. In a letter written by Yusef's last Chief Minister, there is a sad commentary on the old Bashaw: 'As for our old Master, he has become incapable even of getting to his feet. He is no longer capable of speaking or thinking clearly. His situation would move even a stone. He is no longer anything but a shell of a man. Those who knew him formerly would say today that it is not he.'

His situation moved the old consul Warrington to call on him. In this interview, which Warrington reported briefly to the Colonial Office in December 1835, the consul found the old Bashaw living half-starved and virtually in rags, utterly neglected by the new Bashaw: 'He took me by the hand,' wrote Warrington, 'and cried like a child. He lamented that he had ever abdicated'. They were the last recorded words of the once great Yusef Bashaw, who died three years later almost unnoticed and unmourned.

For Warrington too, things had now changed. He no longer played a leading rôle in the affairs of the country. The French consul was in the ascendant with the new Bashaw. Sadly he wrote to the Governor of Malta lamenting his loss of prestige. In reply, the Governor Sir F. Hankey, wrote consolingly:

You must not mind the influence of the French Consul, but continue to go on with British affairs confined to you with the same zeal and activity for which you have always been remarkable. You say that the French consul is now Bashaw. I remember when you filled that office much to the advantage of British interests. Times will change, and you will get back to your old office, perhaps. In the meantime, my old, disreputable, Mediterranean fellow-labourer, I sincerely wish you health. . . .

Times for Tripoli were about to change, but in a manner unexpected by anyone in the Regency. French influence had been noted elsewhere than in Downing Street. On May 20th 1835, a Turkish brig arrived in the harbour carrying an envoy from the Sultan, Shaker Effendi. He bore despatches from the Grand Vizier at the Porte announcing that the Sultan, alarmed at the civil war in the Regency, was sending troops to help Ali Bashaw to maintain order and overcome the rebels in the *menshia*. Five days later, a Turkish squadron of ten warships and ten troop transports arrived. Salutes were fired from both the town, and the *menshia*, but the Turkish gunners only replied to those of the city batteries.

Courtesy visits were now exchanged between ships and shore, and when these were over, the troop transports were evacuated and 5000 troops ferried ashore, where they took up positions at the shore and land batteries of the city.

On May 28th, the Turkish commander Nejib Pasha, sent a message from his flagship to the Castle announcing a courtesy visit ashore, and inviting the Bashaw and Chief Minister aboard the flagship to accompany him officially to the Castle.

At 9 a.m. Ali Bashaw, accompanied by Mohammed d'Ghies as Chief Minister, left the Marine in a state barge, and went aboard the Turkish flagship. At 11 a.m., the state barge left the flagship once more, but those ashore could see only Nejib Pasha and Mohammed d'Ghies sitting in it. As it drew into the landing place at the Marine, the lines of Turkish troops lining the city walls and strategic points in the City, brandished their arms and shouted. Surprise was complete. The Bashaw of Tripoli by a ruse worthy of Turkish tradition, had been banished. The Karamanli dynasty, after a hundred and thirty-five years, had ended as it had begun, by a *coup de main.*

In the Castle, Nejib Pasha entered the audience chamber where no Turkish envoy had sat for a century and a quarter, the Ministers of State and Ulema were summoned and the Turkish Pasha read out to them the Sultan's new commands. Tripoli no longer held the rank of an Ottoman province; Nejib Pasha was appointed Governor-General until a new nominee of the Sultan's was appointed, and by this *firman*, he now assumed control. The Arab historian records that, with one voice, the assembled company gave the famous cry in Arabic, reminiscent of the days of Haroun el Rashid, *Semiaan wa taatan*, we hear and obey!

A day later, the *menshia* submitted, but not before Warrington was able to help some of the leaders of the revolt, in danger of their lives, to escape in a British corvette which was lying offshore.

Two days later, the new Governor-General addressed an official Note to the Consular Corps, announcing his installation, and his instructions, which were to maintain those friendly relations between the Porte and their countries, which had previously existed with the former régime:

By the present, we give you notice of our arrival here, carrying instructions from the Sublime Porte, to put an end to the disorders which, for a long time, have afflicted the country, and to govern it and its dependencies, as long as it shall please our August Master and Sovereign, the Sultan Mahmud. It is to us, therefore, that you should now in future address yourselves. Be persuaded for our part, that we are always anxious to maintain the friendly relations which happily reign between the Sublime Porte, and the Christian powers resident in Tripoli. Nejib Pasha. June 2nd 1835.

The same day, the frigate carrying the deposed Ali Karamanli, his son Suleiman, his white nephews and servants and slaves, set sail for Constantinople. Two of the former Bashaw's mulatto sons, Amura and Ibrahim, were allowed to remain in Tripoli, and a third son, also a mulatto, Osman, was permitted to retain a small post as nominal governor of Cyrenaica. The old man, Yusef Bashaw, now completely senile remained alive, in circumstances of great poverty, in Tripoli. Here, he died on August 4th 1838, so reduced in circumstances that the remaining members of his family were unable to afford to give him the usual funeral rites. The Turkish government paid, and the old man was inhumed with his ancestors in the Karamanli mosque.

Thus, in the words of Féraud 'the Regency of Tripoli, in the space of one day, became a simple Turkish Vilayet'.

The reasons for the Ottoman decision to take over the control of the Regency once more and remove the shaky régime, can be most likely explained by their growing fear of French influence. After a short and bloody war, Algeria had been occupied by the French in 1830, and there were growing reports of their influence spreading eastwards to Tunisia and so to the borders of Tripolitania. The known pro-French sentiments of the young Bashaw Ali, and his Chief Minister, and the Minister's brother Hassuna d'Ghies, disturbed the Sultan and his Divan. No doubt the powerful British Ambassador to the Porte, Sir Stratford de Redcliffe, who shared with Lord Palmerston, now Foreign Secretary in London, a fear of the extension of French influence, played a part in influencing the Turks to act decisively in Tripoli. For the same reason, an initial attempt by the Turks to get Warrington removed as consul in Tripoli for his activities in the *menshia*, was also dropped, and the old consul remained.

Warrington was to linger on as consul-general in Tripoli for another seven years. His relations with the new Ottoman administrators were to remain no more than formal in those years. But the restless, independent spirit of the Englishman who, for over twenty years had played a by no means minor rôle in the affairs of the Regency, could still burst into life. He was always regarded by the *Kuloghlis* of the *menshia* and the Beduin tribesmen as a sort of defender of their rights, and they still flocked to his house in the *menshia* for consultation. Indeed, on the appointment by the Turks in 1858 of a singularly ruthless and cruel administrator as Governor in Tripoli, whose exactions and repressions equalled the notorious Ali Burghol of former days, Warrington defied him, wrote violent protests to London, and so disturbed the Foreign Office that Sir Stratford de Redcliffe issued an ultimatum to the Porte that unless the governor, Asker Ali, were removed from Tripoli within twenty-four hours, a British frigate would remove him. It was Warrington's last appearance on the field of major diplomacy.

But, old, irritable and sometimes violent, he still held a position in the country. Apart from his constant struggle to prevent French influence from spreading into areas he still considered a British prerogative, he wrestled ceaselessly with the Foreign Office to help spread the British influence by the opening of vice-consulates all over the country. These he staffed, where possible, from his five remaining sons. Three of them, Henry, Frederick and Osman, were for years the British representatives at Murzuk, Ghadames and Benghazi. Of these, Frederick Warrington, who lingered on in Tripoli until 1880, became almost as famous as his father, but for different reasons. Brought up from childhood in Tripoli, and having spent many years in the *menshia* with his father, he spoke fluent colloquial Arabic. Added to this he had a charming and winning personality, so that Europeans and Arabs equally liked him.

Courteous and gentle, he even charmed the Anglophobe consul and historian, Féraud[1] who grew to know him well. '*N'étant jamais sorti de Tripoli depuis son enfance,*' wrote Féraud, '*il parlait l'Arabe comme un Bedouin.*' Indeed, it was in Arabic, since Féraud spoke no English and Frederick no French, that their amicable dialogues took place.

Of Frederick Warrington also the famous German traveller Barth, could write: '*Ce digne Européen, devenu Arabe, est, pour le voyageur en Afrique le personnage le plus important qui soit à Tripoli.*'

[1] Charles Féraud, the historian, had become French consul in Tripoli in 1878.

During his final years, the old consul Hanmer Warrington spent much time in his garden, leaving the day-to-day work in the consulate to his vice-consul, and occupying his time on entertaining passing travellers, and carrying on petty feuds with his colleagues in the consular corps.

A last glimpse of his famous garden—so soon to vanish that today not even the actual site of it is known—is given by Richardson the English traveller, who sought the help of the old consul on a visit to Tripoli in 1845. Riding near the sea, through the palm trees, the tumbled plots of vegetable gardens, the green patches of pepper plants and lucerne, the irrigation canals and *jabias*, the cactus hedges and sandy lanes lined with pomegranate and orange trees, Richardson reached the garden where the old consul greeted him and led him through the six acre garden: 'The choicest fruit trees of North Africa, with ornamental trees of every shape and hue and foliage—all the growth of thirty years, and the greater part of them planted by the hands of Colonel Warrington himself. . . . The fairest, loveliest garden of Tripoli!'

It would be pleasant to leave old Hanmer Warrington in his garden among the trees, the flowers and the marble statuary. But, alas, it was not to be. Time had not really mellowed that irritable and sometimes violent character. In April 1846, during a dispute with the Neapolitan consul over a trivial matter of some cigars, Warrington struck the man with his cane. A series of diplomatic exchanges, at the highest level now ensued, which proved at last too much for the Foreign Office.[1] In June 1846, in a letter from the Foreign Secretary, Lord Aberdeen, Warrington received the *coup de grace*:

I regret to perceive in the Despatches now under my consideration that your conduct, towards the Consul of a friendly Power has been, and continues to be, most unjustifiable and incomprehensible. If the conduct of the Consular Agent of any other power resident in Tripoli was such as to interfere with the rights and Privileges, accorded by

[1] The Barbary Consulates had come under the supervision of the Foreign Office in 1836.

Treaty and usage to the Consular Agent of Her Majesty, it was your duty to send a full and circumstantial narrative of such conduct to H.M. government—omitting in such a narrative those injurious personal allusions in which you have permitted yourself to indulge in regard to the Consul of Naples. I regret to be compelled to observe that it appears to me that it would be no less for your own future comfort than for the benefit of Her Majesty's service, that you should make up your mind to retire . . .

Warrington made one effort to save his post, pointing out, with perhaps some truth, 'It is no idle vanity to say that I am beloved and respected by Turk, Christian and Jew.'

But it was obviously in vain and he shortly after resigned. The government gave him a retirement pension of £900 a year. Probably because of his former debts, he never returned to England. Instead, he accepted an offer from his daughter Jane, who had married one of his vice-consuls, Thomas Wood, to live with her at Patras, where Wood was now in residence. Mrs. Warrington had long since died, and he was quite alone. The Woods were not burdened with him long. He died on August 17th 1847, and his son-in-law raised an elaborate monument to him which runs:

Sacred to the memory of Lieut Colonel Hanmer Warrington
who died at the British Consulate, Patras,
on the 17th August 1847, aged 70.
The life of this gallant officer was devoted
to the service of his country.
32 years of which he was employed,
as H.M.'s Agent & Consul General at Tripoli.
And long will his name be remembered in that land
Where the slaves and the free were equally
Objects of his protecting care
He was a kind and affectionate
Husband and Father
An unflinching friend and Noble Defender of the Rights of Man.

With the death of Yusef Karamanli in 1838, and the exile and death of Consul Hanmer Warrington in 1847, the last and certainly the most picturesque of the figures in the Karamanli legend leave the stage. Both are equally well remembered in oral tradition.

The returning Turks relegated Tripolitania administratively to the status of a mere Ottoman *vilayet*, and it was thus as a backwater of the Turkish empire, with a succession of Turkish governors and moderately discreet European consuls that it remained until 1911.

In 1911 during the course of the Italo-Turkish war, Tripoli was invaded by Italy, and subsequently annexed as an Italian colony. It remained a part of Italy's colonial empire until 1943, when, after the defeat of the Italian and German armies in the western desert, it was occupied by British troops, and placed under British military administration. (The Fezzan was placed under French control.)

In 1948, a four Power Commission was set up to determine its future status, with that of the other former Italian colonies. The result in 1951 was independence. It is as an independent country that Libya, enriched by vast oil resources, faces the world.

The first British officers who entered the Castle of Tripoli in 1943, found that it had been turned by the Italians into a museum whose principal object was to extol the achievements of the Romans—the progenitors of their own Latin past. Beautiful mosaics and marbles from the excavations at Sabratha and Leptis Magna filled the rooms where once the Karamanlis had held their courts. In a small room, near the centre of the Castle, was found a disintegrating mass of mouldy papers, piled in disorder from floor to ceiling. They were the archives of the Ottoman and Karamanli secretariats—the correspondence, memoranda, treaties, reports of more than 250 years. It was in this condition that the present writer saw them in 1947. The Libyans explained their state by relating that when the Italian troops in 1911 had occupied the Castle, they had thrown all the archives from the Castle walls into the sea. They had been rescued by a young Italian officer who found them floating in the harbour. He had no time to do more than order their rescue and retention, and thus they had remained for more than thirty years.

They have now been, with much care, examined, sorted and tabulated, and it is one of the ironies of history that the official who took on this labour in 1948 was one of the last remaining members of the Karamanli family, Sayyid Bahjat Karamanli.

Appendices
Glossary
Bibliography
Index

APPENDIX I

There is a later and somewhat curious footnote to the history of the Karamanli family.

In 1855, there arrived in Tripoli a certain James Hamilton, traveller and adventurer. He carried a passport from the British Ambassador in Constantinople, Sir Stratford de Redcliffe.[1] At Tripoli, under the guise of travelling, he made his way into the interior and got into touch with the Arab leader Ghouma, at that time in open rebellion with the Turkish authorities. He brought with him messages from the exiled Ahmed Karamanli, still living in Constantinople, the tenor of which was, that if Ghouma would lead a rising in Ahmed Karamanli's favour, the Prince might return to Tripoli with his adherents and overturn the Turks.

Hamilton was in fact arrested and handed over to Hermann the British consul in Tripoli who imprisoned him for a time before expelling him from the province. Although Hamilton seems from the evidence to have been a somewhat mentally unstable adventurer, the point of interest in his attempt to recruit Ghouma, is that in Constantinople he had persuaded Richard Burton, later Sir Richard Burton the famous traveller, to assist him.

Burton eventually had the good sense not to accompany Hamilton to Tripoli, and to extricate himself from the project before it took place. But Hamilton must have publicised Burton's interest, for Burton received a severe reprimand from the Military Secretary at the India Office. In a reply, Burton explained that he had met Hamilton in Egypt in 1854,[2] and again in Constantinople in 1855, when he himself was returning from the Crimea.

Burton wrote, in a letter of April 1856, to the Military Secretary:

> We met at the British Embassy, Therapia. There he informed me that the British Ambassador had commissioned him to restore in Tripoli the old hereditary dynasty of the Caramanly (Turkish) Beys. . . . I had no reason to doubt Mr. James Hamilton; he was

[1] Féraud, who briefly mentions this episode, says that Hamilton was described on his passport as M. l' Abbé Hamilton.

[2] Probably on Burton's return from his pilgrimage to Mecca.

received by H.B.M.'s Ambassador, with whom he appeared to be on the best of terms. He was intimate with the present Chief of the Caramanly family and he had no difficulty of access to him. . . .

Burton, who seems to have overlooked the fact that Britain was at that time an ally of Turkey in a war with Russia, at first agreed to join this hare-brained expedition, and withdrew, 'fearing the preposterous nature of his project . . .' It was well for his career that he did so.

There seem to be no evidence that Sir Stratford de Redcliffe ever lent himself to such a political gamble as the return of a Karamanli to the throne of Tripoli.

APPENDIX II

An idea of the size, composition and *lingua-franca* of the Bashaw of Tripoli's Court may be drawn from the list of Palace staff, to whom presents had to be given on the arrival of a new consul. It was prepared by Consul Fraser in 1767 (P.R.O. F.O. 76). Titles of the posts are presumably Fraser's own.

After the Bashaw, the Bey, and their families, it continues:

Dullatli. Probably chef de protocol.
Kehya Grande. Judge at the Gate.
Khasnadar. Chamberlain.
Rais del Marine. Captain of the Port.
Captana. Admiral.
Patrono. Vice-Admiral.
Reale. Rear-Admiral.
Shual el fitrise. Master of ceremonies.
Kehya el Hakim. Vice-Kehya.
Aga el Spahi. General of Horse.
Bash Shaus Spahi. Aid Major Domo.
Defterdar Bashh Khoja. Turkish Secretary.
Bash Khatib. Arabic Secretary.
Aga el Zindana. Captain of the Town Guard.
Shaikh. Lord Mayor.
Katib el Bey. Bey's secretary.
Guardiana Bash el Medina. Liet. of the Town Guard.
Kaid el Khubz. Commissary for Bread.
Kaid el Khandok. Commissary for Stores.
Kaid el Barud. Commissary for Powder.
Zentuti. Paymaster General.
Agha el Kursi. President of the Council.
Agha el Gunsoutsi (unreadable).
Bash Topje. First Canoneer.
Khoja el Diwan. Clerk of Council.
Seli Afshar. General of country Horse.
Caid el Shayl (probably Khayl). Master of Horse.
Khasnadar thani. Vice-Chamberlain.

Caid Biri Caid Amore	(unexplained) but Biri is probably Miri, or chief of govt. stores).
Ali Agha Hassan Agha Kadib Agha Ali bin Mirza	Captains of the Bashaw's personal guard who take their posts alternately.

GLOSSARY

(*Ar.*) Arabic.
(*T.*) Turkish.
(*P.*) Persian.
(*It.*) Italian.
(*Sp.*) Spanish.

Adan. (*Ar.*) Morning call to prayer.
Agha. (*T.*) Senior military officer.
Akhdar. (*Ar.*) Green.
Bashaw. (*T.*) A title given to Turkish rulers of high rank by English consuls, since the 16th century. Deriving from the Turkish 'Bash', meaning 'Head Man', or, 'Chief'.
Baraka. (*Ar.*) Blessing.
Bagnio. (*It.*) Prison for slaves.
Bastinado. (*Sp.*) Punishment by beating the soles of the feet.
Bey. (*T.*) A title of rank. In Tripoli most frequently used to describe the eldest son of the Bashaw.
Bashasha. (*Ar.*) Smiling or welcoming countenance.
Caftan. (*T.*) Ceremonial cloak; gift of the Sultan.
Capudan Pasha. (*T.*) Title of the Admiral of the Turkish fleet.
Capigi Bashi. (*T.*) The Sultan's official envoy.
Doganier. (*It.*) Customs officer.
Diwan. (*P.*) Council of State.
Dey. (*T.*) 'Uncle', a title given by the *janissaries* to their own leaders.
Dira. (*Ar.*) Beduin tribal area, or circuit of pasturage.
Firman. (*T.*) Decree of the Sultan.
Funduk. (*Ar.*) Caravanserai or barracks.
Ghibli. (*Ar.*) South wind.
Ghurfa. (*Ar.*) Room or privy chamber.
Hampas. (*T.*) 'Helpers'; black slaves of special status.
Harim. (*Ar.*) Women's quarters in a Moslem household.
Hijab. (*Ar.*) Protective amulet, often a Qur'anic quotation.
Inbat. (*Ar.*) A wind which causes growth.
Istislam. (*Ar.*) Submission to Islamic doctrine.

Jabia. (Ar.) Water trough.
Jebel. (*Ar.*) Mountain.
Jefara. (*Ar.*) A low, wide plain.
Janissary. (*T.*) From *yeni ceri*, Turkish 'new troops'.
Jaffareah. (*Ar.*) Divination by semi-divine afflatus.
Jebel. (*Ar.*) Mountain.
Jeleck. (*T.*) Waistcoat.
Kuloghli. (*T.*) Son of a slave, i.e. official servant of the Sultan.
Kehya. (*T.*) Steward or chamberlain.
Khoja. (*T.*) A clerk.
Khasnadar. (*T.*) Treasurer.
Kaid. (*Ar.*) Leader.
Leben. (*Ar.*) Sour milk; diet of the Beduin.
Marabut. (*Ar.*) A holy man; also a saint.
Menshia. (*Ar.*) Place of growth, or of sweet scents.
Mumineen. (*Ar.*) 'The faithful ones' (Qur'an) i.e. Moslems.
Mughteseb. (*Ar.*) Usurper.
Nubar. (*Ar.*) Military band, personal to the Bashaw.
Samiaan wa taatan. (*Ar.*) 'We hear and obey'. From the 1001 Arabian Nights.
Sahel. (*Ar.*) Wide, desert plain.
Saquiffa. (*Ar.*) Covered passage-way.
Sandanar. (*T.*) Police, post, or guard house.
Selectar. (*T.*) Ceremonial sword bearer to the Bashaw.
Shaqiq. (*Ar.*) Brothers by both parents; i.e. from a 'divided seed'.
Sultan Rasu. (*Ar.*) Literally, 'Sultan by his own head'.
Taiffa. (*Ar.*) Corporation of sea captains.
Turba. (*Ar.*) Tomb.
Teskera. (*T.*) Passport.
Wadi. (*Ar.*) Valley or water-course.

While Turkish and Arabic must have been both spoken at the Bashaw's Court, it seems as if the *lingua franca* was a sort of bastard Italian.

Money

The external exchange rate in Tripoli was most frequently in Spanish dollars, i.e. payment for redemption of slaves and for subsidies. A variety of coins was used for internal exchange.

Rates were approximately as follows:

I Spanish dollar = 33 N.P.
I Venetian sequin = 60 N.P.
I Tripoli sequin =43 N.P.
I Tripoli piastre = $7\frac{1}{2}$ N.P.
I Kharrouba = 32 piastres.
I Mahboub = 30 N.P.
I Bu khamseen = $\frac{1}{2}$ N.P.

Note. Both the Mahboub and Kharrouba were imaginary money units based on weight. Kharroubas were, in fact, carob seeds.

BIBLIOGRAPHY

Allen, G. W. *Our Navy & the Barbary Corsairs.* Archon Books, Connecticut, 1965.

Barbary Wars. Vols. IV, V and VI. U.S. Government Printing office.

Barth, Henry. *Travels in North Africa.* Longman Brown, London, 1857–58.

Beechey, F. W. *Proceedings from the Expedition to Explore the Northern coast of Africa.* J. Murray, London, 1828.

Bergna, R. C. *Tripoli dal 1510 al 1850.* Rome, 1925.

Bernard, Augustin. *Un Memoir inedit de Pellissier de Reynaud.* Paris, 1928.

Blaquière, Edward. *Letters from the Mediterranean.* J. Murray, London, 1813.

Bono, Salvatore. *I Corsari Barbareschi.* Edizione R.A.I., Turin, 1964.

Bovill, E. W. (Editor). *Missions to the Niger.* 3 vols. Hakluyt Society, 1967.

Boyde, Henry. *Voyages to Barbary.* Oliver Payne, London, 1736.

Corbett, J. S. *England in the Mediterranean.* Longmans, 1904.

Cowper, H. S. *The Hill of Graces.* Methuen, London, 1897.

Dan, Pére. *Histoire de Barbarie et de ses Corsaires.* Paris, 1637.

Della Cella, P. *Viaggio de Tripoli di Barbaria alla frontiere dell' Egitto.* Rome, 1819.

Denham, D. and Clapperton, H. *Narrative of Travels in North Africa.* J. Murray, London, 1826.

Féraud, Charles. *Annales Tripolitaines.* Librairie Vuibert, Paris, 1927.

Horn, D. B. *British Diplomatic Service.* 1689–1789. Clarendon Press, 1961.

Hubac, P. *Les Barbaresque.* Editions Berger Levrault. Paris, 1949.

Lane Poole, S. *The Barbary Corsairs.* Fisher Unwin, London, 1890.

Lyon, G. F. *Narrative of Travels in North Africa.* J. Murray, London, 1826.

Mackesy, Piers. *The War in the Mediterranean.* 1803–1810. Longmans, 1957.

Masson, P. *Histoire des Etablissements et de Commerce Français dans l'Afrique Barbaresque.* Paris, 1903.

Mathuisieulx, M. de. *A Travers la Tripolitanie.* Hachette, Paris, 1903.

Micacchi, Rodolfo. *La Tripolitania sotto il dominio dei Caramanli.* Collezione Riccioli, Rome, 1936.

Morgan, J. *Historical Memoir of Barbary*. Gale, London, 1816.

Nash, Howard P. *The Forgotten Wars*. A. S. Barnes, London, 1968.

Pacho, M. J. R. *Voyage dans la Marmarique* . . . Paris, 1827.

Pananti, F. *Narrative of a Residence in Algiers*. Colburn, London, 1817.

Perk, A. *Zes Jaren te Tripoli in Barbariji*. Amsterdam, 1875.

Playfair, R. L. *The Scourge of Christendom*. Smith & Elder, London, 1884.

Rennell Rodd (Lord Rennell). *General William Eaton*. Routledge, London, 1932.

Rycaut, Paul. *History of the Ottoman Empire*. London, 1686.

Richardson, James. *Travels in the Sahara*. Bentley, London, 1857–58.

Roux, F. Charles. *Bonaparte et la Tripolitanie*. Paris, 1929.

Russell, M. *The Barbary States*. Oliver & Boyd, Edinburgh, 1835.

Shaw, Thomas. *Travels in Barbary*. A. Millar, London, 1757.

Todd, Mabel L. *Tripoli the Mysterious*. Grant Richards, London, 1912.

Tully, Richard. *Narrative of Ten Years Residence at Tripoli*. Colburn, London, 1819. New Limited Edition, edited by Seton Dearden. Arthur Barker, 1957.

Wright and Macleod. *The first Americans in North Africa*. Princeton, U.P., 1945.

Welch, Galbraith. *North African Prelude*. Morrow, New York, 1949.

Grosvenor, Lord. Journal. *Travels in Barbary*. Privately Printed for Chester Infirmary, 1830.

Biographical Dictionary of Eminent Scotsmen (Gordon Laing). Robert Chambers, Edinburgh, 1835.

Hertzlet's *Treaties*, Vol. I. H. Butterworth, London, 1840.

Revue des deux Mondes. Paris, Oct. 1855.

Revue Tunisiennes. XIII & XIV. Tunis, 1906–7.

Revue Africaine. LV. Paris, 1911.

Oriente Moderno. XII. Rome, 1932.

Rivista della Colonia Italiana. VI. Rome, 1930–32.

Quarterly Review, 1823, 1828, 1845. (Laing controversy.)

Gentleman's Magazine, vol. 64 (Tully's debts), 1794.

Bulletin of Historical Research, No. 23. Supervising of the Barbary Consuls, 1756–1836. Hilda Lee.

Tripoli Archives. Public Record Office (State Papers Foreign), No. 71, 76 vol. 9. 7–43. C.O. 83.

INDEX

Index

Index